940! As the world teetered on the brink of global war, frail Steve Rogers entered a secret laboratory and was transformed into the American Super-Soldier! For five thrilling years, he fought the Axis Powers--until a freak stroke of fate threw him into suspended animation. When he awoke, he was a man decades out of his time! Since that fateful day, Steve Rogers sought his destiny in this brave new world!

But that was a long time ago...

PROMISED LAND

CAPTAIN AMERICA BY MARK WAID: PROMISED LAND. Contains material originally published in magazine form as CAPTAIN AMERICA #701-704. First printing 2018. ISBN 978-1-302-90993-2. Published by MARVEL WORLDWIDE, INC., a subsidiary of MARVEL ENTERTAINMENT, LLC. OFFICE OF PUBLICATION: 135 West 50th Street, New York, NY 10020. Copyright © 2018 MARVEL No similarity between any of the names, characters, persons, and/or institutions in this magazine with those of any living or dead person or institution is intended, and any such similarity which may exist is purely coincidental. Printed in Canada. DAN BUCKLEY, President, Marvel Entertainment; JOHN NEE, Publisher; JOE QUESADA, Chief Creative Officer; TOM BREVOORT, SVP of Publishing; DAVID BOGART, SVP of Business Affairs & Operations, Publishing & Partnership; DAVID GABRIEL, SVP of Sales & Marketing, Publishing; JEFF YOUNGQUIST, VP of Production & Special Projects; DAN CARR, Executive Director of Publishing Technology; ALEX MORALES, Director of Publishing Operations; DAN EDINGTON, Managing Editor; SUSAN CRESPI, Production Manager; STAN LEE, Chairman Emeritus. For information regarding advertising in Marvel Comics or on Marvel.com, please contact Vit DeBellis, Custom Solutions & Integrated Advertising Manager, at vdebellis@marvel.com. For Marvel subscription inquiries, please call 888-511-5480. Manufactured between 7/6/2018 and 8/7/2018 by SOLISCO PRINTERS, SCOTT, QC, CANADA.

10 9 8 7 6 5 4 3 2 1

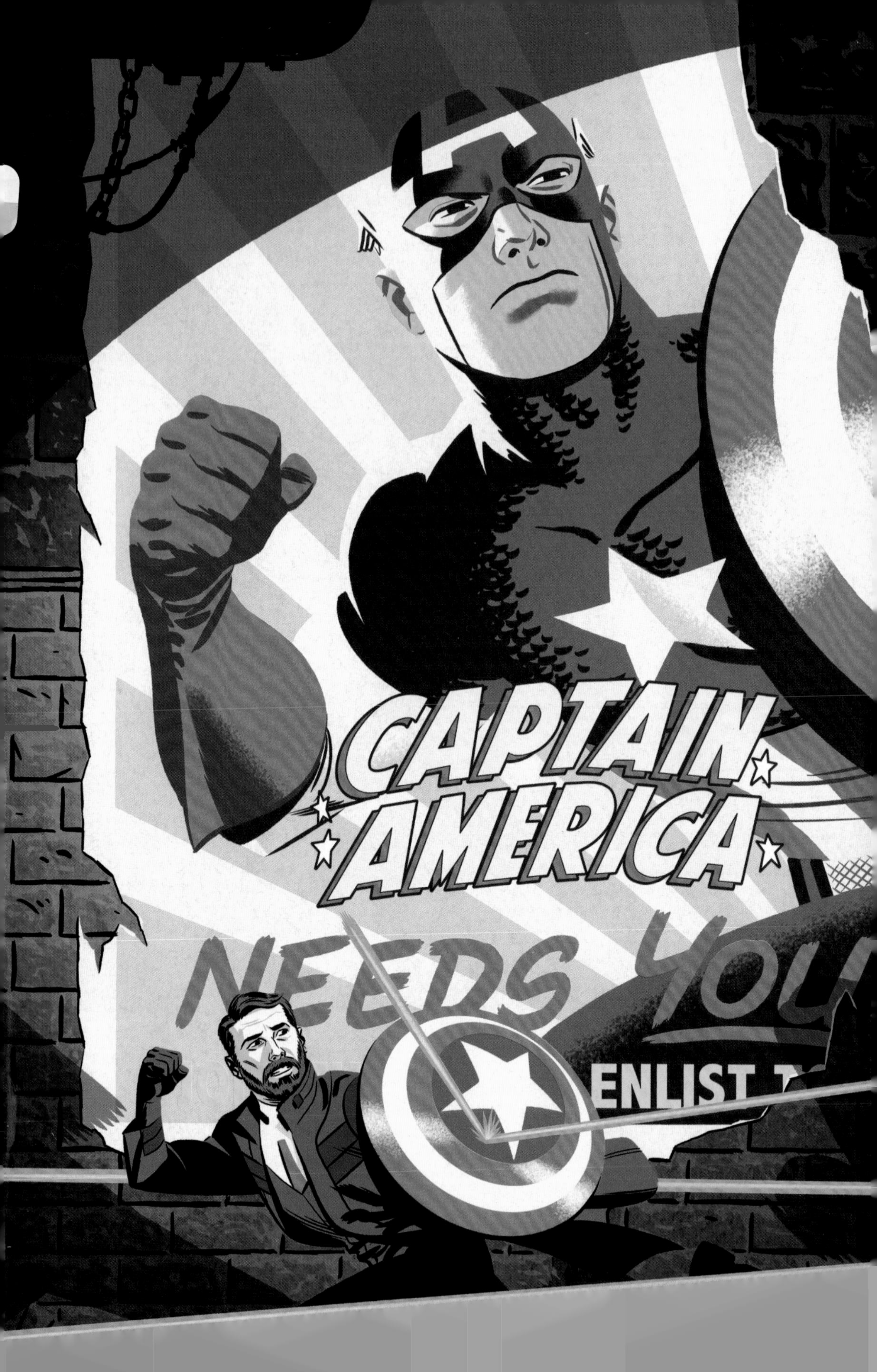
CAPTAIN
AMERICA
NEEDS YOU
ENLIST

PROMISED LAND

WRITER: **MARK WAID**

ARTISTS: **LEONARDO ROMERO** (#701-704)
WITH ADAM HUGHES & J.G. JONES (#701),
ROD REIS & HOWARD CHAYKIN (#702)
AND ALAN DAVIS & MARK FARMER(#703)

COLOR ARTISTS: **JORDIE BELLAIRE** (#701-704)
WITH ADAM HUGHES & PAUL MOUNTS(#701),
ROD REIS & JESUS ABURTOV (#702)
AND IRMA KNIIVILA (#703)

LETTERER: VC'S JOE CARAMAGNA
COVER: MICHAEL CHO
ASSOCIATE EDITOR: ALANNA SMITH
EDITOR: TOM BREVOORT

Captain America created by Joe Simon & Jack Kirby

COLLECTION EDITOR: MARK D. BEAZLEY
ASSISTANT EDITOR: CAITLIN O'CONNELL
ASSOCIATE MANAGING EDITOR: KATERI WOODY
SENIOR EDITOR, SPECIAL PROJECTS: JENNIFER GRÜNWALD
VP PRODUCTION & SPECIAL PROJECTS: JEFF YOUNGQUIST
SVP PRINT, SALES & MARKETING: DAVID GABRIEL
GRAPHIC DESIGNER: CARLOS LAO

EDITOR IN CHIEF: C.B. CEBULSKI CHIEF CREATIVE OFFICER: JOE QUESADA
PRESIDENT: DAN BUCKLEY EXECUTIVE PRODUCER: ALAN FINE

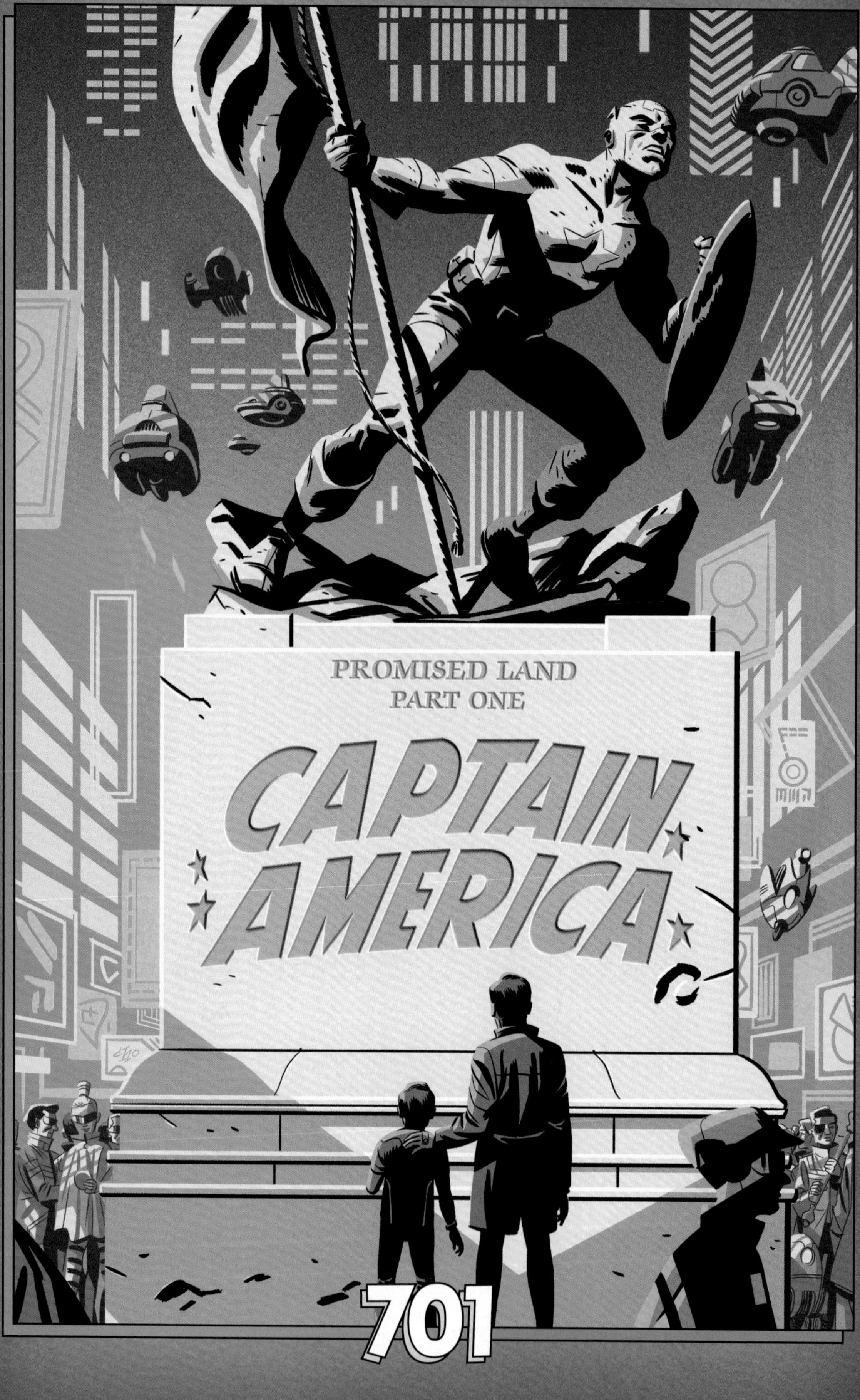
PROMISED LAND
PART ONE
CAPTAIN AMERICA
701

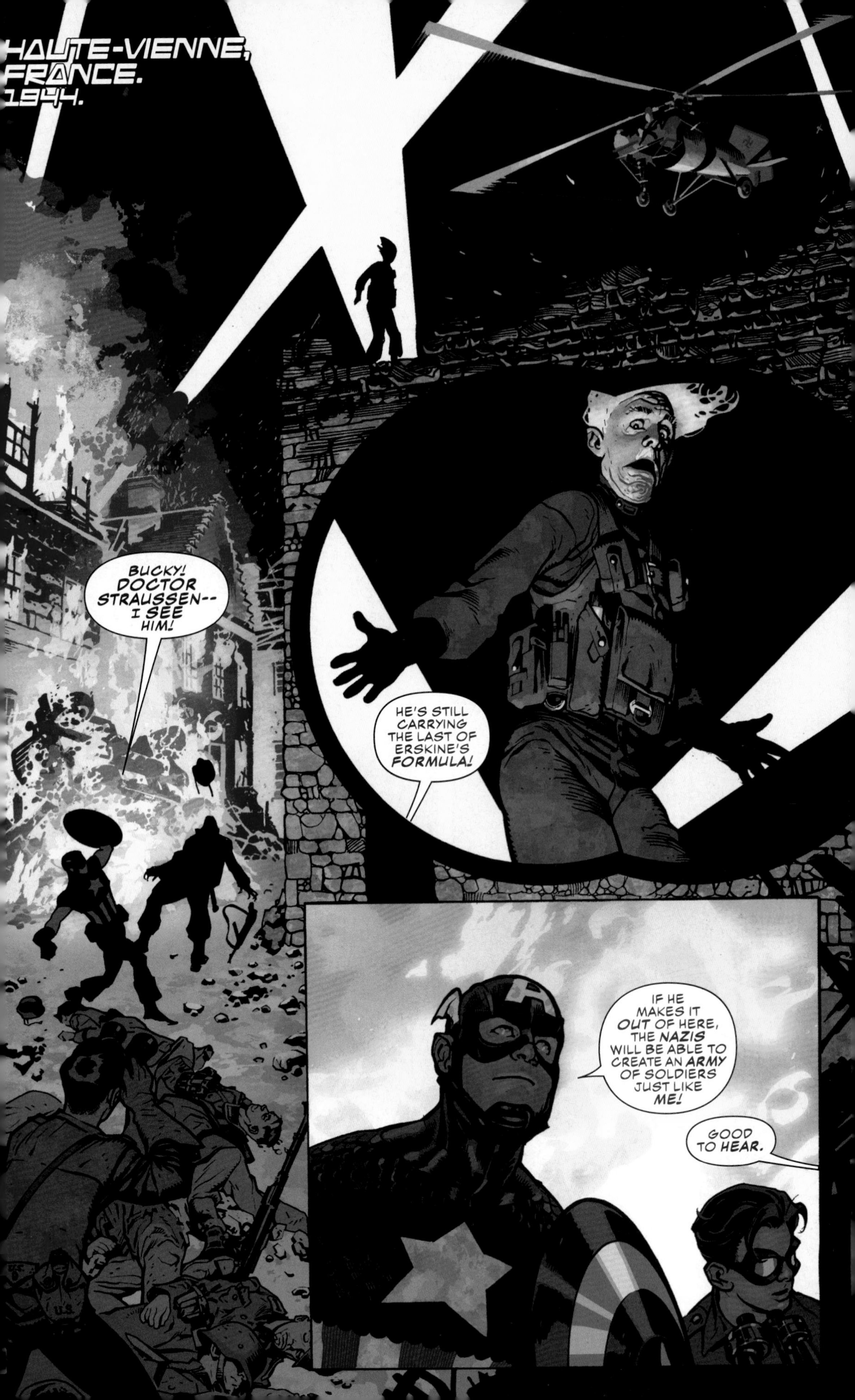
HAUTE-VIENNE, FRANCE. 1944.
BUCKY! DOCTOR STRAUSSEN-- I SEE HIM!
HE'S STILL CARRYING THE LAST OF ERSKINE'S FORMULA!
IF HE MAKES IT OUT OF HERE, THE NAZIS WILL BE ABLE TO CREATE AN ARMY OF SOLDIERS JUST LIKE ME!
GOOD TO HEAR.

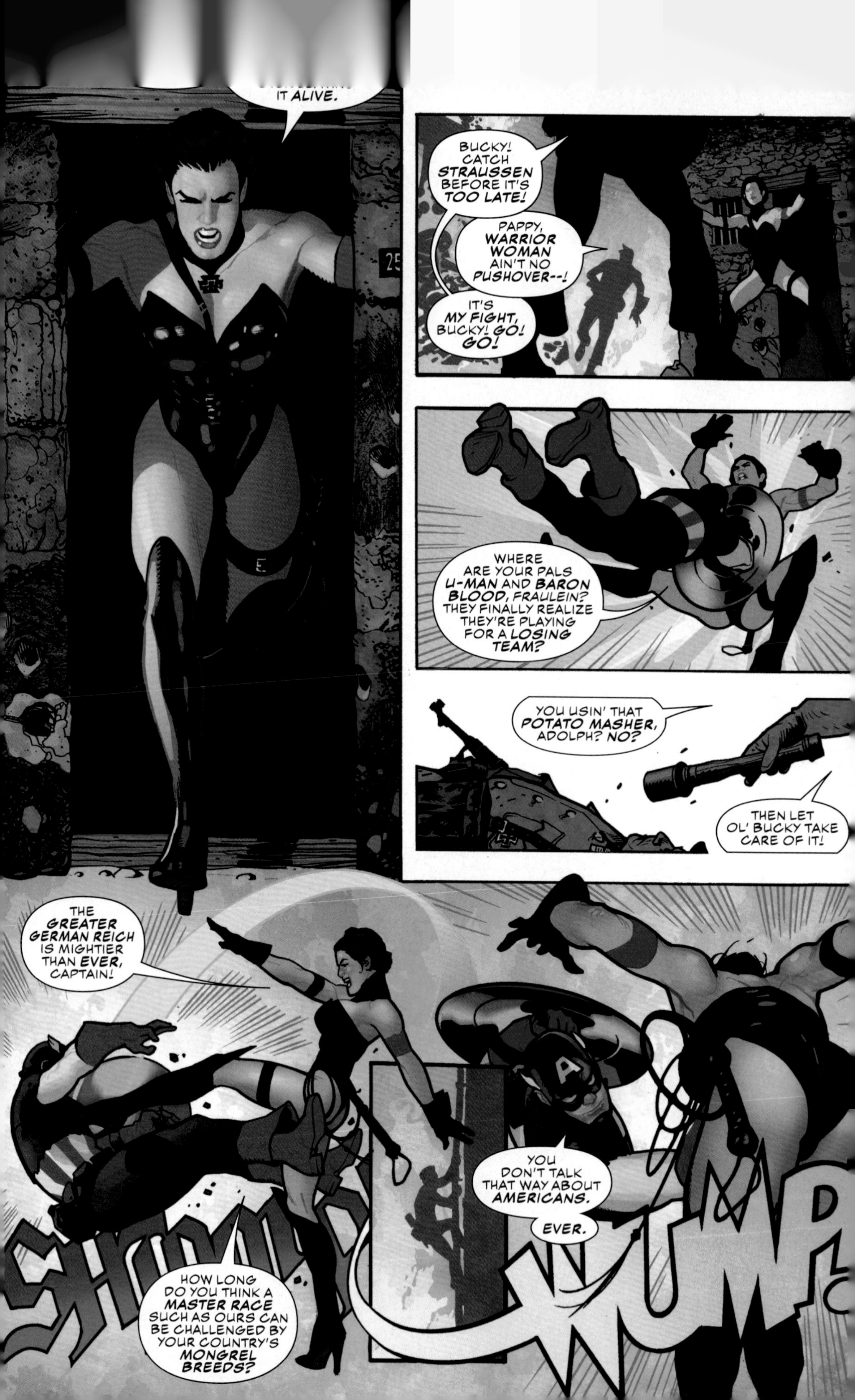
IT ALIVE.
BUCKY! CATCH STRAUSSEN BEFORE IT'S TOO LATE!
PAPPY, WARRIOR WOMAN AIN'T NO PUSHOVER--!
IT'S MY FIGHT, BUCKY! GO! GO!
WHERE ARE YOUR PALS U-MAN AND BARON BLOOD, FRAULEIN? THEY FINALLY REALIZE THEY'RE PLAYING FOR A LOSING TEAM?
YOU USIN' THAT POTATO MASHER, ADOLPH? NO?
THEN LET OL' BUCKY TAKE CARE OF IT!
THE GREATER GERMAN REICH IS MIGHTIER THAN EVER, CAPTAIN!
HOW LONG DO YOU THINK A MASTER RACE SUCH AS OURS CAN BE CHALLENGED BY YOUR COUNTRY'S MONGREL BREEDS?
YOU DON'T TALK THAT WAY ABOUT AMERICANS.
EVER.

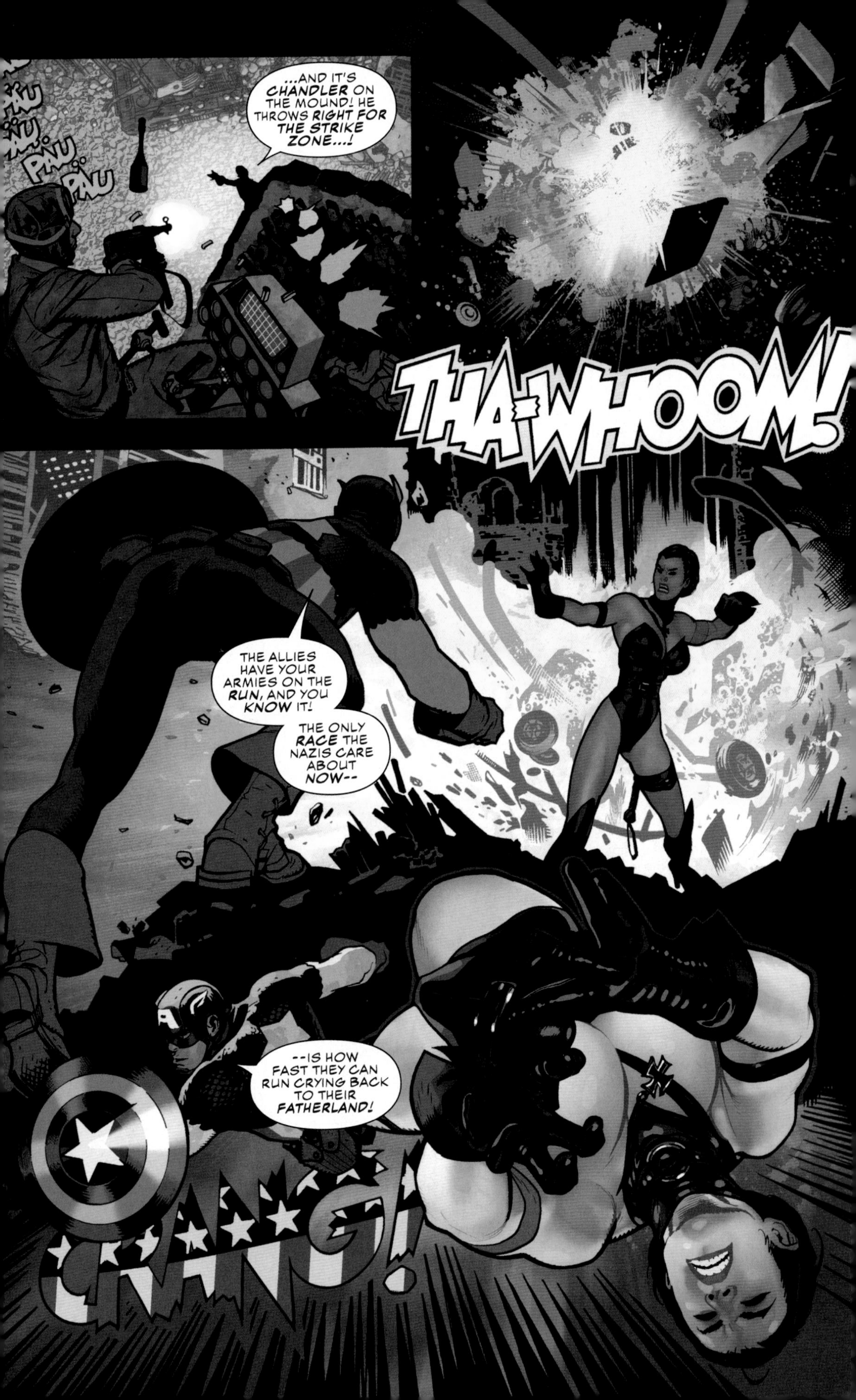
PAU
PAU
PAU
PAU
...AND IT'S CHANDLER ON THE MOUND! HE THROWS RIGHT FOR THE STRIKE ZONE...!
THA-WHOOM!
THE ALLIES HAVE YOUR ARMIES ON THE RUN, AND YOU KNOW IT!
THE ONLY RACE THE NAZIS CARE ABOUT NOW--
--IS HOW FAST THEY CAN RUN CRYING BACK TO THEIR FATHERLAND!
CRANG!

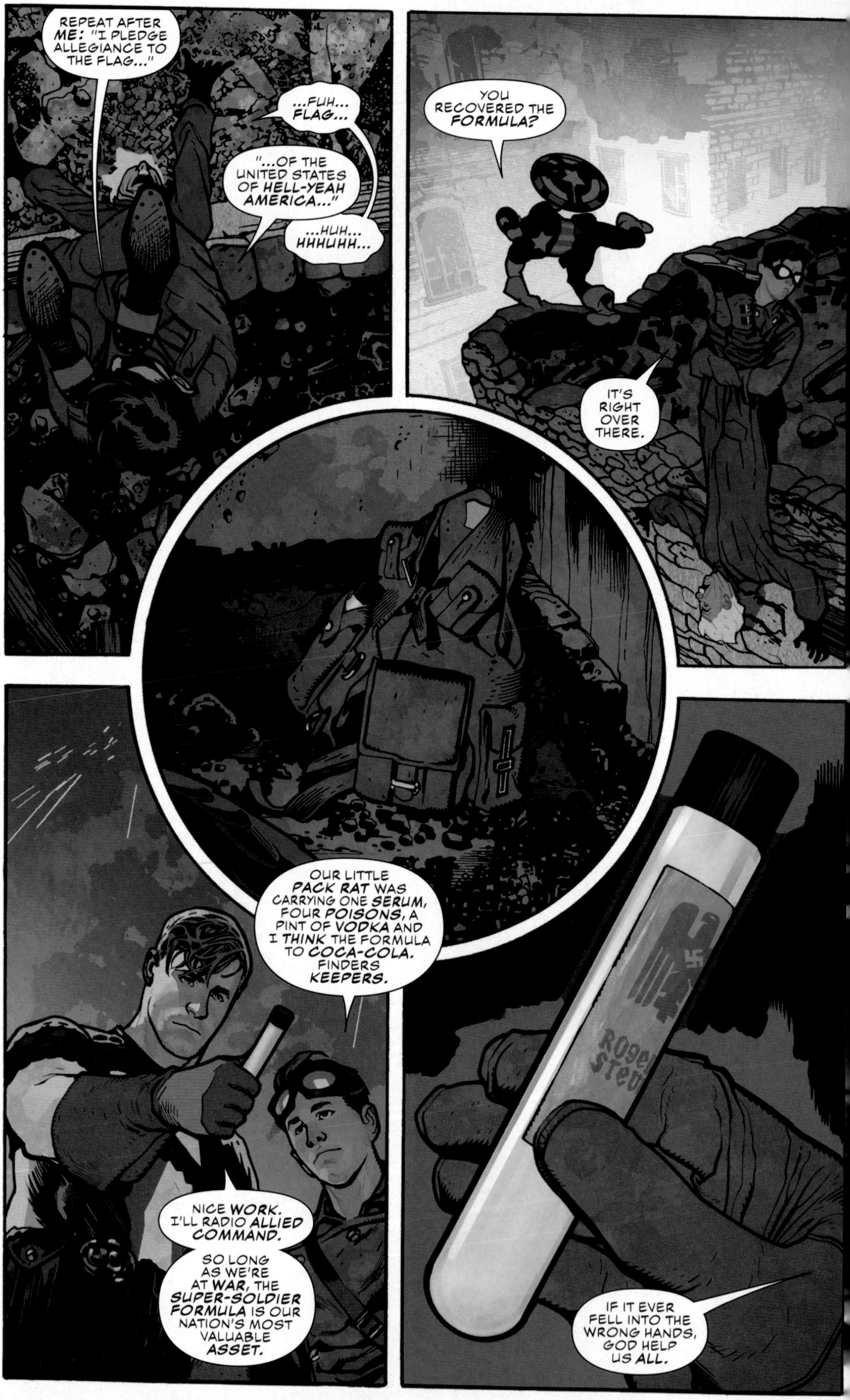
REPEAT AFTER ME: "I PLEDGE ALLEGIANCE TO THE FLAG..."
...FUH... FLAG...
"...OF THE UNITED STATES OF HELL-YEAH AMERICA..."
...HUH... HHHUHH...
YOU RECOVERED THE FORMULA?
IT'S RIGHT OVER THERE.
OUR LITTLE PACK RAT WAS CARRYING ONE SERUM, FOUR POISONS, A PINT OF VODKA AND I THINK THE FORMULA TO COCA-COLA. FINDERS KEEPERS.
NICE WORK. I'LL RADIO ALLIED COMMAND.
SO LONG AS WE'RE AT WAR, THE SUPER-SOLDIER FORMULA IS OUR NATION'S MOST VALUABLE ASSET.
IF IT EVER FELL INTO THE WRONG HANDS, GOD HELP US ALL.

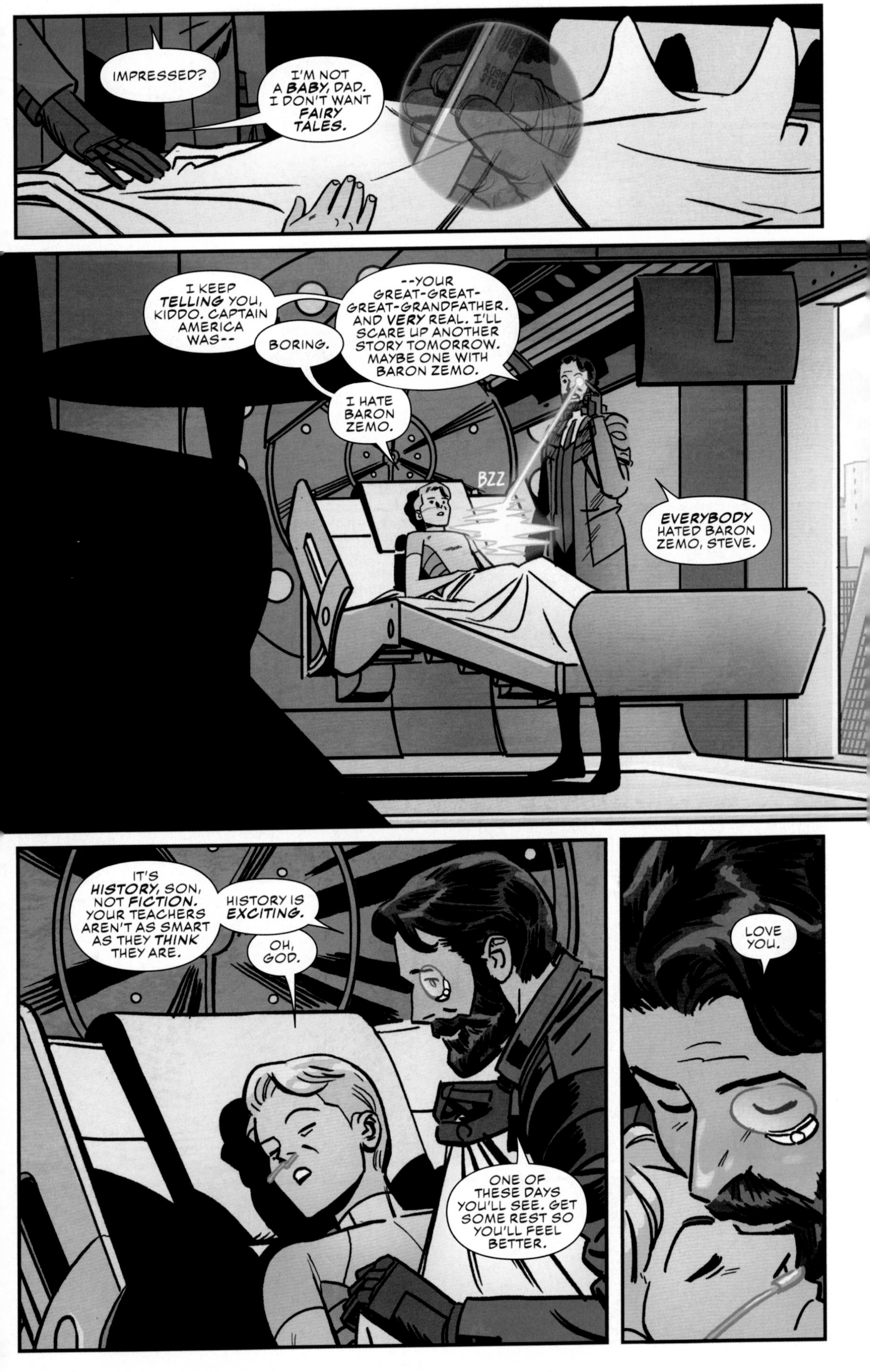

IMPRESSED?
I'M NOT A BABY, DAD. I DON'T WANT FAIRY TALES.
I KEEP TELLING YOU, KIDDO. CAPTAIN AMERICA WAS--
BORING.
--YOUR GREAT-GREAT-GREAT-GRANDFATHER. AND VERY REAL. I'LL SCARE UP ANOTHER STORY TOMORROW. MAYBE ONE WITH BARON ZEMO.
I HATE BARON ZEMO.
BZZ
EVERYBODY HATED BARON ZEMO, STEVE.
IT'S HISTORY, SON, NOT FICTION. YOUR TEACHERS AREN'T AS SMART AS THEY THINK THEY ARE.
HISTORY IS EXCITING.
OH, GOD.
ONE OF THESE DAYS YOU'LL SEE. GET SOME REST SO YOU'LL FEEL BETTER.
LOVE YOU.

HOW IS HE, JACK?

WHY DON'T *YOU* TELL *ME*, DOCTOR?

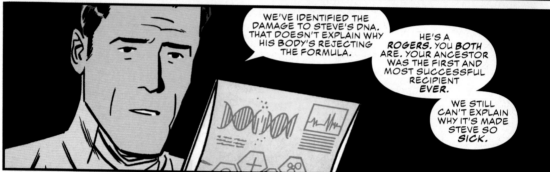

WE'VE IDENTIFIED THE DAMAGE TO STEVE'S DNA. THAT DOESN'T EXPLAIN WHY HIS BODY'S REJECTING THE FORMULA.

HE'S A *ROGERS.* YOU *BOTH* ARE. YOUR ANCESTOR WAS THE FIRST AND MOST SUCCESSFUL RECIPIENT *EVER.*

WE STILL CAN'T EXPLAIN WHY IT'S MADE STEVE SO *SICK.*

TRY. I'VE BEEN GETTING THE RUNAROUND FOR A *YEAR* NOW. THERE HAS TO BE *SOMEONE* AT THIS HOSPITAL WHO CAN CUT THROUGH ALL THIS BUREAUCRATIC--

BLAM

WE WORK WITH THE DATA WE *HAVE.* IN CONSIDERATION OF YOUR *LINEAGE,* WE'VE PRIORITIZED STEVE'S CASE. IF YOU WANT FASTER SERVICE, YOU'LL JUST HAVE TO TAKE IT UP WITH 1600.

THEN STAY BY YOUR COMM. YOU'LL BE GETTING A CALL.

SO MUCH FOR AN ADVANCED SOCIETY.

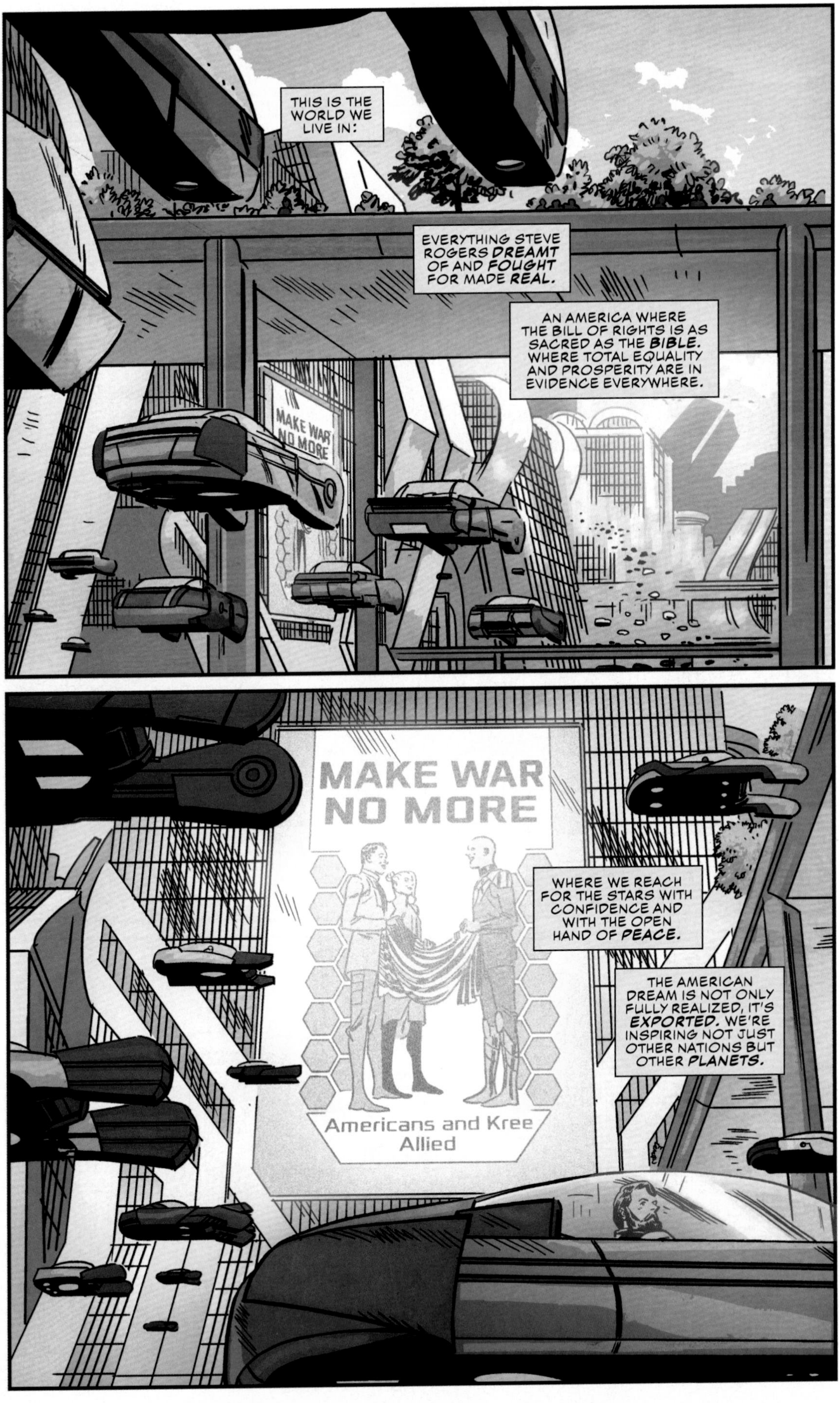
THIS IS THE WORLD WE LIVE IN:
EVERYTHING STEVE ROGERS **DREAMT** OF AND **FOUGHT** FOR MADE **REAL.**
AN AMERICA WHERE THE BILL OF RIGHTS IS AS SACRED AS THE **BIBLE.** WHERE TOTAL EQUALITY AND PROSPERITY ARE IN EVIDENCE EVERYWHERE.
MAKE WAR NO MORE
MAKE WAR NO MORE
Americans and Kree Allied
WHERE WE REACH FOR THE STARS WITH CONFIDENCE AND WITH THE OPEN HAND OF **PEACE.**
THE AMERICAN DREAM IS NOT ONLY FULLY REALIZED, IT'S ***EXPORTED.*** WE'RE INSPIRING NOT JUST OTHER NATIONS BUT OTHER ***PLANETS.***

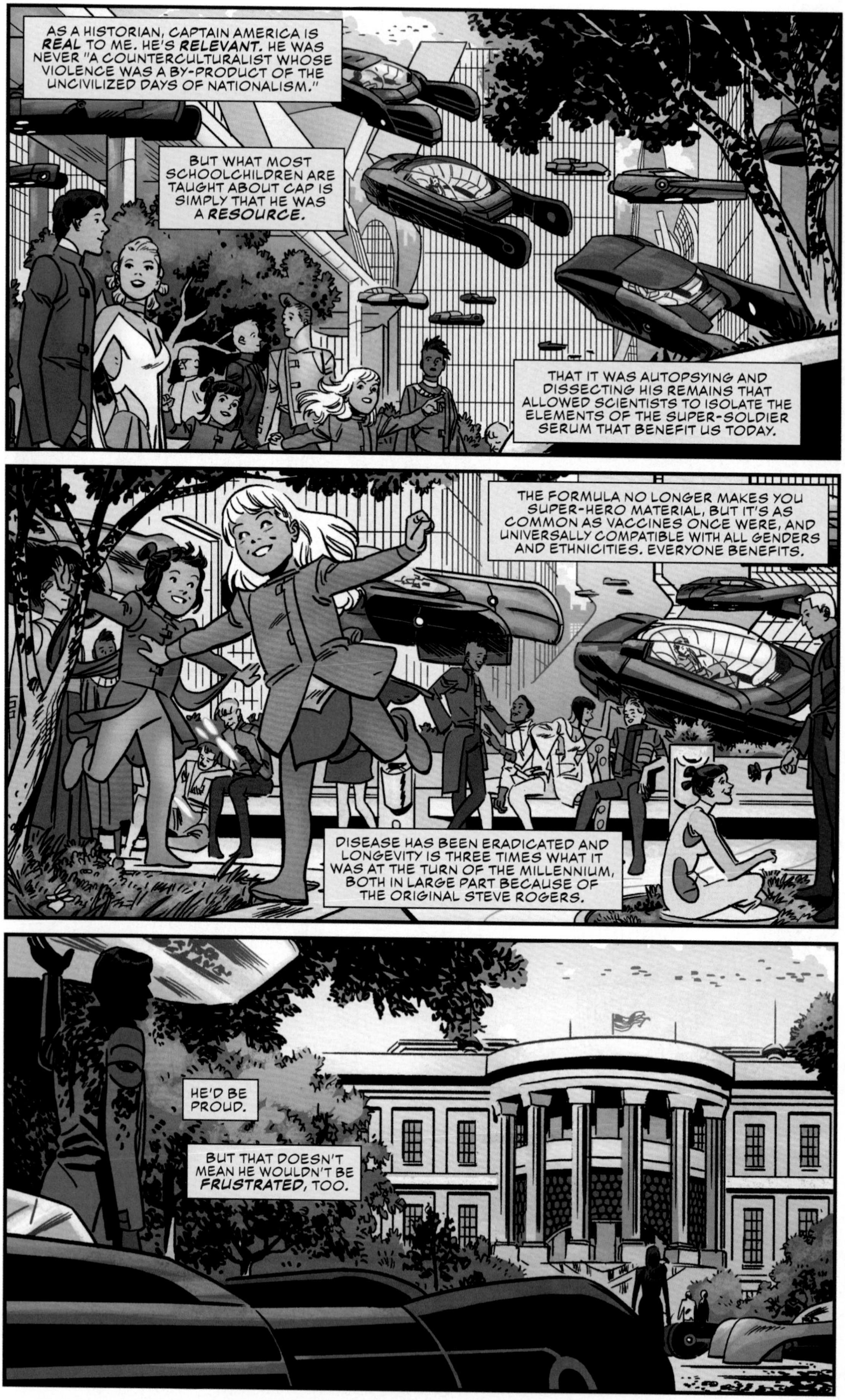
AS A HISTORIAN, CAPTAIN AMERICA IS REAL TO ME. HE'S RELEVANT. HE WAS NEVER "A COUNTERCULTURALIST WHOSE VIOLENCE WAS A BY-PRODUCT OF THE UNCIVILIZED DAYS OF NATIONALISM."
BUT WHAT MOST SCHOOLCHILDREN ARE TAUGHT ABOUT CAP IS SIMPLY THAT HE WAS A RESOURCE.
THAT IT WAS AUTOPSYING AND DISSECTING HIS REMAINS THAT ALLOWED SCIENTISTS TO ISOLATE THE ELEMENTS OF THE SUPER-SOLDIER SERUM THAT BENEFIT US TODAY.
THE FORMULA NO LONGER MAKES YOU SUPER-HERO MATERIAL, BUT IT'S AS COMMON AS VACCINES ONCE WERE, AND UNIVERSALLY COMPATIBLE WITH ALL GENDERS AND ETHNICITIES. EVERYONE BENEFITS.
DISEASE HAS BEEN ERADICATED AND LONGEVITY IS THREE TIMES WHAT IT WAS AT THE TURN OF THE MILLENNIUM, BOTH IN LARGE PART BECAUSE OF THE ORIGINAL STEVE ROGERS.
HE'D BE PROUD.
BUT THAT DOESN'T MEAN HE WOULDN'T BE FRUSTRATED, TOO.

MR. PRESIDENT, THANK YOU FOR SEEING ME.

THE DOOR IS ALWAYS OPEN FOR A *HISTORIAN*, JACK. YOU KNOW THAT.

HOW'S STEVE?

GETTING *WORSE*, SIR. IT'S JUST THE TWO OF US NOW. I... I CAN'T LOSE MY SON.

THE DOCTORS ARE EITHER HELPLESS OR HOPELESS. THEY CLAIM THEY'RE BEING STONEWALLED FOR LACK OF DATA.

I'VE NEVER ASKED YOU FOR *ANYTHING*, MR. PRESIDENT, BUT I NEED YOU TO DECLASSIFY ALL THE FORMULA DEVELOPMENT RECORDS JUST THIS ONCE. PLEASE.

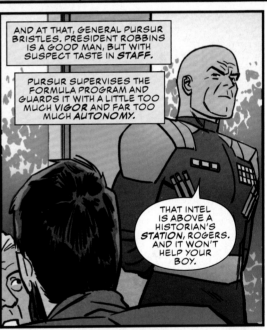

AND AT THAT, GENERAL PURSUR BRISTLES. PRESIDENT ROBBINS IS A GOOD MAN, BUT WITH SUSPECT TASTE IN *STAFF*.

PURSUR SUPERVISES THE FORMULA PROGRAM AND GUARDS IT WITH A LITTLE TOO MUCH *VIGOR* AND FAR TOO MUCH *AUTONOMY*.

THAT INTEL IS ABOVE A HISTORIAN'S *STATION*, ROGERS. AND IT WON'T HELP YOUR BOY.

ARE YOU SUDDENLY A *DOCTOR*? I'M NOT ASKING TO EVEN *LOOK* AT THE DATA! BUT HIS *MEDTECHS*--

IT'S A MATTER OF NATIONAL SECURITY. WE *CANNOT* HAVE THE FORMULA GOING INTERSTELLAR.

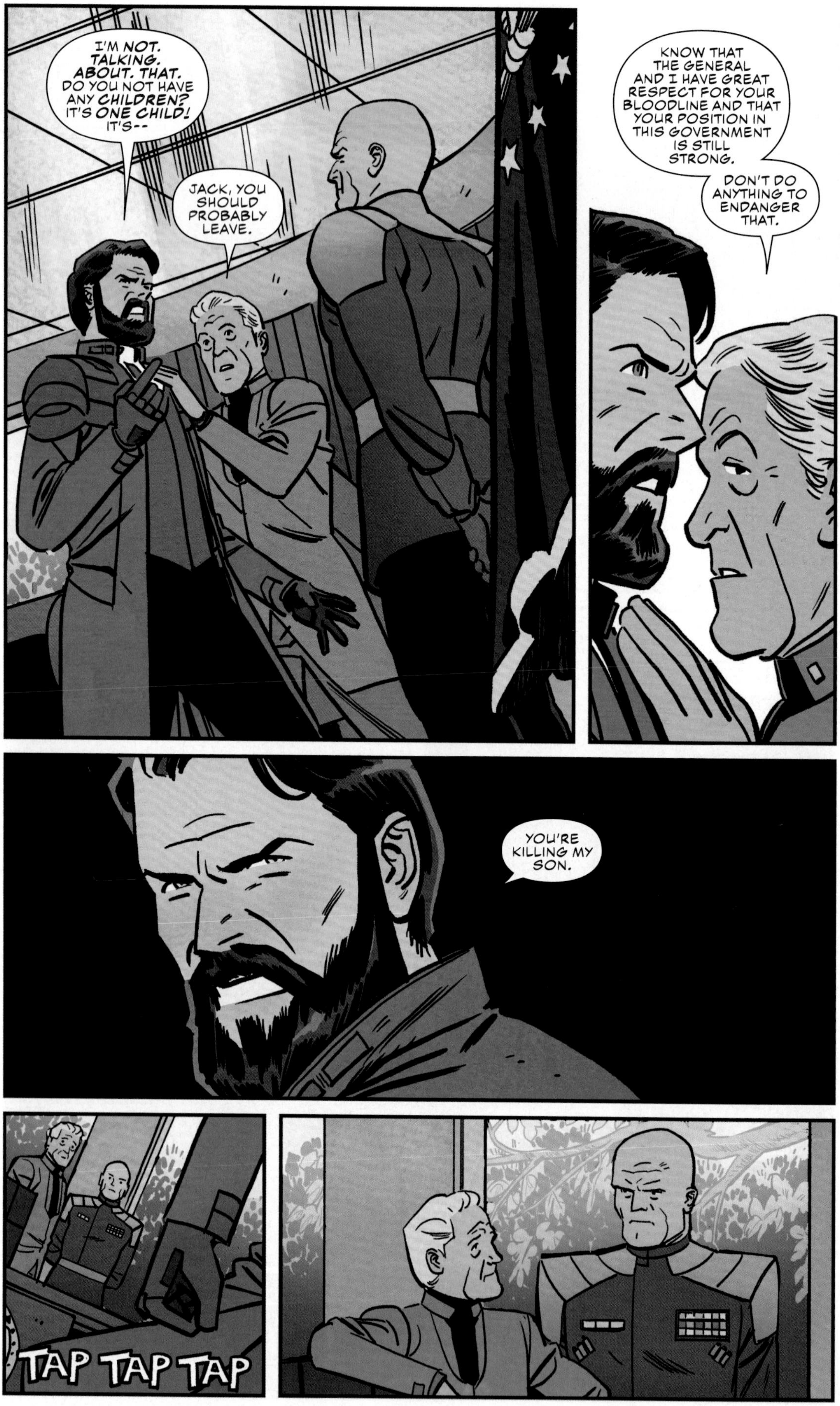

I'M NOT. TALKING. ABOUT. THAT. DO YOU NOT HAVE ANY CHILDREN? IT'S ONE CHILD! IT'S--
JACK, YOU SHOULD PROBABLY LEAVE.
KNOW THAT THE GENERAL AND I HAVE GREAT RESPECT FOR YOUR BLOODLINE AND THAT YOUR POSITION IN THIS GOVERNMENT IS STILL STRONG.
DON'T DO ANYTHING TO ENDANGER THAT.
YOU'RE KILLING MY SON.
TAP TAP TAP

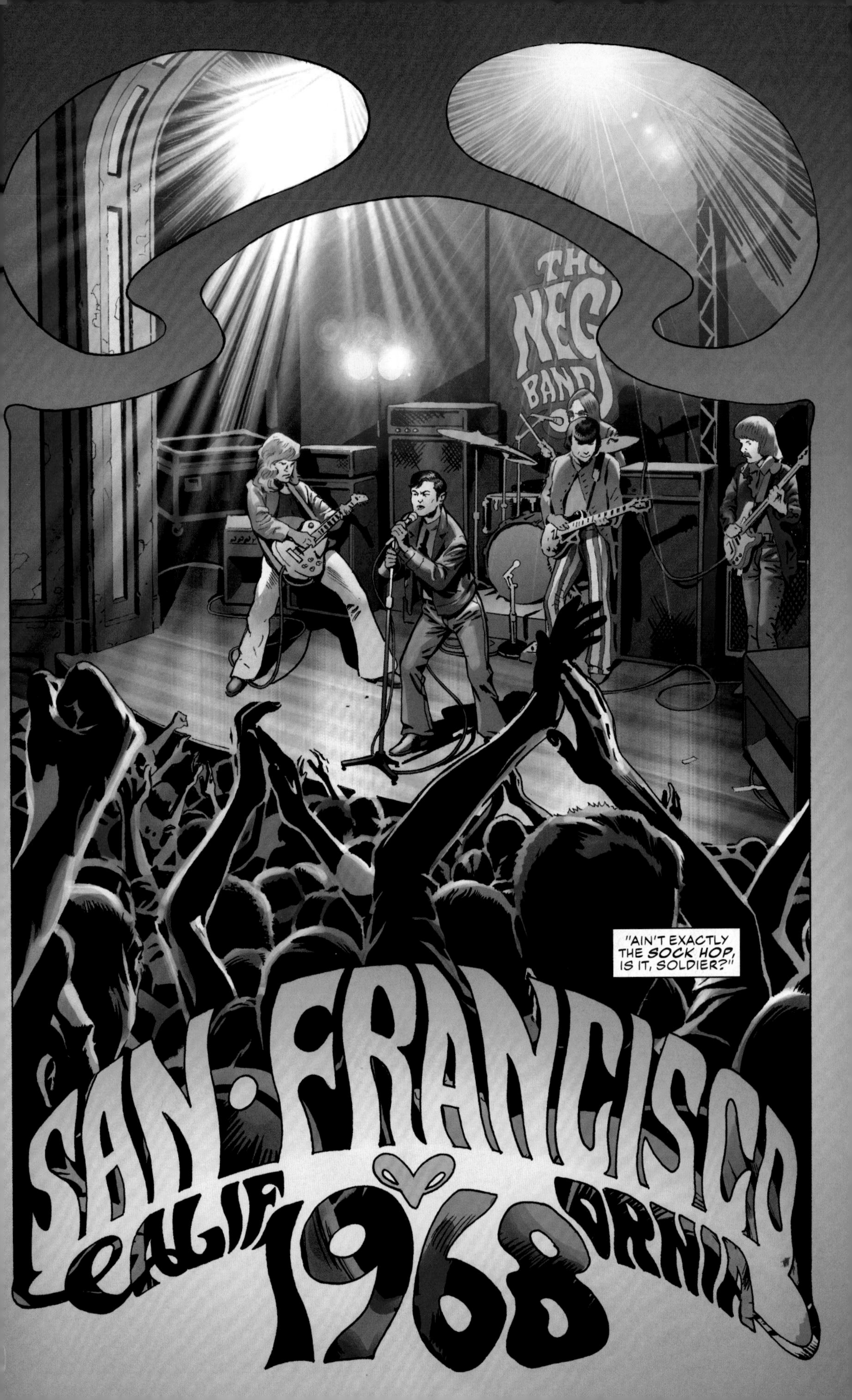
"AIN'T EXACTLY THE SOCK HOP, IS IT, SOLDIER?"
SAN FRANCISCO
CALIFORNIA
1968

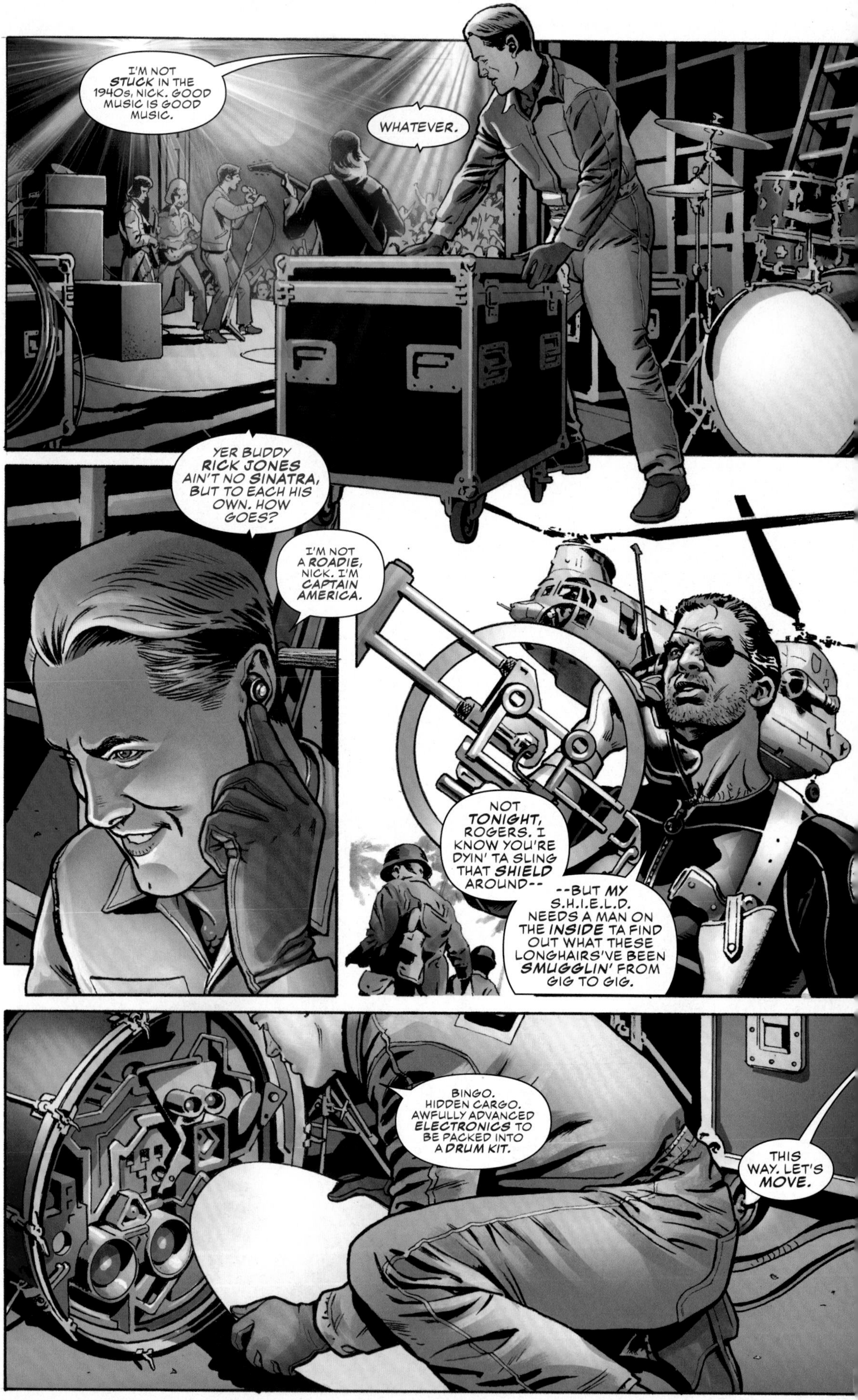
I'M NOT STUCK IN THE 1940s, NICK. GOOD MUSIC IS GOOD MUSIC.
WHATEVER.
YER BUDDY RICK JONES AIN'T NO SINATRA, BUT TO EACH HIS OWN. HOW GOES?
I'M NOT A ROADIE, NICK. I'M CAPTAIN AMERICA.
NOT TONIGHT, ROGERS. I KNOW YOU'RE DYIN' TA SLING THAT SHIELD AROUND--
--BUT MY S.H.I.E.L.D. NEEDS A MAN ON THE INSIDE TA FIND OUT WHAT THESE LONGHAIRS'VE BEEN SMUGGLIN' FROM GIG TO GIG.
BINGO. HIDDEN CARGO. AWFULLY ADVANCED ELECTRONICS TO BE PACKED INTO A DRUM KIT.
THIS WAY. LET'S MOVE.

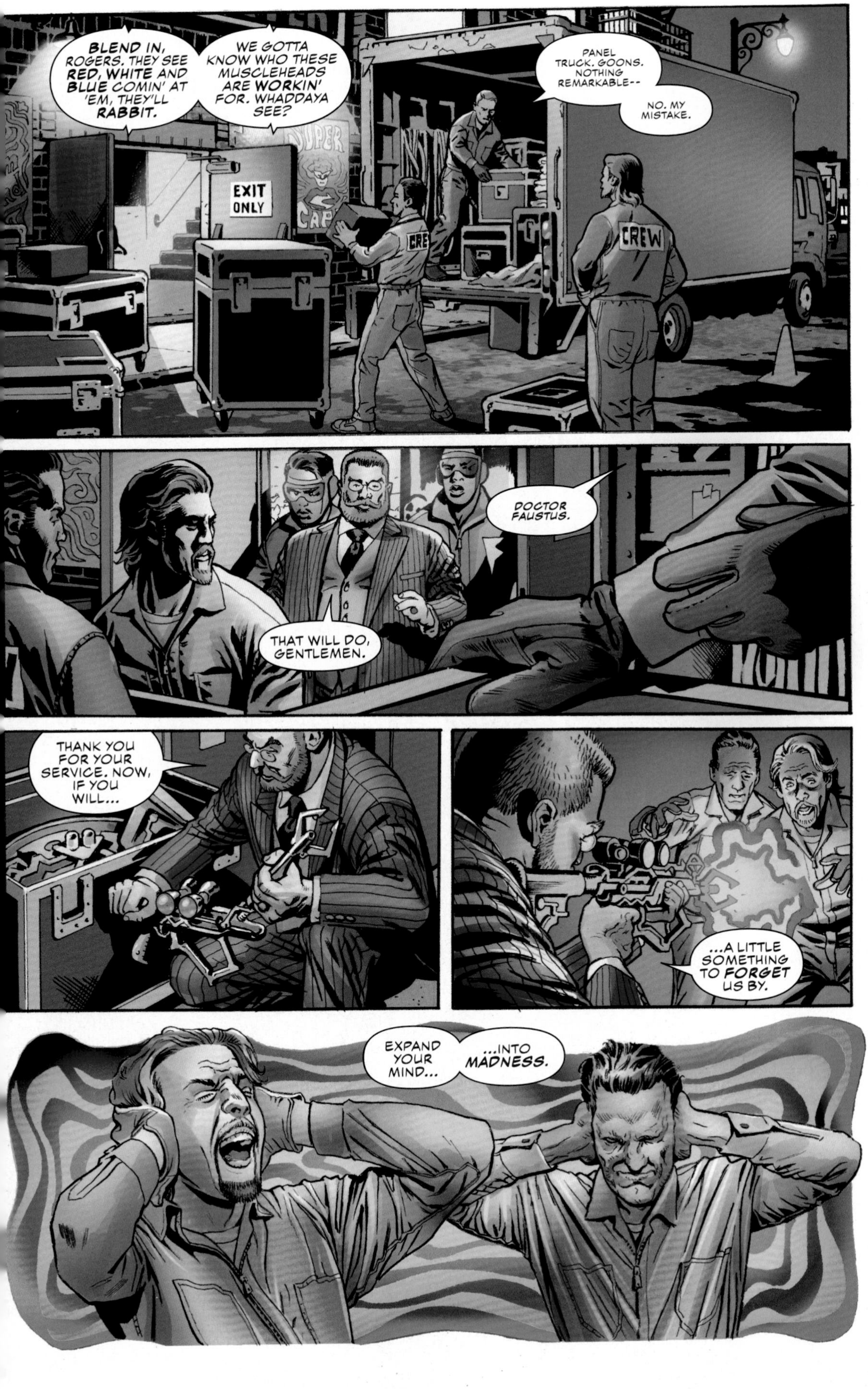
BLEND IN, ROGERS. THEY SEE RED, WHITE AND BLUE COMIN' AT 'EM, THEY'LL RABBIT.
WE GOTTA KNOW WHO THESE MUSCLEHEADS ARE WORKIN' FOR. WHADDAYA SEE?
PANEL TRUCK. GOONS. NOTHING REMARKABLE--
NO. MY MISTAKE.
EXIT ONLY
CREW
DOCTOR FAUSTUS.
THAT WILL DO, GENTLEMEN.
THANK YOU FOR YOUR SERVICE. NOW, IF YOU WILL...
...A LITTLE SOMETHING TO FORGET US BY.
EXPAND YOUR MIND...
...INTO MADNESS.

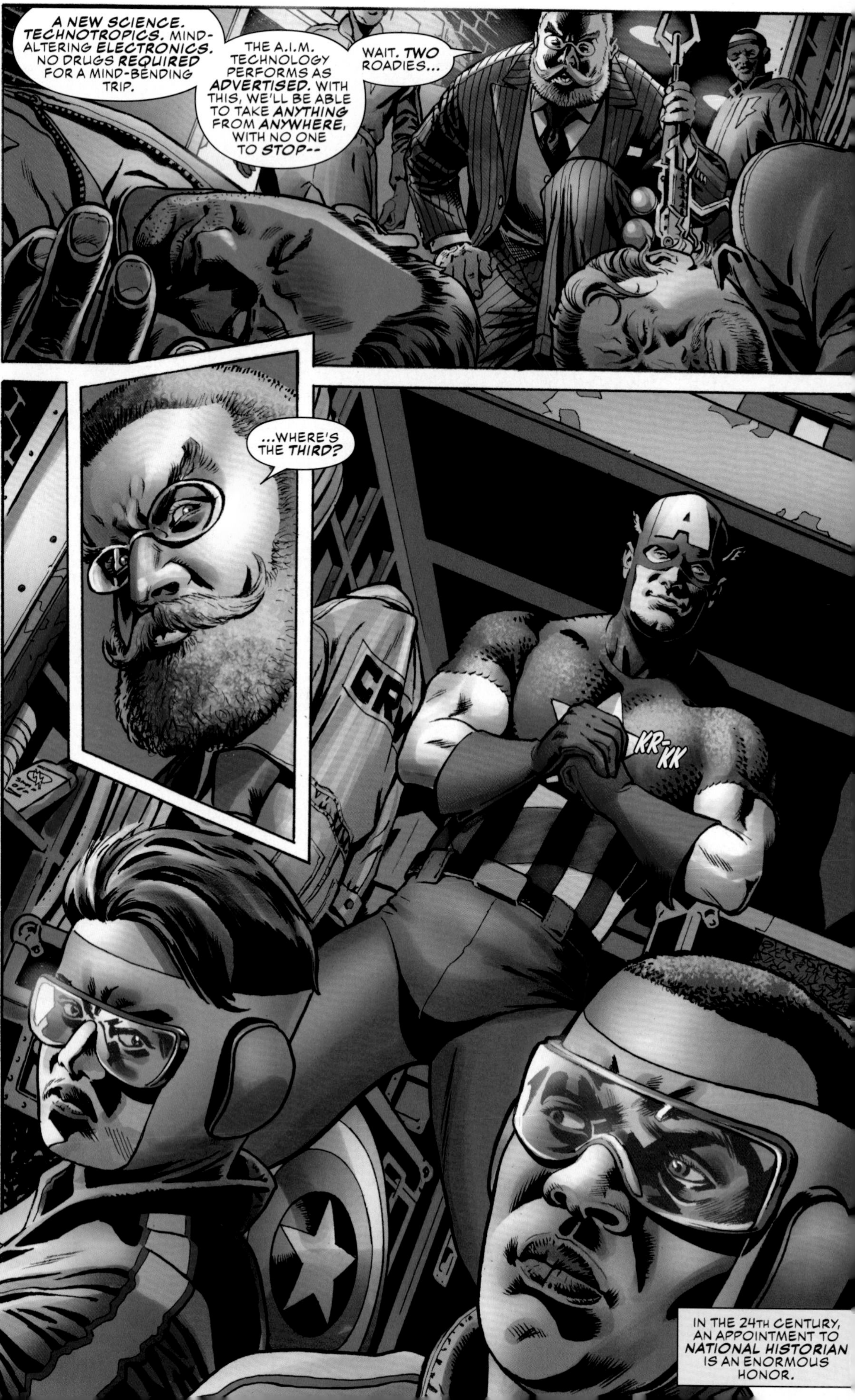

A NEW SCIENCE. TECHNOTROPICS. MIND-ALTERING ELECTRONICS. NO DRUGS REQUIRED FOR A MIND-BENDING TRIP.
THE A.I.M. TECHNOLOGY PERFORMS AS ADVERTISED. WITH THIS, WE'LL BE ABLE TO TAKE ANYTHING FROM ANYWHERE, WITH NO ONE TO STOP--
WAIT. TWO ROADIES...
...WHERE'S THE THIRD?
KR-KK
IN THE 24TH CENTURY, AN APPOINTMENT TO NATIONAL HISTORIAN IS AN ENORMOUS HONOR.

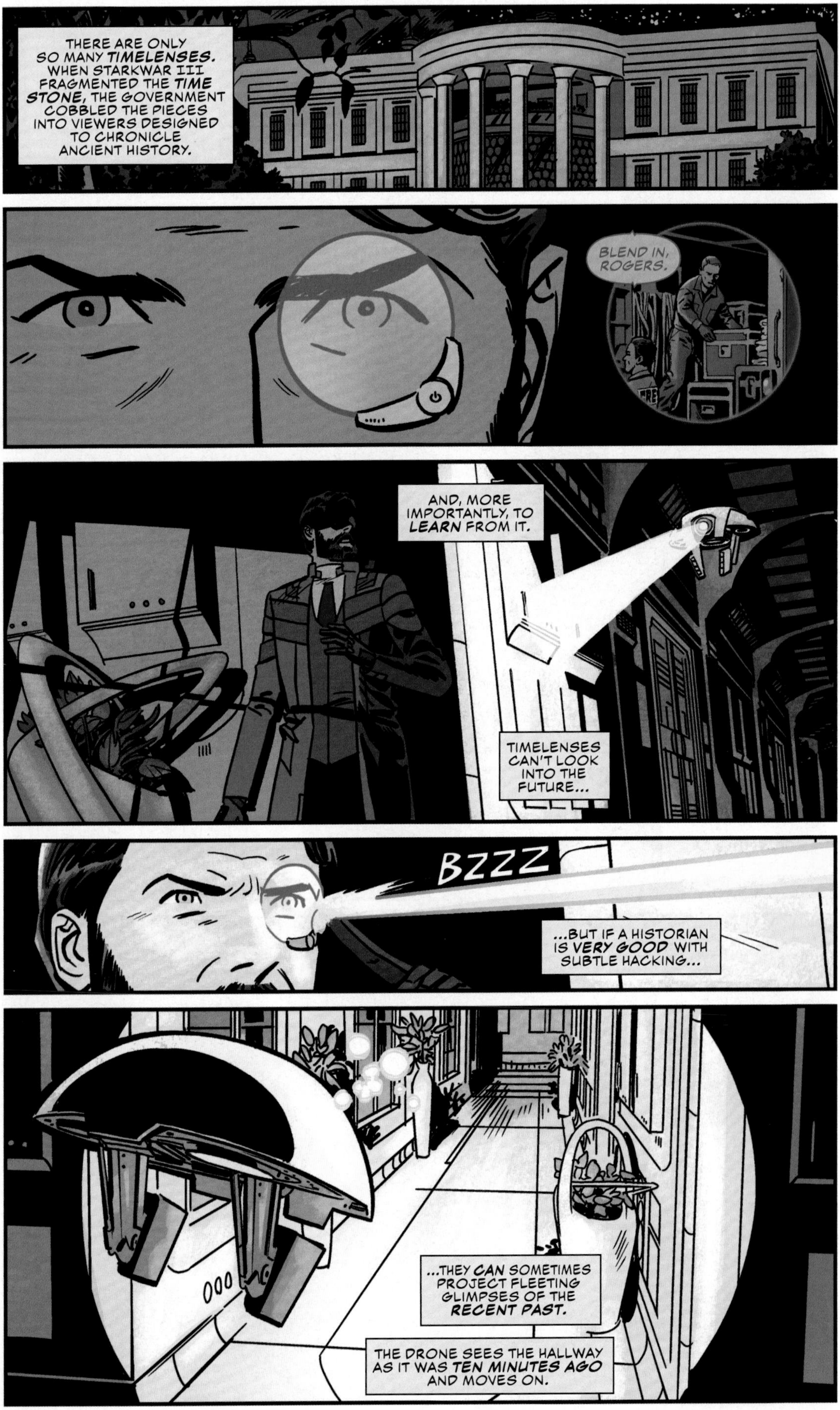

THERE ARE ONLY SO MANY TIMELENSES. WHEN STARKWAR III FRAGMENTED THE TIME STONE, THE GOVERNMENT COBBLED THE PIECES INTO VIEWERS DESIGNED TO CHRONICLE ANCIENT HISTORY.
BLEND IN, ROGERS.
AND, MORE IMPORTANTLY, TO LEARN FROM IT.
TIMELENSES CAN'T LOOK INTO THE FUTURE...
BZZZ
...BUT IF A HISTORIAN IS VERY GOOD WITH SUBTLE HACKING...
...THEY CAN SOMETIMES PROJECT FLEETING GLIMPSES OF THE RECENT PAST.
THE DRONE SEES THE HALLWAY AS IT WAS TEN MINUTES AGO AND MOVES ON.

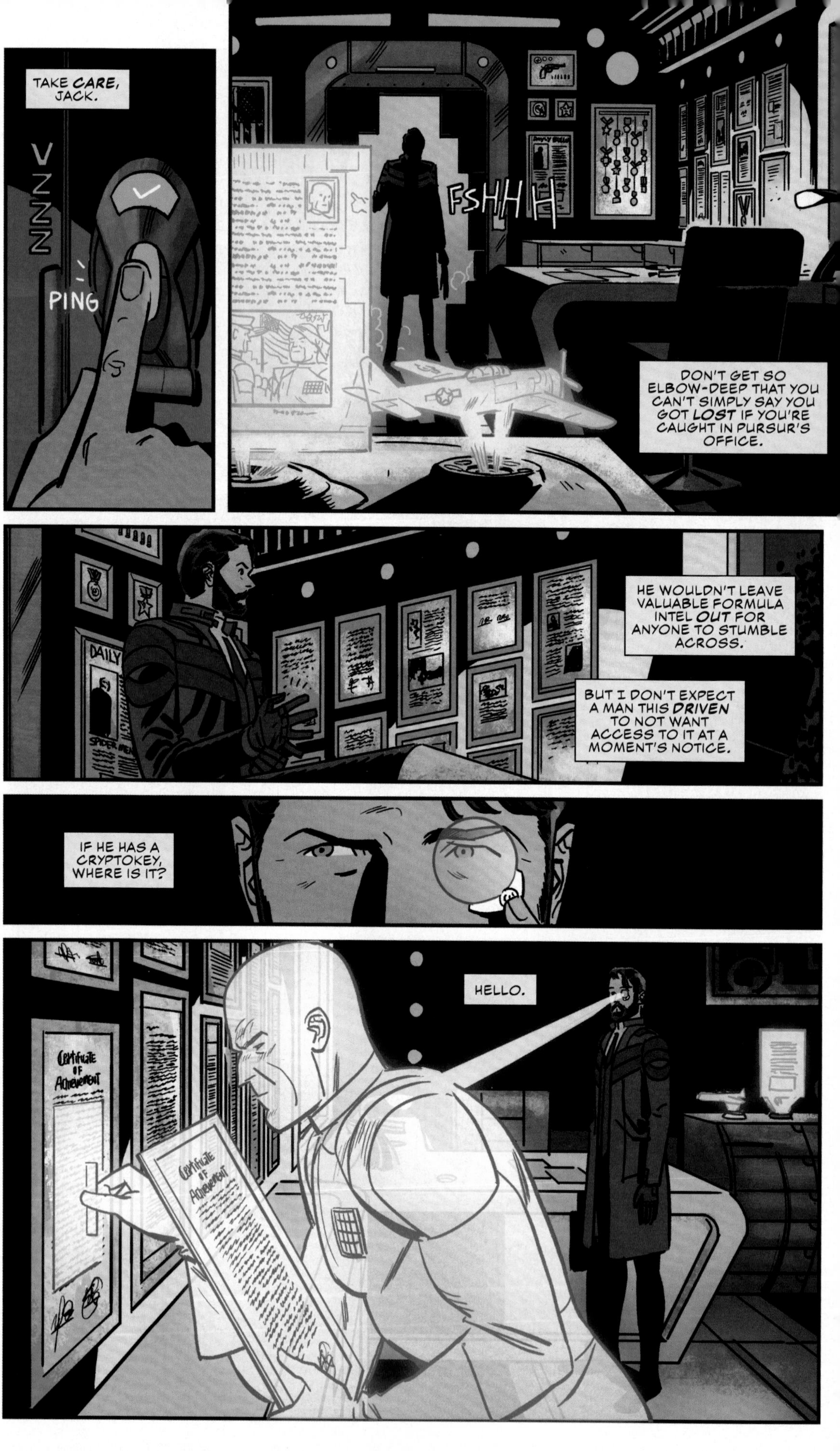

TAKE CARE, JACK.
VZZZ
PING
FSHHH
DON'T GET SO ELBOW-DEEP THAT YOU CAN'T SIMPLY SAY YOU GOT LOST IF YOU'RE CAUGHT IN PURSUR'S OFFICE.
HE WOULDN'T LEAVE VALUABLE FORMULA INTEL OUT FOR ANYONE TO STUMBLE ACROSS.
BUT I DON'T EXPECT A MAN THIS DRIVEN TO NOT WANT ACCESS TO IT AT A MOMENT'S NOTICE.
IF HE HAS A CRYPTOKEY, WHERE IS IT?
HELLO.
Certificate of Achievement
Certificate of Achievement

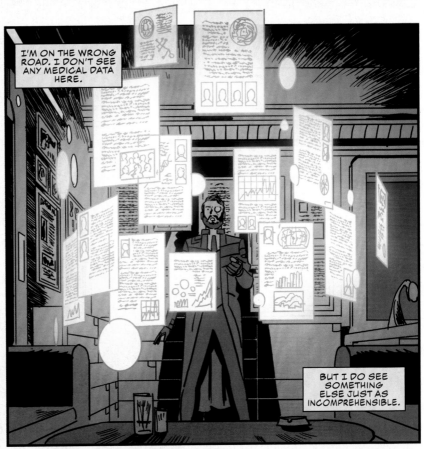

I'M ON THE WRONG ROAD. I DON'T SEE ANY MEDICAL DATA HERE.

BUT I DO SEE SOMETHING ELSE JUST AS INCOMPREHENSIBLE.

RECORDS IN THE *KREE* LANGUAGE.

I DON'T GET IT. PURSUR IS SO PARANOID ABOUT THE FORMULA FINDING ITS WAY *OFF-WORLD.* WHAT'S THE *CONNECTION* HERE TO AN *ALIEN RACE?*

I STUDIED KREE IN OVERSCHOOL. I'M NOT A *LINGUIST,* BUT I CAN IMMEDIATELY MAKE OUT THE WORDS *"OPERATION STARMARCH."* SOME SORT OF...

...

NO. NOT "SOME SORT OF." A PLAN.

THE *TRUTH* BEHIND THE *FORMULA.*

NO.

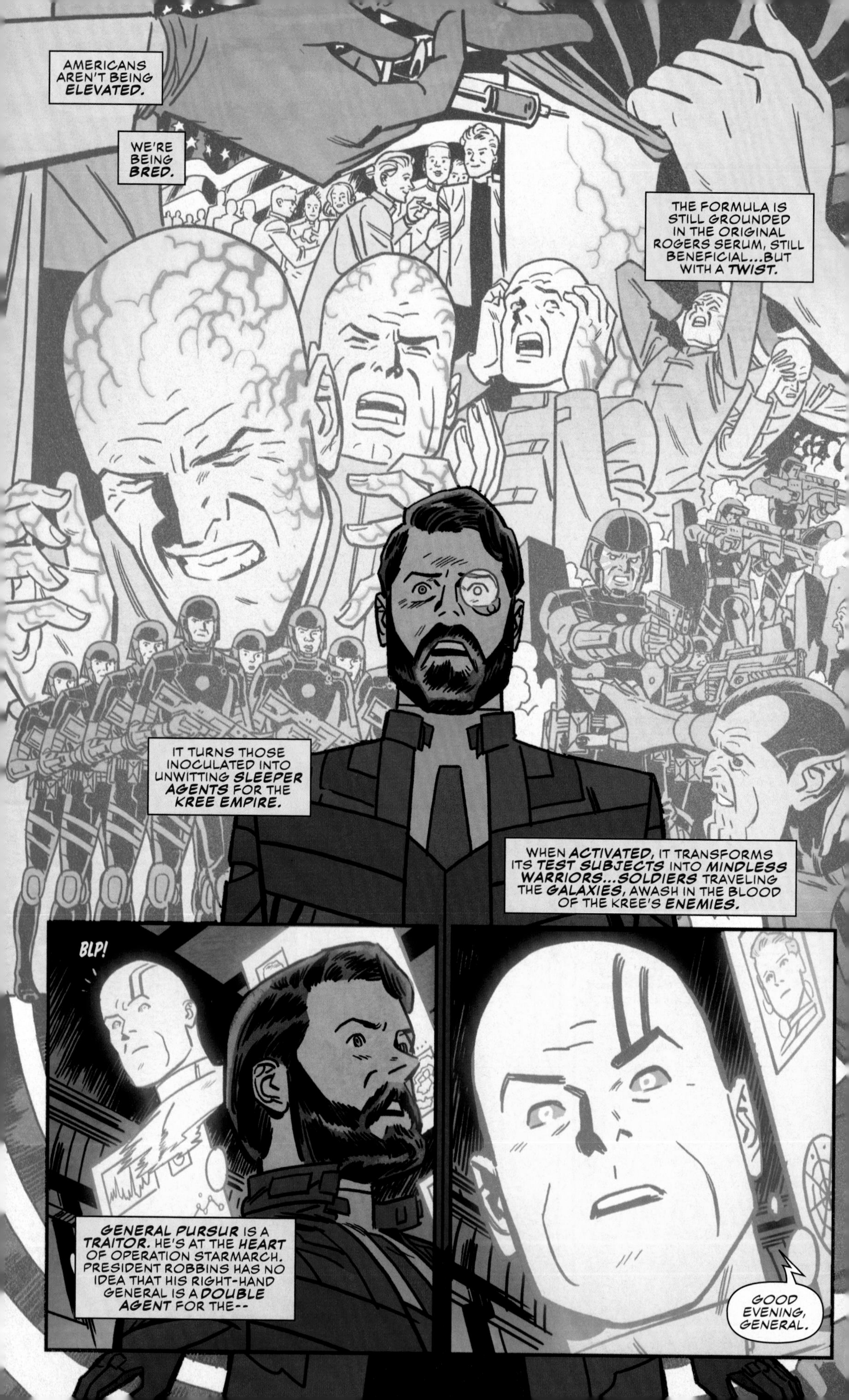
AMERICANS AREN'T BEING ELEVATED.
WE'RE BEING BRED.
THE FORMULA IS STILL GROUNDED IN THE ORIGINAL ROGERS SERUM, STILL BENEFICIAL...BUT WITH A TWIST.
IT TURNS THOSE INOCULATED INTO UNWITTING SLEEPER AGENTS FOR THE KREE EMPIRE.
WHEN ACTIVATED, IT TRANSFORMS ITS TEST SUBJECTS INTO MINDLESS WARRIORS...SOLDIERS TRAVELING THE GALAXIES, AWASH IN THE BLOOD OF THE KREE'S ENEMIES.
BLP!
GENERAL PURSUR IS A TRAITOR. HE'S AT THE HEART OF OPERATION STARMARCH. PRESIDENT ROBBINS HAS NO IDEA THAT HIS RIGHT-HAND GENERAL IS A DOUBLE AGENT FOR THE--
GOOD EVENING, GENERAL.

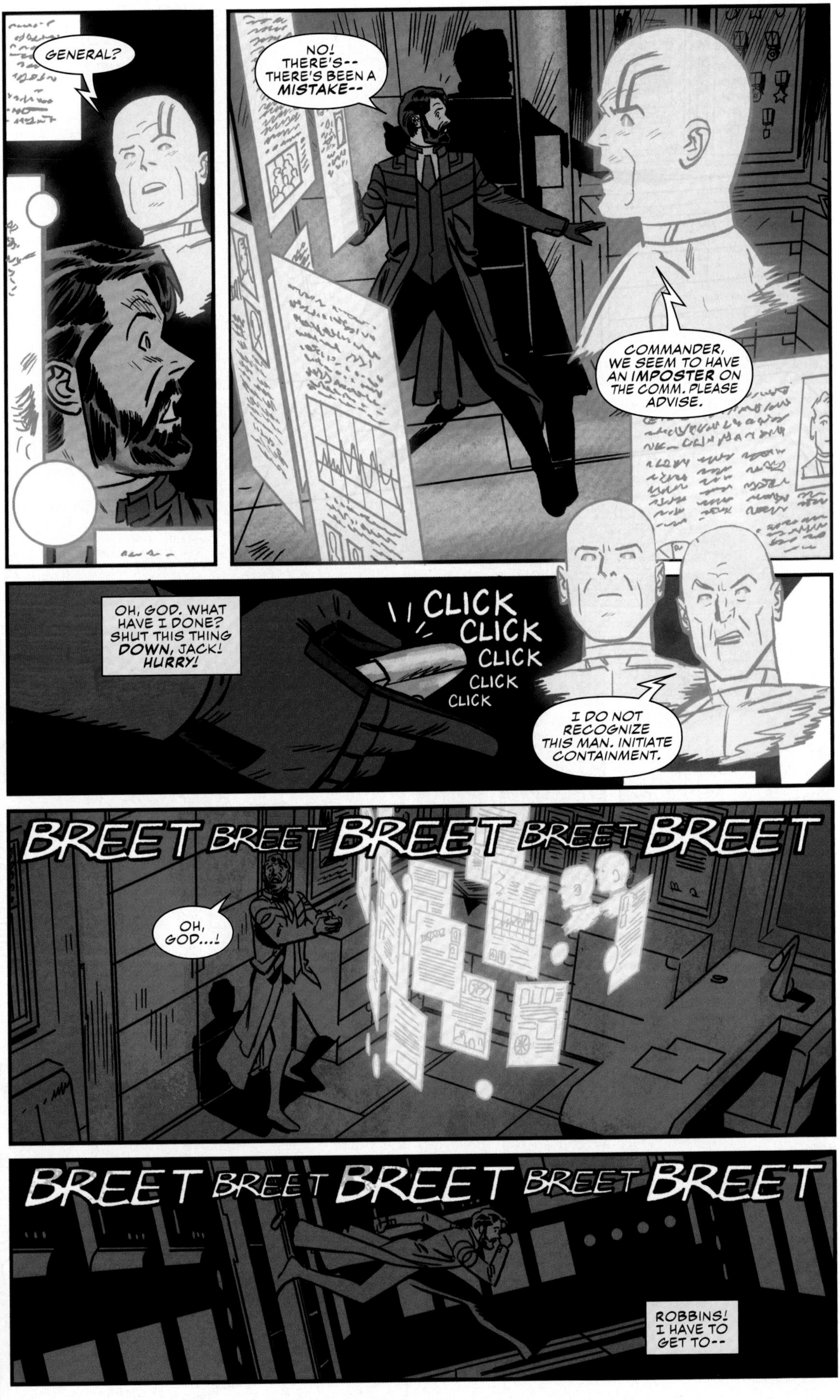
GENERAL?
NO! THERE'S-- THERE'S BEEN A MISTAKE--
COMMANDER, WE SEEM TO HAVE AN IMPOSTER ON THE COMM. PLEASE ADVISE.
OH, GOD. WHAT HAVE I DONE? SHUT THIS THING DOWN, JACK! HURRY!
CLICK CLICK CLICK CLICK CLICK
I DO NOT RECOGNIZE THIS MAN. INITIATE CONTAINMENT.
BREET BREET BREET BREET BREET
OH, GOD...!
BREET BREET BREET BREET BREET
ROBBINS! I HAVE TO GET TO--

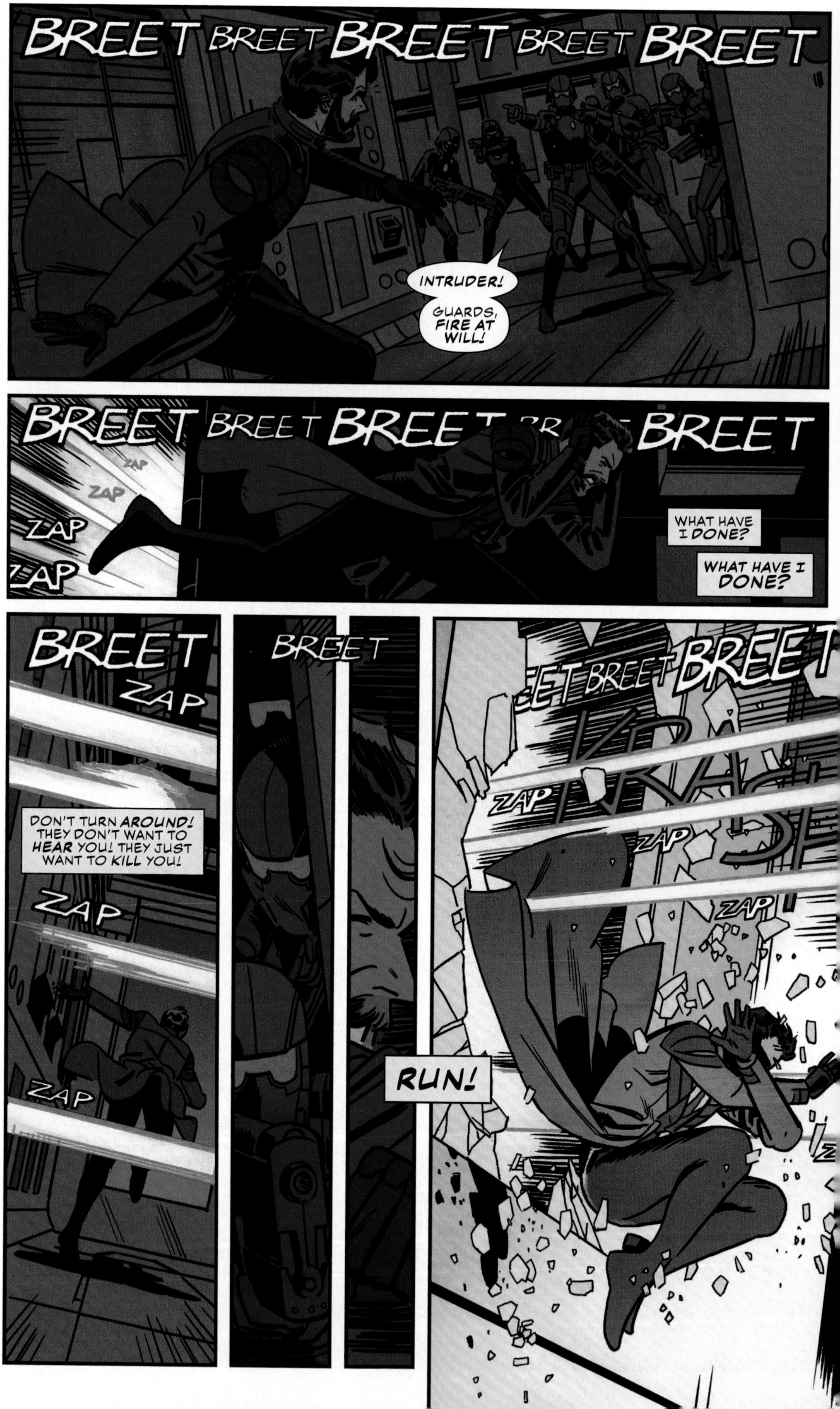
BREET breet BREET breet BREET
INTRUDER!
GUARDS, FIRE AT WILL!
BREET BREET BREET BREET
ZAP
ZAP
ZAP
ZAP
WHAT HAVE I DONE?
WHAT HAVE I DONE?
BREET
ZAP
DON'T TURN AROUND! THEY DON'T WANT TO HEAR YOU! THEY JUST WANT TO KILL YOU!
ZAP
ZAP
BREET
BREET BREET
ZAP
ZAP
ZAP
RUN!

YOU *IDIOT.*

YOUR SON *NEEDS* YOU, AND NOW--

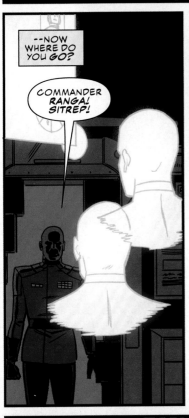

--NOW WHERE DO YOU *GO?*

COMMANDER *RANGA!* SITREP!

GENERAL *PURSUR* WILL *KNOW* YOU WERE IN HIS *OFFICE.*

HE'LL *KNOW* WHAT YOU'VE *LEARNED.*

AND HE'LL STOP AT *NOTHING* TO KEEP YOU *SILENT.*

ATTENTION, ALL PEACEKEEPERS WITHIN RANGE OF THIS MESSAGE!

THE WHITE HOUSE HAS BEEN *ATTACKED* BY A *TERRORIST SPY,* IDENTIFICATION *JACKSON ROGERS,* CITIZEN GF-35667!

"FIND HIM. *MUZZLE* HIM.

"AND *BRING HIM TO ME.*"

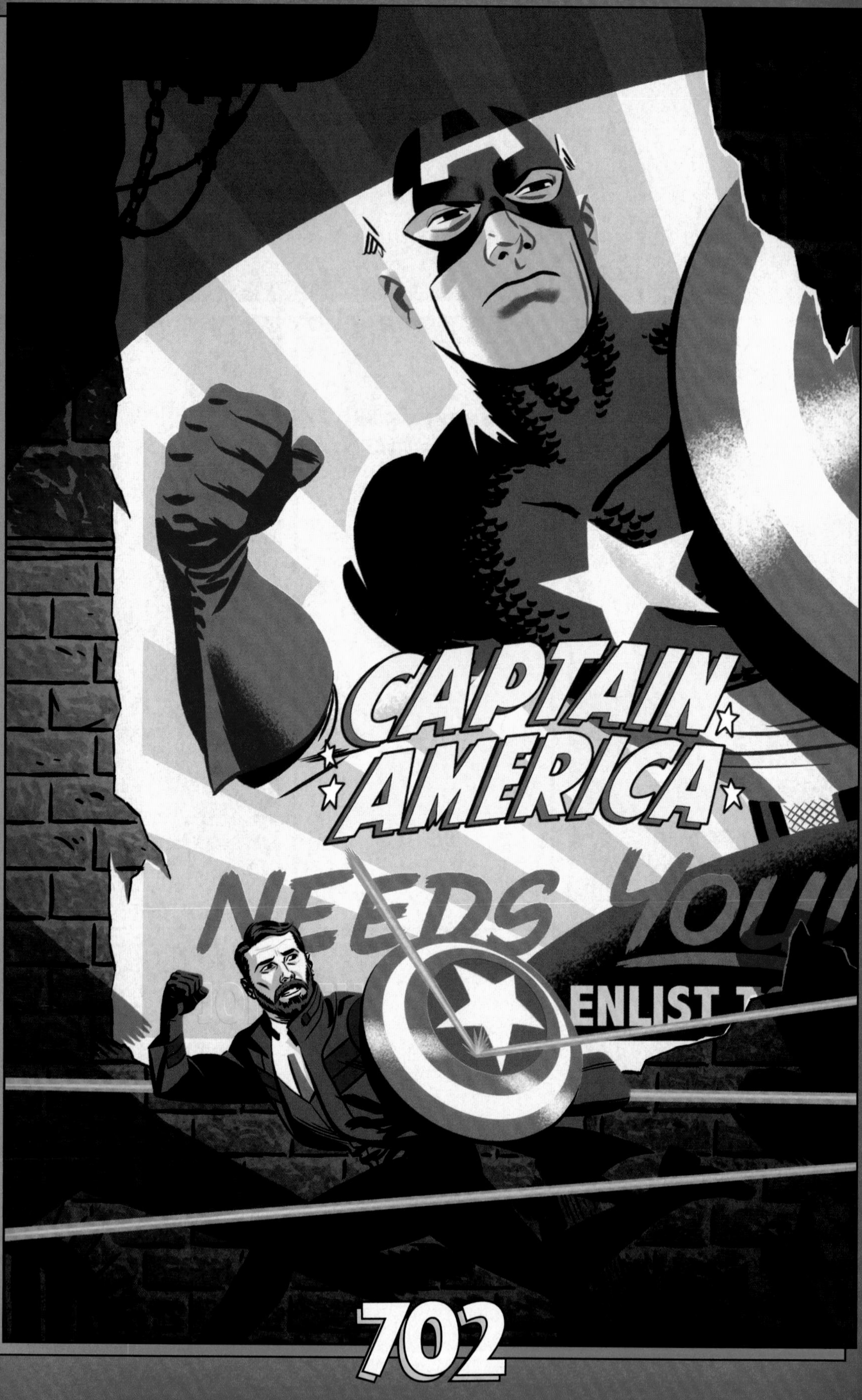
CAPTAIN AMERICA
NEEDS YOU
ENLIST
702

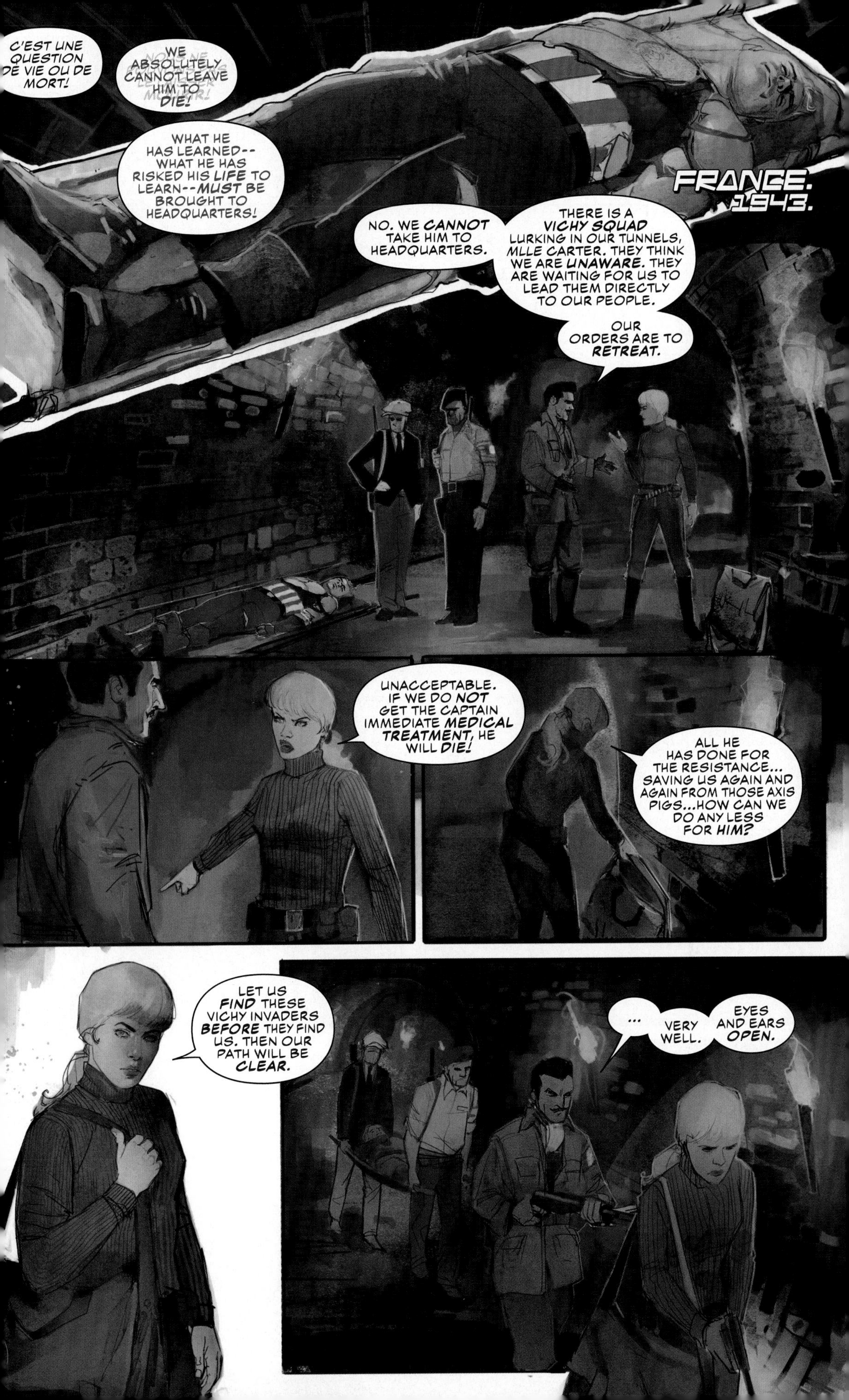

C'EST UNE QUESTION DE VIE OU DE MORT!
WE ABSOLUTELY CANNOT LEAVE HIM TO DIE!
WHAT HE HAS LEARNED--WHAT HE HAS RISKED HIS LIFE TO LEARN--MUST BE BROUGHT TO HEADQUARTERS!
FRANCE. 1943.
NO. WE CANNOT TAKE HIM TO HEADQUARTERS.
THERE IS A VICHY SQUAD LURKING IN OUR TUNNELS, MLLE CARTER. THEY THINK WE ARE UNAWARE. THEY ARE WAITING FOR US TO LEAD THEM DIRECTLY TO OUR PEOPLE.
OUR ORDERS ARE TO RETREAT.
UNACCEPTABLE. IF WE DO NOT GET THE CAPTAIN IMMEDIATE MEDICAL TREATMENT, HE WILL DIE!
ALL HE HAS DONE FOR THE RESISTANCE... SAVING US AGAIN AND AGAIN FROM THOSE AXIS PIGS...HOW CAN WE DO ANY LESS FOR HIM?
LET US FIND THESE VICHY INVADERS BEFORE THEY FIND US. THEN OUR PATH WILL BE CLEAR.
...
VERY WELL.
EYES AND EARS OPEN.

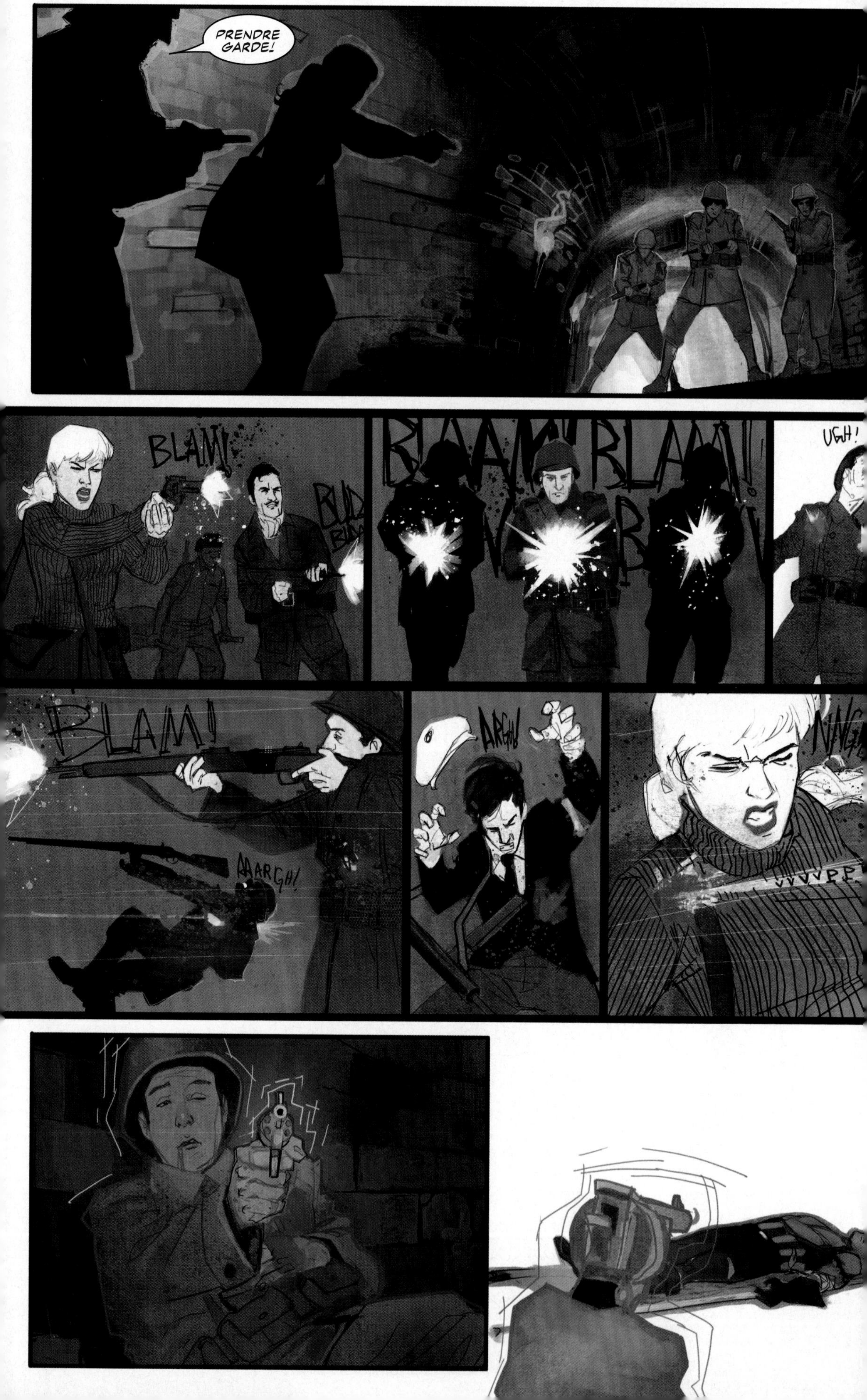
PRENDRE GARDE!
BLAM!
BLAAM! BLAAM!
UGH!
BLAM!
AAARGH!
ARGH!

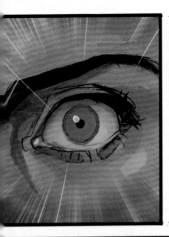

SP-TANNG!

BLED OUT. WE'RE CLEAR.

GET THE CAPTAIN TO SAFETY! GO!

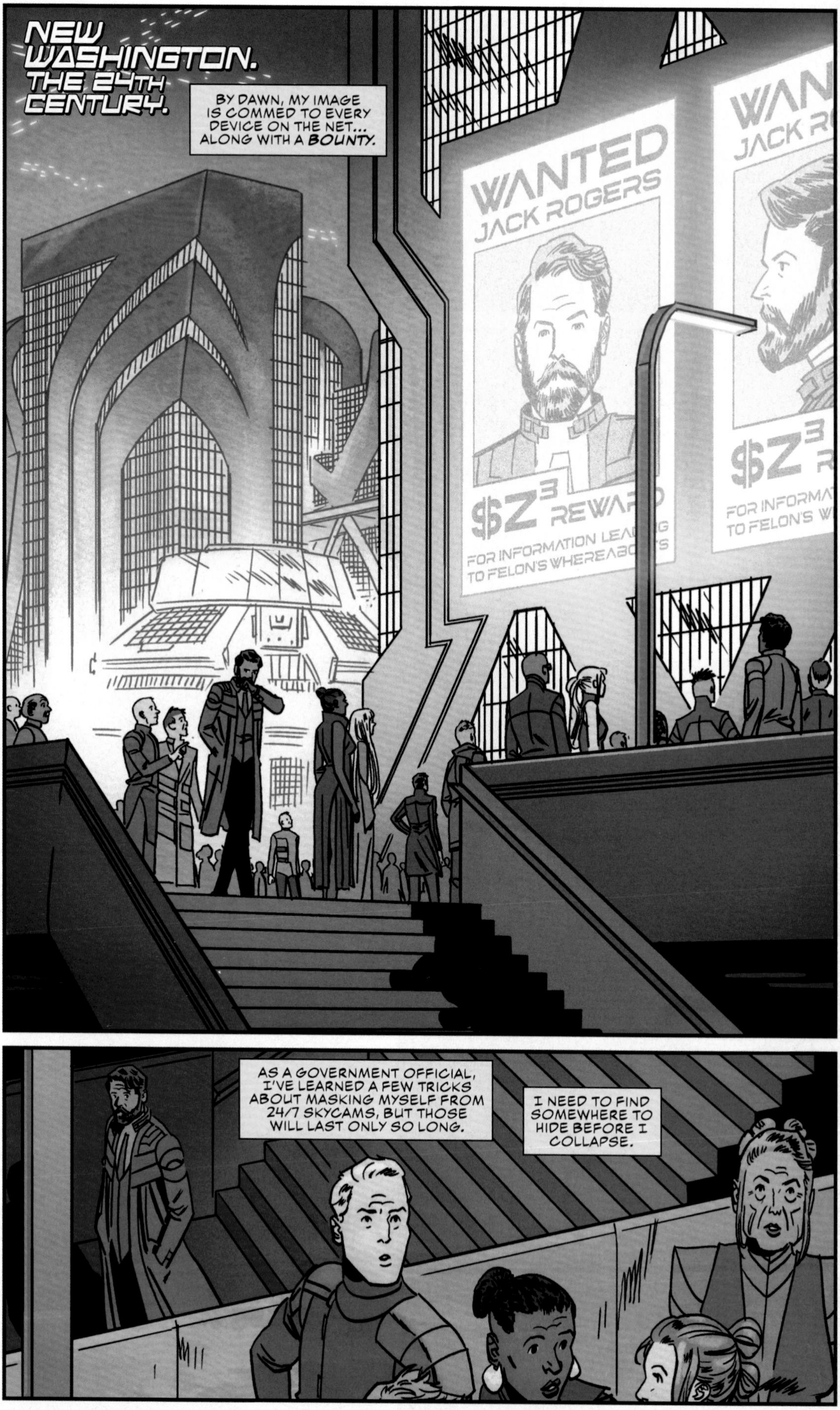
NEW WASHINGTON. THE 24TH CENTURY.
BY DAWN, MY IMAGE IS COMMED TO EVERY DEVICE ON THE NET... ALONG WITH A BOUNTY.
WANTED
JACK ROGERS
FOR INFORMATION
TO FELON'S WHEREABOUTS
AS A GOVERNMENT OFFICIAL, I'VE LEARNED A FEW TRICKS ABOUT MASKING MYSELF FROM 24/7 SKYCAMS, BUT THOSE WILL LAST ONLY SO LONG.
I NEED TO FIND SOMEWHERE TO HIDE BEFORE I COLLAPSE.

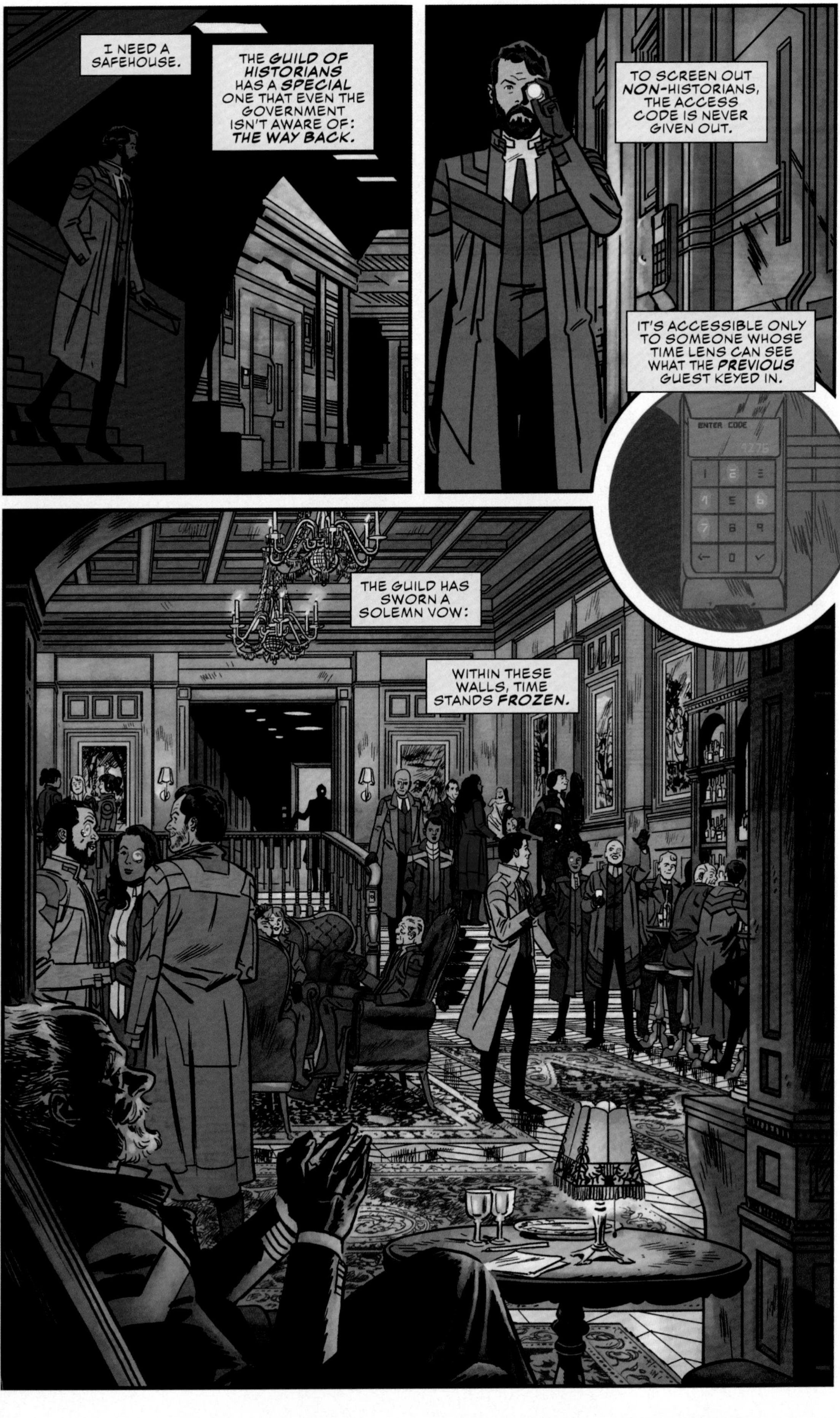
I NEED A SAFEHOUSE.
THE GUILD OF HISTORIANS HAS A SPECIAL ONE THAT EVEN THE GOVERNMENT ISN'T AWARE OF: THE WAY BACK.
TO SCREEN OUT NON-HISTORIANS, THE ACCESS CODE IS NEVER GIVEN OUT.
IT'S ACCESSIBLE ONLY TO SOMEONE WHOSE TIME LENS CAN SEE WHAT THE PREVIOUS GUEST KEYED IN.
ENTER CODE
THE GUILD HAS SWORN A SOLEMN VOW:
WITHIN THESE WALLS, TIME STANDS FROZEN.

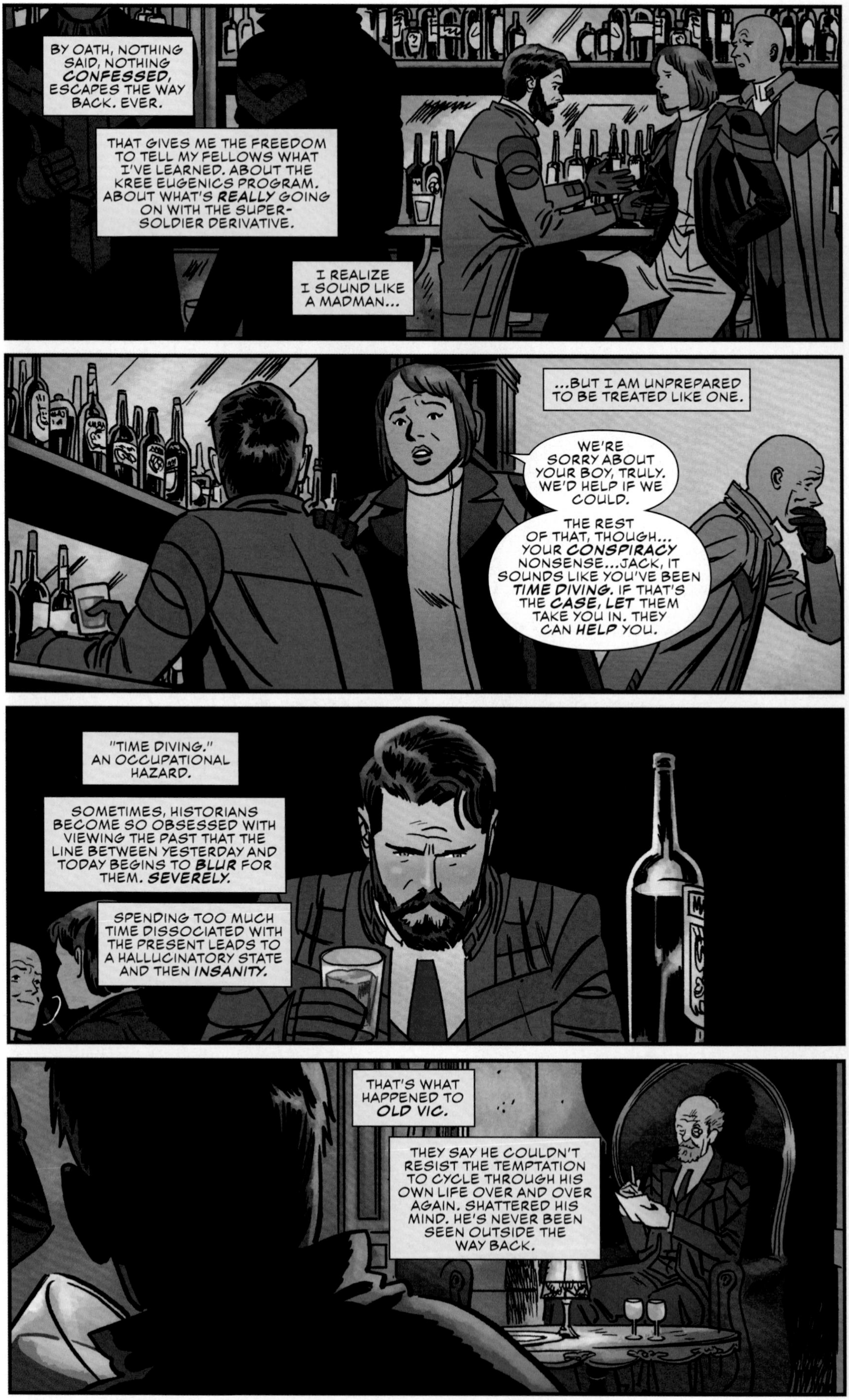
BY OATH, NOTHING SAID, NOTHING CONFESSED, ESCAPES THE WAY BACK. EVER.
THAT GIVES ME THE FREEDOM TO TELL MY FELLOWS WHAT I'VE LEARNED. ABOUT THE KREE EUGENICS PROGRAM. ABOUT WHAT'S REALLY GOING ON WITH THE SUPER-SOLDIER DERIVATIVE.
I REALIZE I SOUND LIKE A MADMAN...
...BUT I AM UNPREPARED TO BE TREATED LIKE ONE.
WE'RE SORRY ABOUT YOUR BOY, TRULY. WE'D HELP IF WE COULD.
THE REST OF THAT, THOUGH... YOUR CONSPIRACY NONSENSE...JACK, IT SOUNDS LIKE YOU'VE BEEN TIME DIVING. IF THAT'S THE CASE, LET THEM TAKE YOU IN. THEY CAN HELP YOU.
"TIME DIVING." AN OCCUPATIONAL HAZARD.
SOMETIMES, HISTORIANS BECOME SO OBSESSED WITH VIEWING THE PAST THAT THE LINE BETWEEN YESTERDAY AND TODAY BEGINS TO BLUR FOR THEM. SEVERELY.
SPENDING TOO MUCH TIME DISSOCIATED WITH THE PRESENT LEADS TO A HALLUCINATORY STATE AND THEN INSANITY.
THAT'S WHAT HAPPENED TO OLD VIC.
THEY SAY HE COULDN'T RESIST THE TEMPTATION TO CYCLE THROUGH HIS OWN LIFE OVER AND OVER AGAIN. SHATTERED HIS MIND. HE'S NEVER BEEN SEEN OUTSIDE THE WAY BACK.

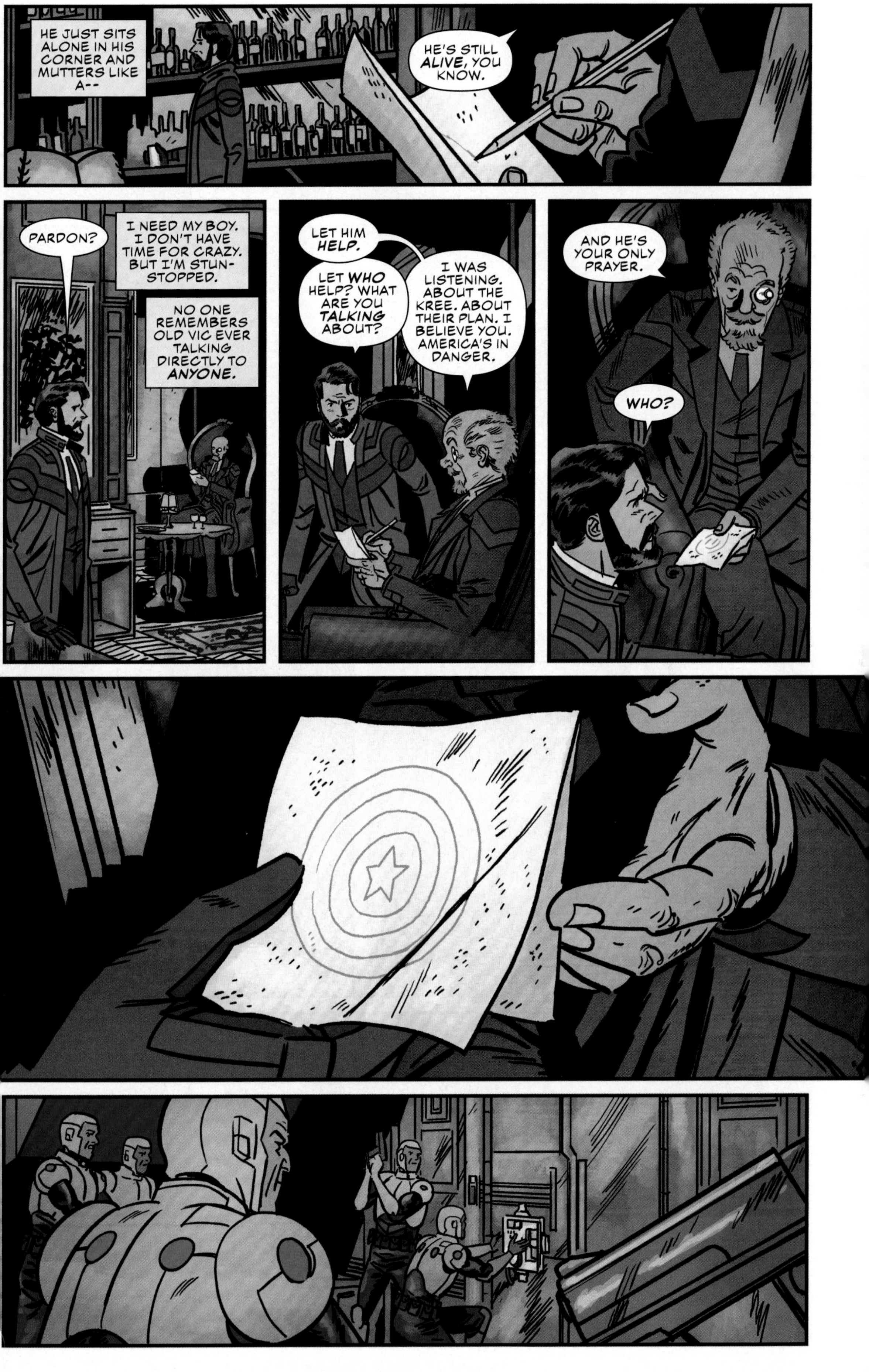
HE JUST SITS ALONE IN HIS CORNER AND MUTTERS LIKE A--
HE'S STILL ALIVE, YOU KNOW.
PARDON?
I NEED MY BOY. I DON'T HAVE TIME FOR CRAZY. BUT I'M STUN-STOPPED.
NO ONE REMEMBERS OLD VIC EVER TALKING DIRECTLY TO ANYONE.
LET HIM HELP.
LET WHO HELP? WHAT ARE YOU TALKING ABOUT?
I WAS LISTENING. ABOUT THE KREE. ABOUT THEIR PLAN. I BELIEVE YOU. AMERICA'S IN DANGER.
AND HE'S YOUR ONLY PRAYER.
WHO?

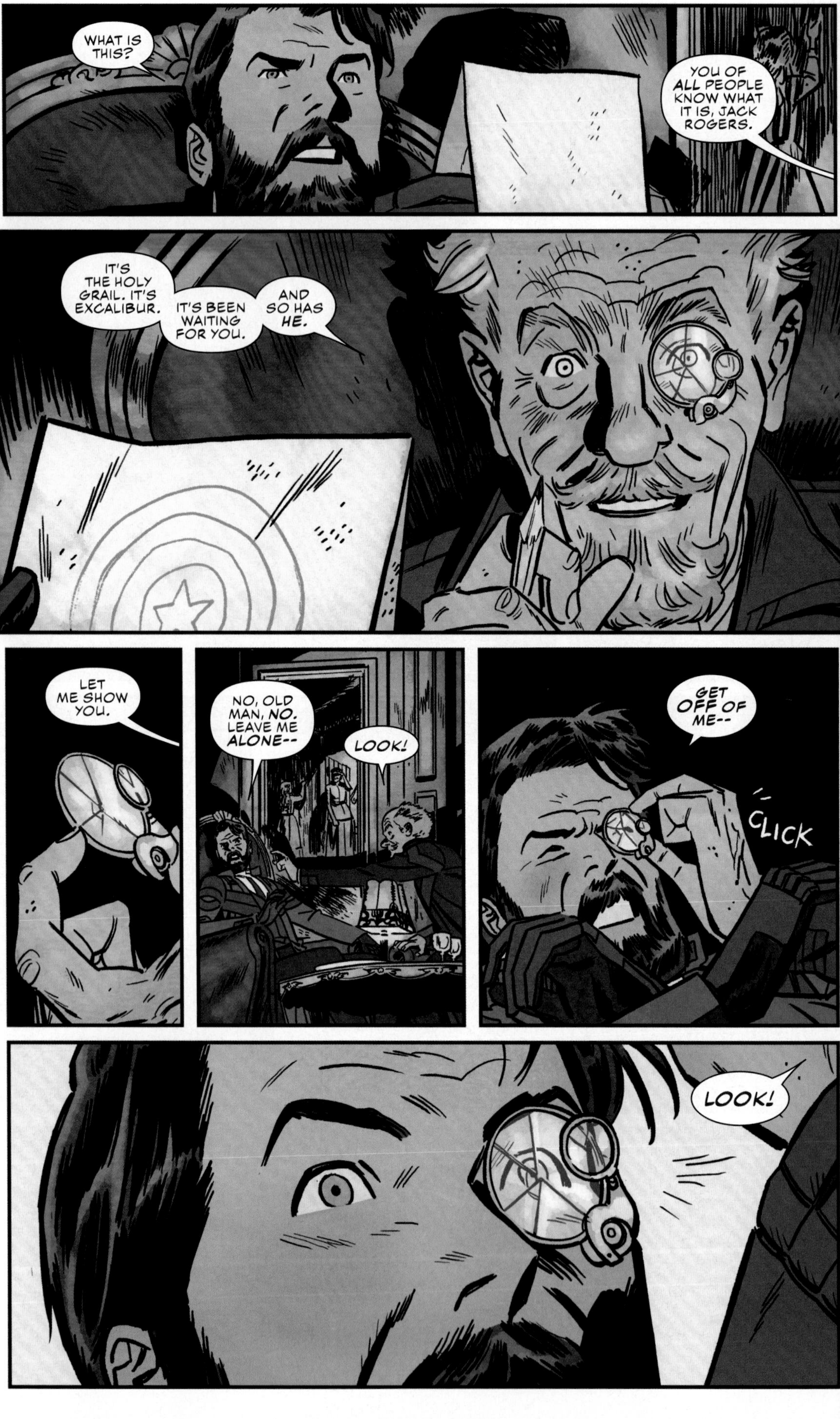
WHAT IS THIS?
YOU OF ALL PEOPLE KNOW WHAT IT IS, JACK ROGERS.
IT'S THE HOLY GRAIL. IT'S EXCALIBUR.
IT'S BEEN WAITING FOR YOU.
AND SO HAS HE.
LET ME SHOW YOU.
NO, OLD MAN, NO. LEAVE ME ALONE--
LOOK!
GET OFF OF ME--
CLICK
LOOK!

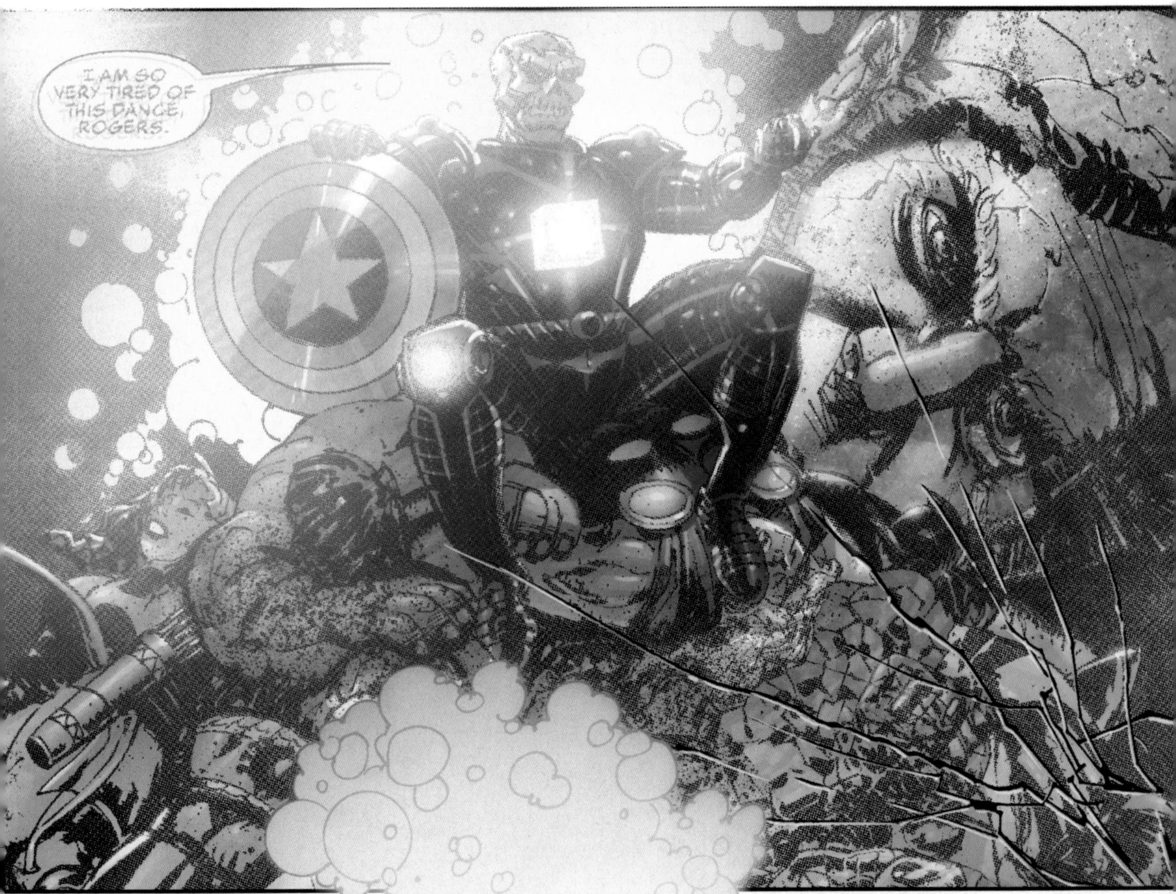
I AM SO VERY TIRED OF THIS DANCE, ROGERS.
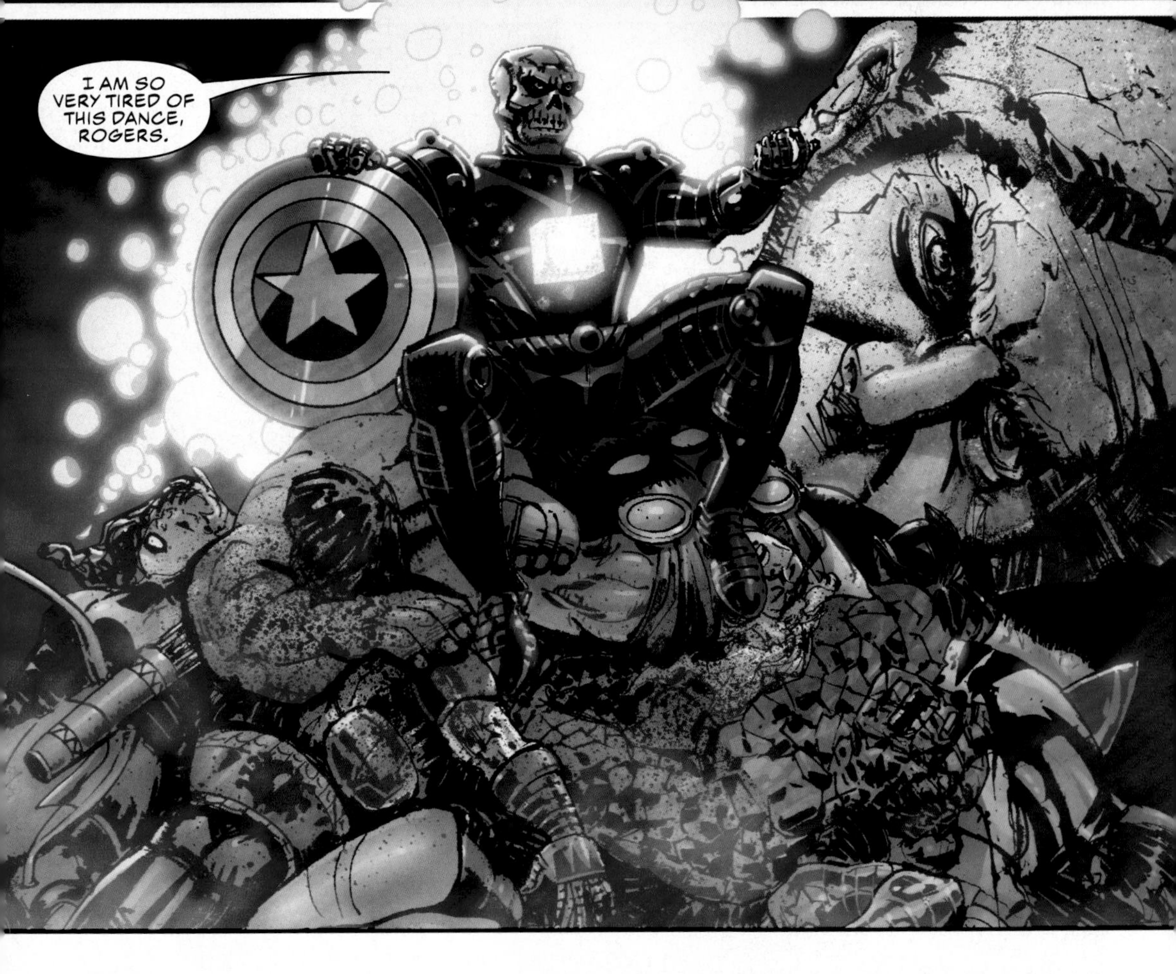
I AM SO VERY TIRED OF THIS DANCE, ROGERS.

THE TWO OF US, ENTWINED FOR OVER A *CENTURY*.

NEITHER OF US EVER IN CONTROL *LONG* ENOUGH TO *ELIMINATE* THE OTHER.

UNTIL NOW.

YOUR PEOPLE--YOUR NATION--ARE *MINE*, CAPTAIN! TRAPPED FOREVER WITHIN THE UNENDING HELL INSIDE MY COSMIC CUBE!

NOW THAT I CAN, AT *LAST*, BASK IN THE *LONG-OVERDUE* PLEASURE OF AWARDING YOU AND YOUR PITIFUL *WAR BANNER* THE SIGNIFICANCE YOU BOTH DESERVE.

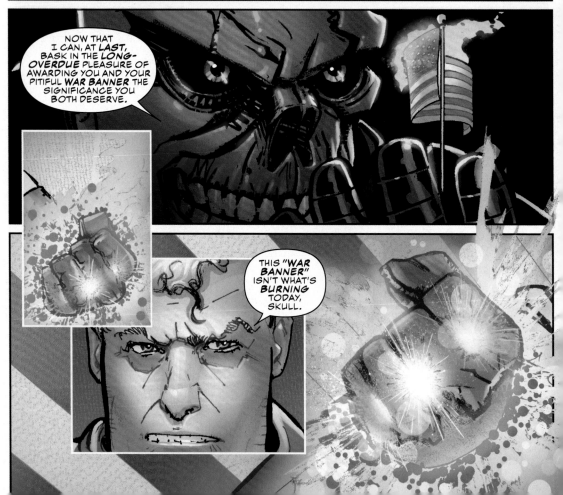

THIS "*WAR BANNER*" ISN'T WHAT'S *BURNING* TODAY, SKULL.

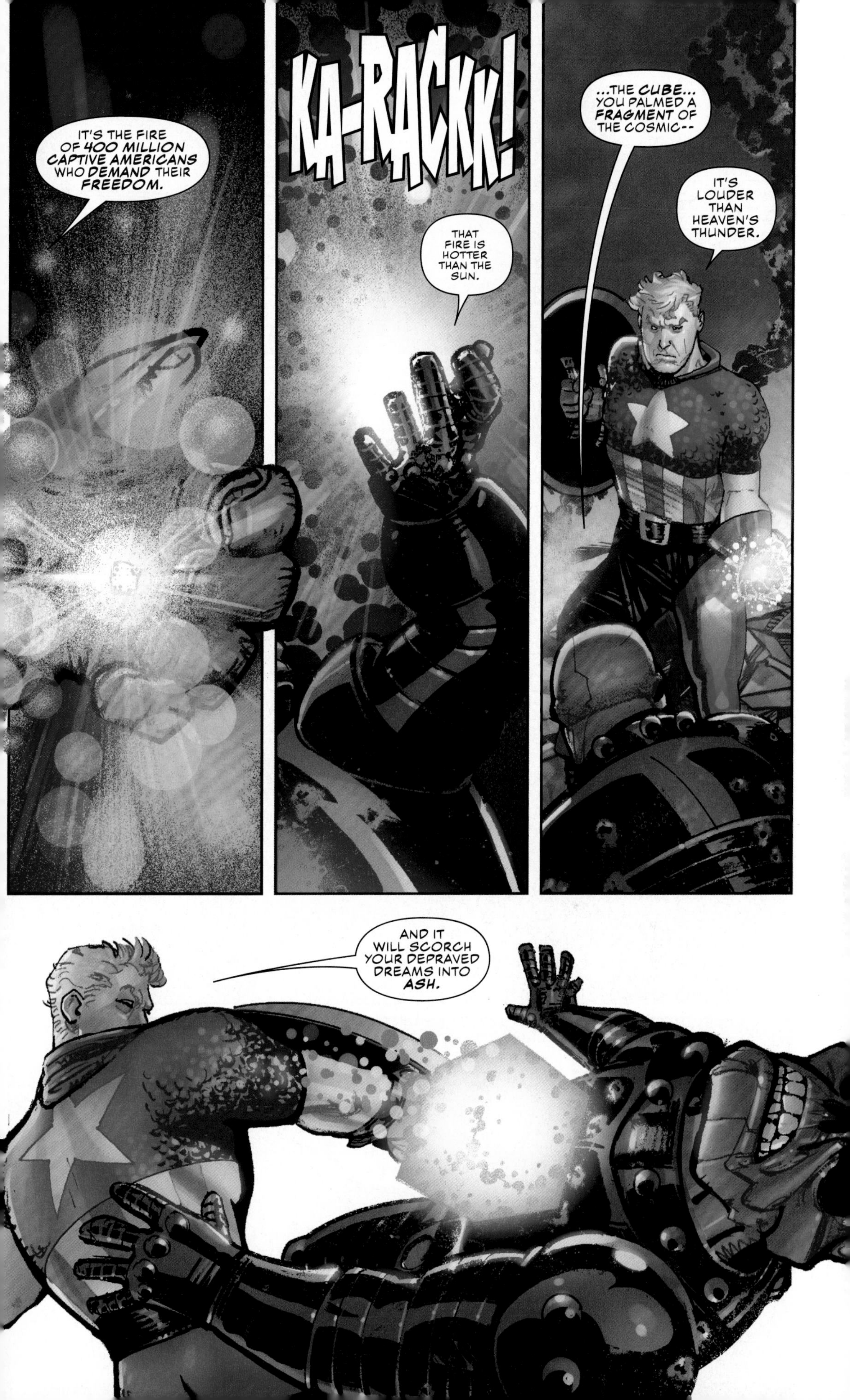
IT'S THE FIRE OF 400 MILLION CAPTIVE AMERICANS WHO DEMAND THEIR FREEDOM.
KA-RACKK!
THAT FIRE IS HOTTER THAN THE SUN.
...THE CUBE... YOU PALMED A FRAGMENT OF THE COSMIC--
IT'S LOUDER THAN HEAVEN'S THUNDER.
AND IT WILL SCORCH YOUR DEPRAVED DREAMS INTO ASH.

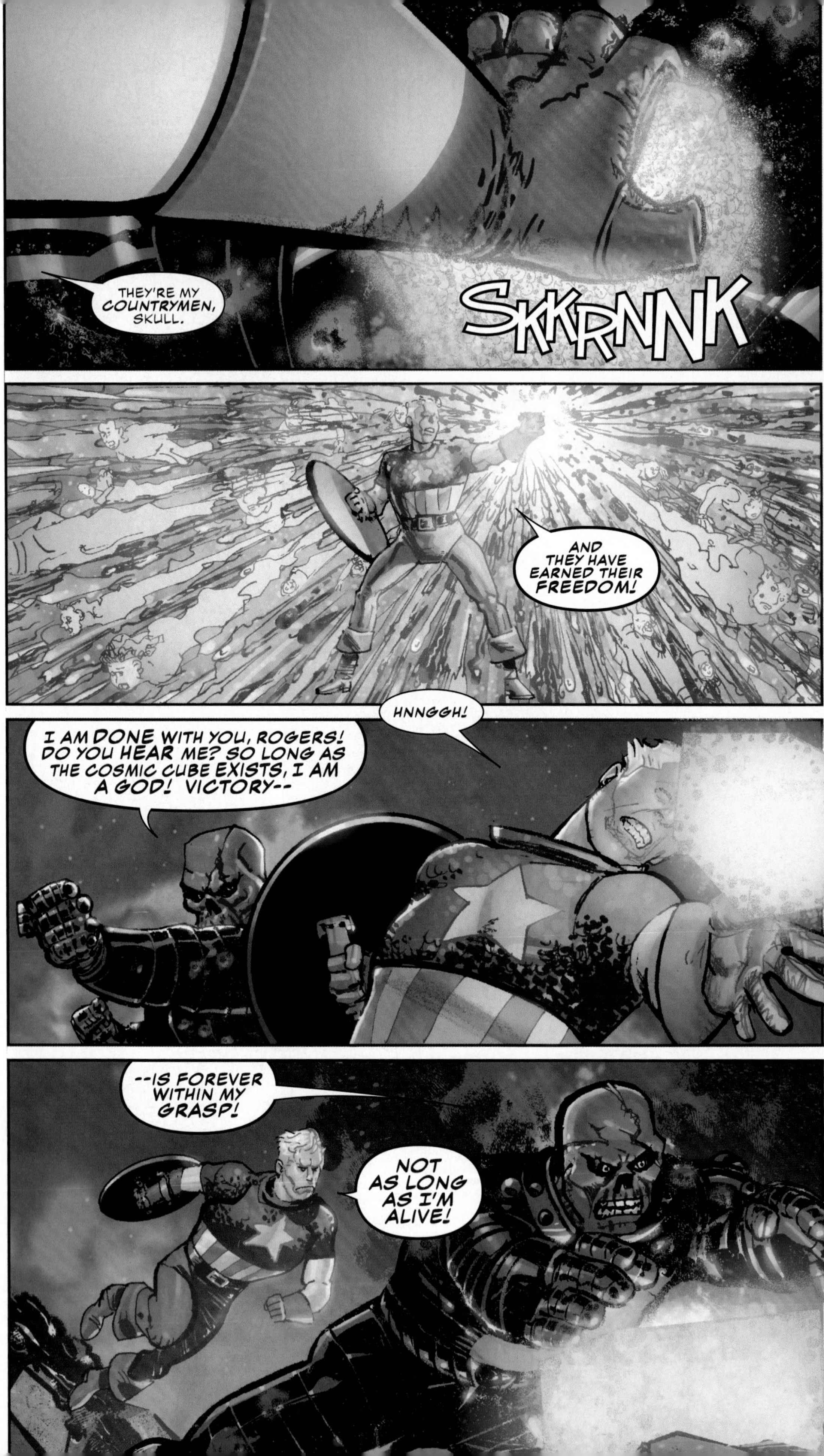
THEY'RE MY COUNTRYMEN, SKULL.
SKKRNNK
AND THEY HAVE EARNED THEIR FREEDOM!
HNNGGH!
I AM DONE WITH YOU, ROGERS! DO YOU HEAR ME? SO LONG AS THE COSMIC CUBE EXISTS, I AM A GOD! VICTORY--
--IS FOREVER WITHIN MY GRASP!
NOT AS LONG AS I'M ALIVE!

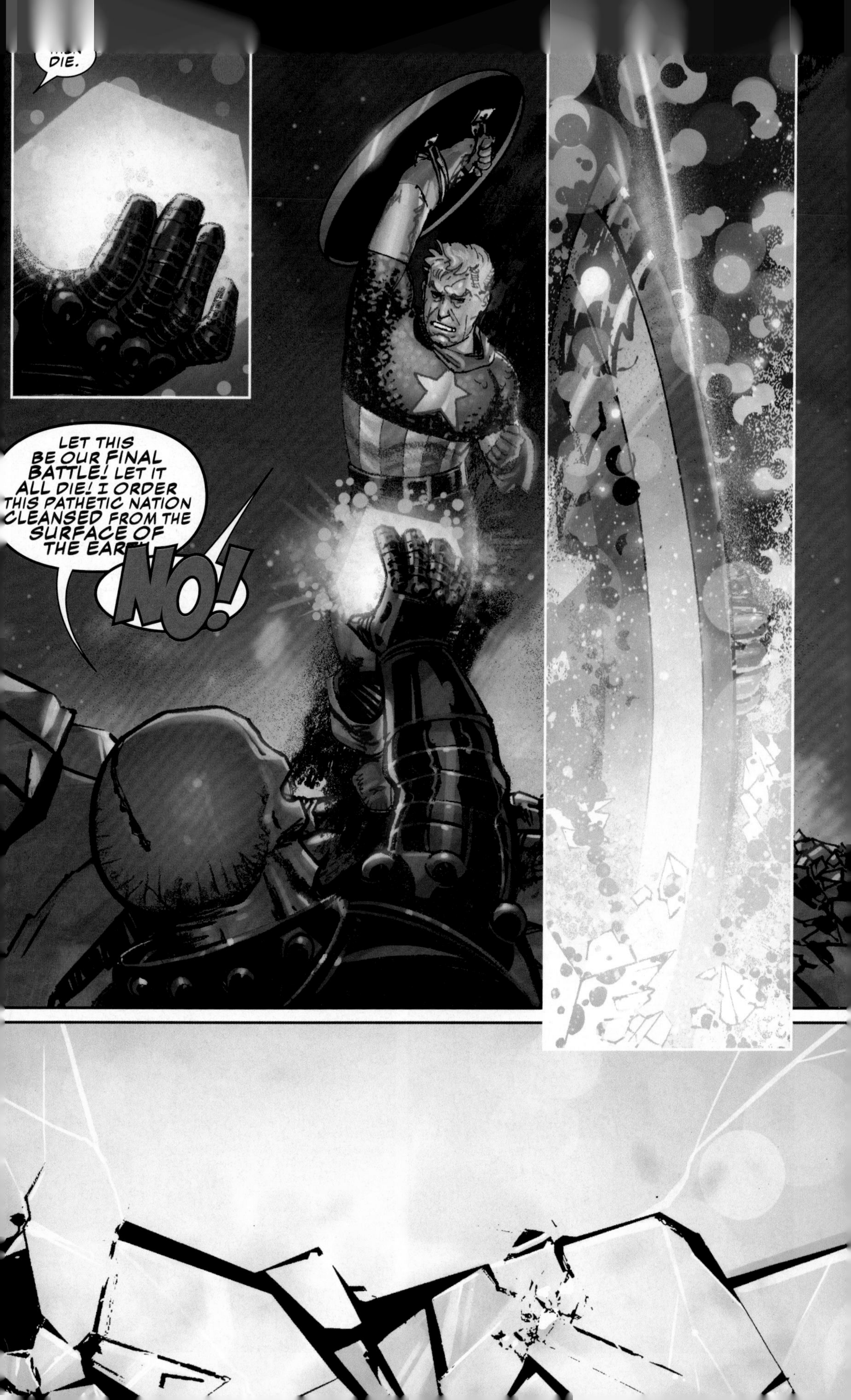
DIE.
LET THIS BE OUR FINAL BATTLE! LET IT ALL DIE! I ORDER THIS PATHETIC NATION CLEANSED FROM THE SURFACE OF THE EAR
NO!

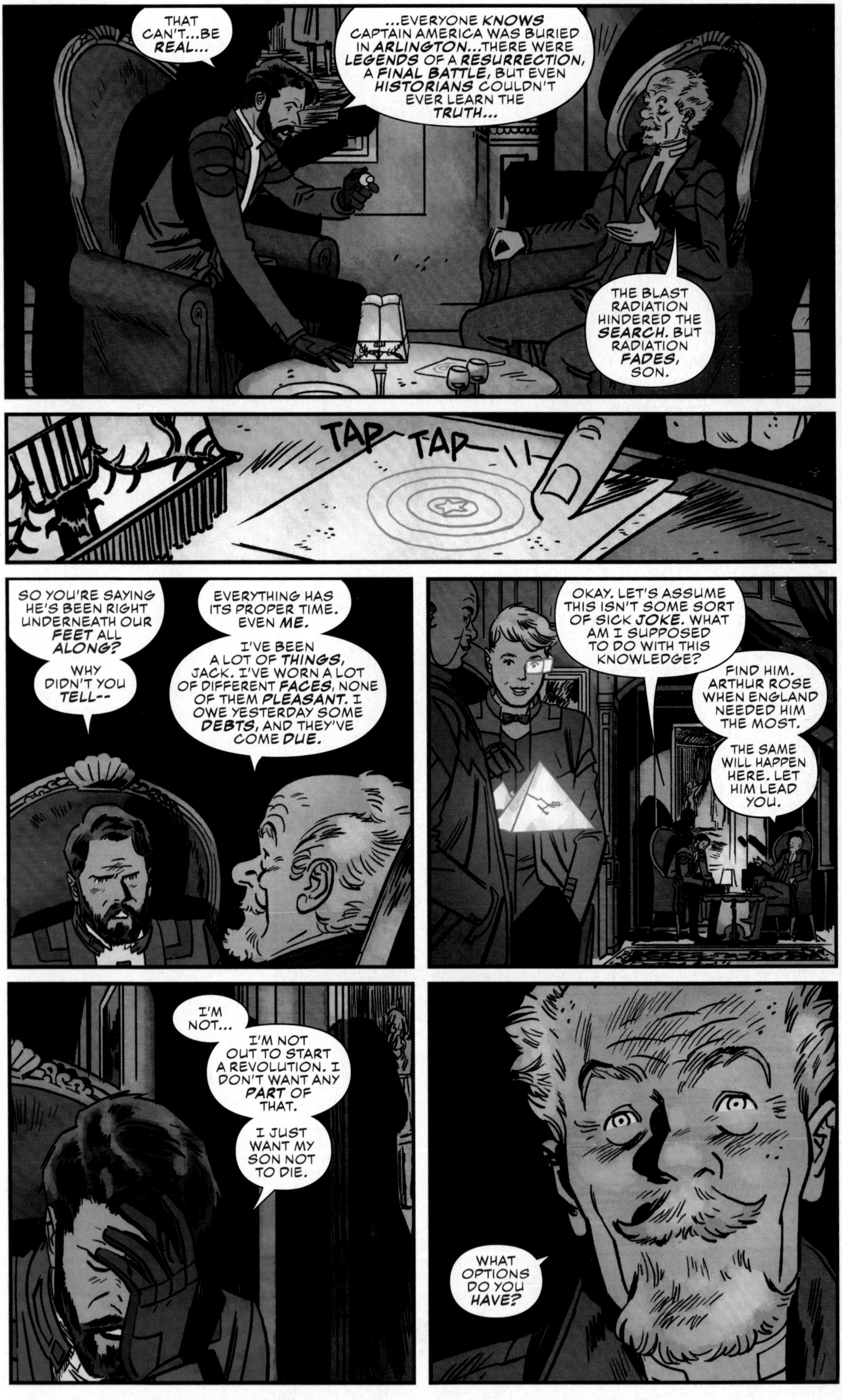
THAT CAN'T...BE REAL...
...EVERYONE KNOWS CAPTAIN AMERICA WAS BURIED IN ARLINGTON...THERE WERE LEGENDS OF A RESURRECTION, A FINAL BATTLE, BUT EVEN HISTORIANS COULDN'T EVER LEARN THE TRUTH...
THE BLAST RADIATION HINDERED THE SEARCH. BUT RADIATION FADES, SON.
TAP TAP
SO YOU'RE SAYING HE'S BEEN RIGHT UNDERNEATH OUR FEET ALL ALONG?
WHY DIDN'T YOU TELL--
EVERYTHING HAS ITS PROPER TIME. EVEN ME.
I'VE BEEN A LOT OF THINGS, JACK. I'VE WORN A LOT OF DIFFERENT FACES, NONE OF THEM PLEASANT. I OWE YESTERDAY SOME DEBTS, AND THEY'VE COME DUE.
OKAY. LET'S ASSUME THIS ISN'T SOME SORT OF SICK JOKE. WHAT AM I SUPPOSED TO DO WITH THIS KNOWLEDGE?
FIND HIM. ARTHUR ROSE WHEN ENGLAND NEEDED HIM THE MOST.
THE SAME WILL HAPPEN HERE. LET HIM LEAD YOU.
I'M NOT...
I'M NOT OUT TO START A REVOLUTION. I DON'T WANT ANY PART OF THAT.
I JUST WANT MY SON NOT TO DIE.
WHAT OPTIONS DO YOU HAVE?

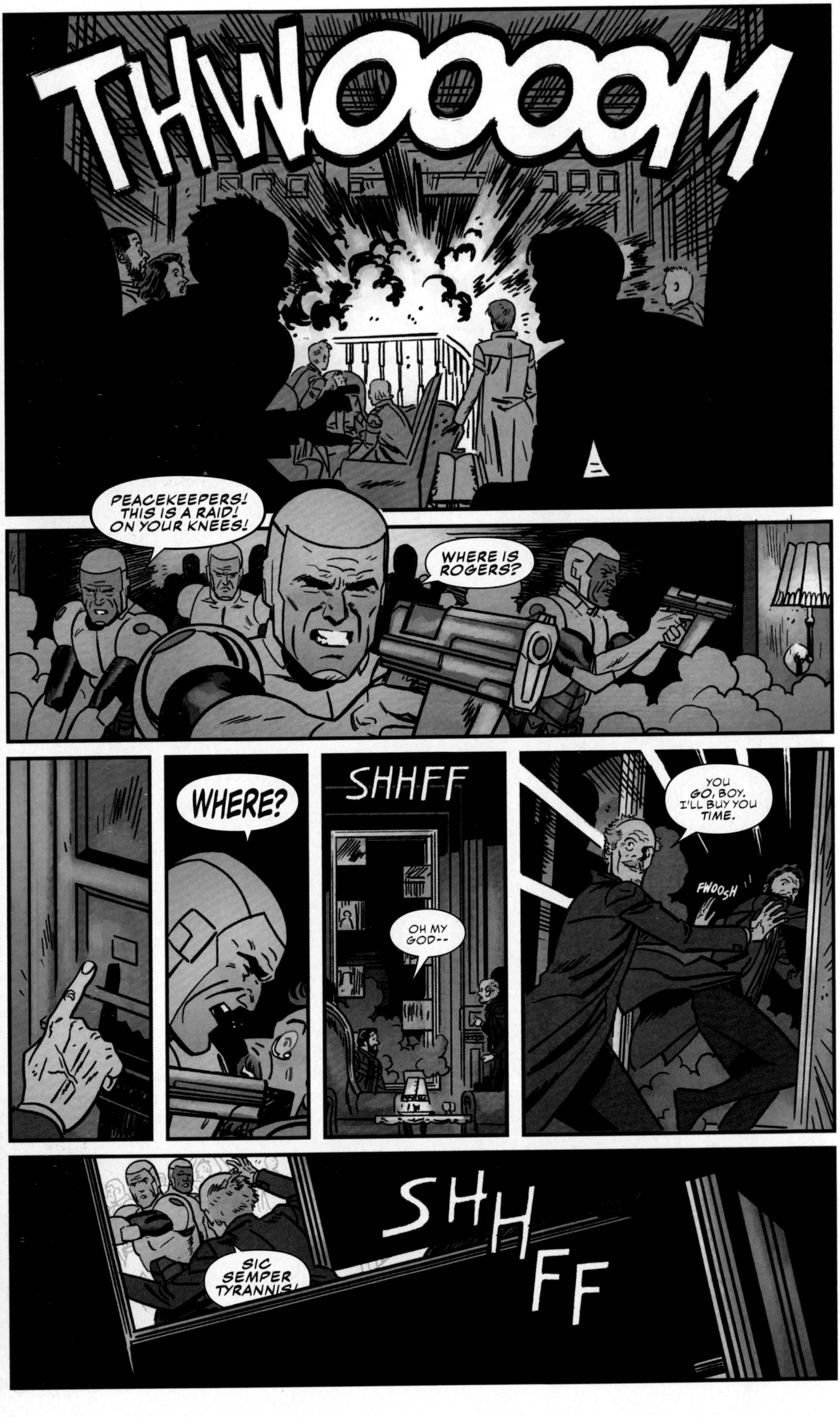
THWOOOOM
PEACEKEEPERS! THIS IS A RAID! ON YOUR KNEES!
WHERE IS ROGERS?
WHERE?
SHHFF
OH MY GOD--
YOU GO, BOY. I'LL BUY YOU TIME.
FWOOSH
SHHFF
SIC SEMPER TYRANNIS!

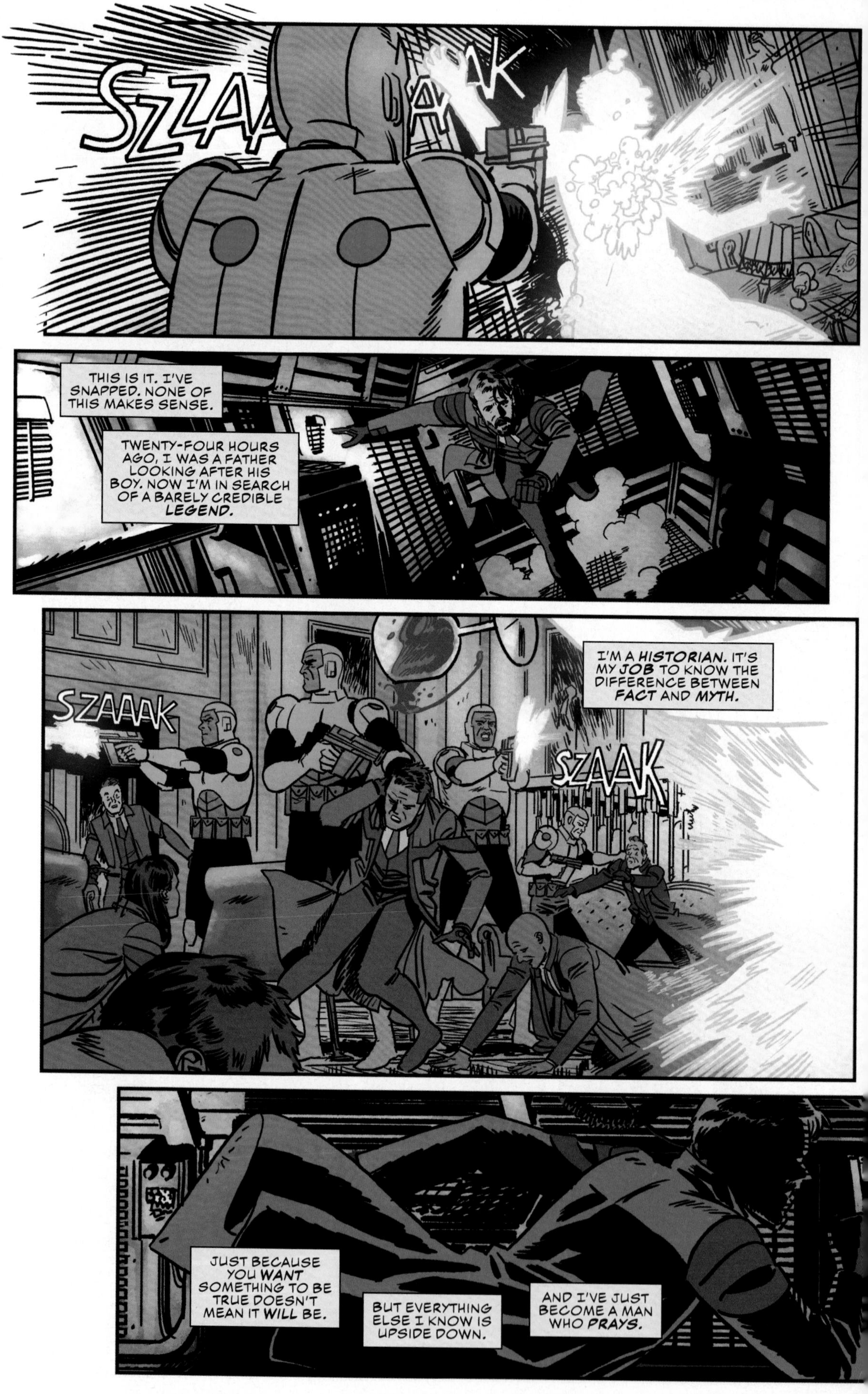
SZZAAAAK
THIS IS IT. I'VE SNAPPED. NONE OF THIS MAKES SENSE.
TWENTY-FOUR HOURS AGO, I WAS A FATHER LOOKING AFTER HIS BOY. NOW I'M IN SEARCH OF A BARELY CREDIBLE LEGEND.
I'M A HISTORIAN. IT'S MY JOB TO KNOW THE DIFFERENCE BETWEEN FACT AND MYTH.
SZAAAK
SZAAK
JUST BECAUSE YOU WANT SOMETHING TO BE TRUE DOESN'T MEAN IT WILL BE.
BUT EVERYTHING ELSE I KNOW IS UPSIDE DOWN.
AND I'VE JUST BECOME A MAN WHO PRAYS.

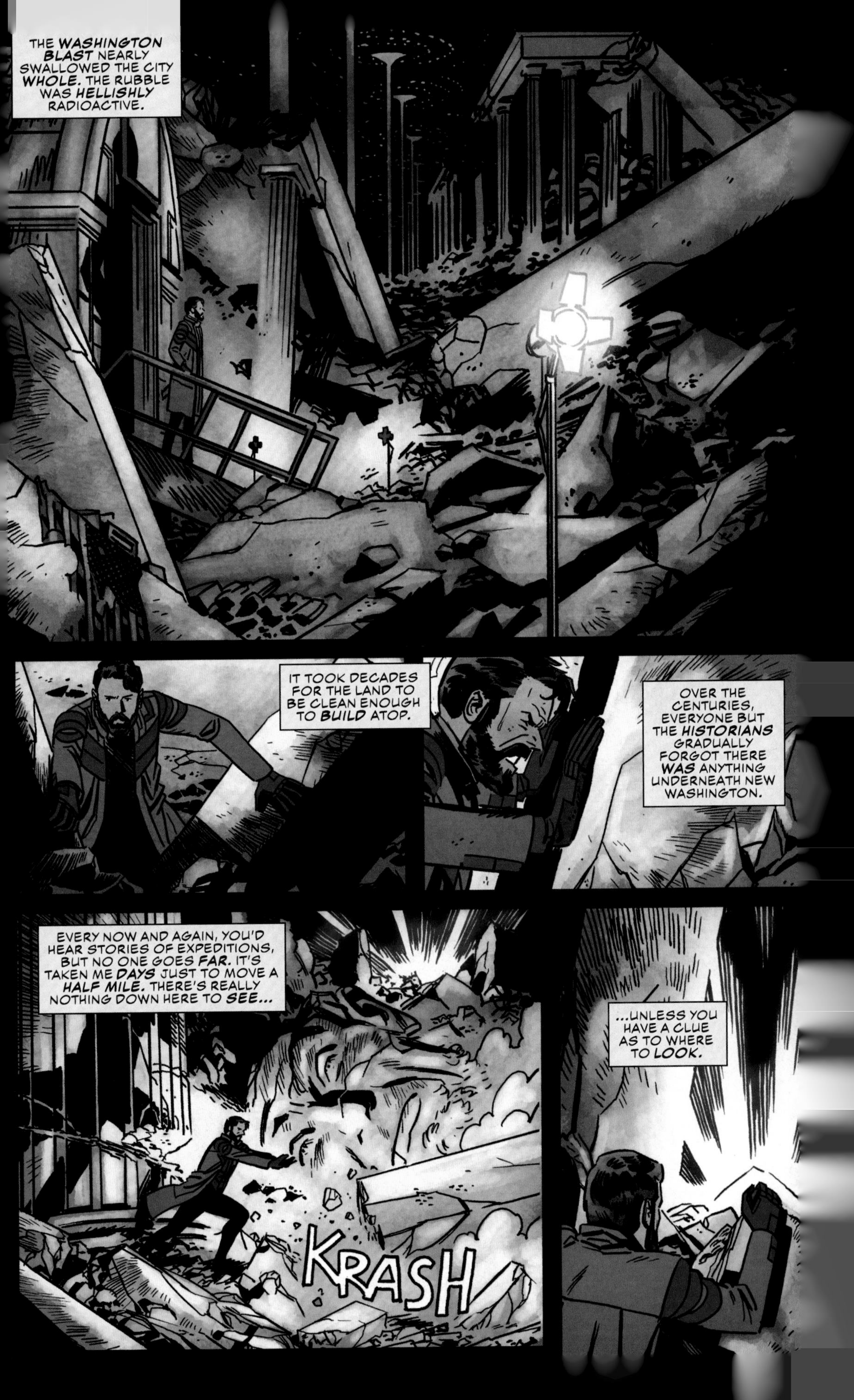
THE WASHINGTON BLAST NEARLY SWALLOWED THE CITY WHOLE. THE RUBBLE WAS HELLISHLY RADIOACTIVE.
IT TOOK DECADES FOR THE LAND TO BE CLEAN ENOUGH TO BUILD ATOP.
OVER THE CENTURIES, EVERYONE BUT THE HISTORIANS GRADUALLY FORGOT THERE WAS ANYTHING UNDERNEATH NEW WASHINGTON.
EVERY NOW AND AGAIN, YOU'D HEAR STORIES OF EXPEDITIONS, BUT NO ONE GOES FAR. IT'S TAKEN ME DAYS JUST TO MOVE A HALF MILE. THERE'S REALLY NOTHING DOWN HERE TO SEE...
KRASH
...UNLESS YOU HAVE A CLUE AS TO WHERE TO LOOK.

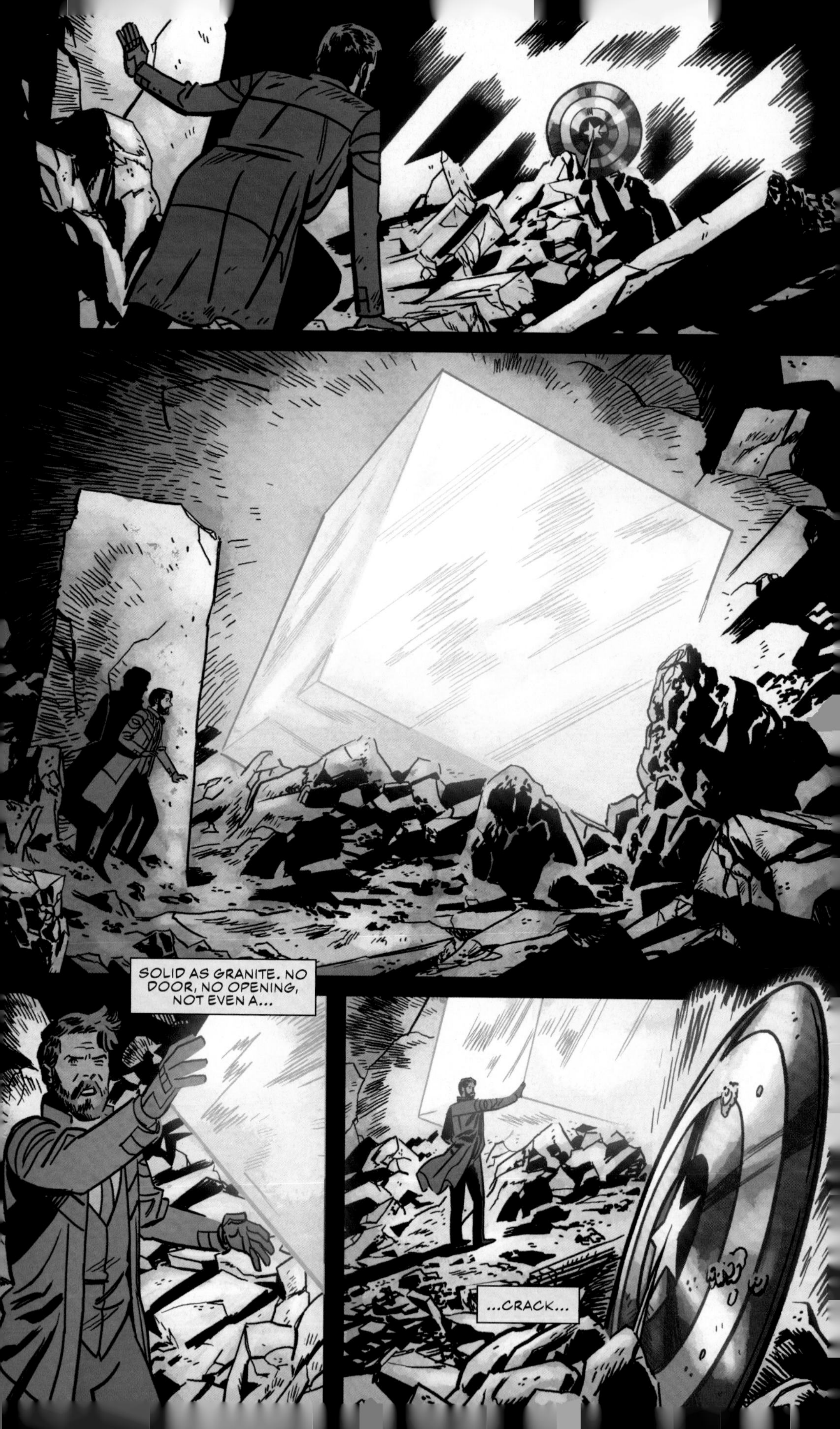
SOLID AS GRANITE. NO DOOR, NO OPENING, NOT EVEN A...
...CRACK...

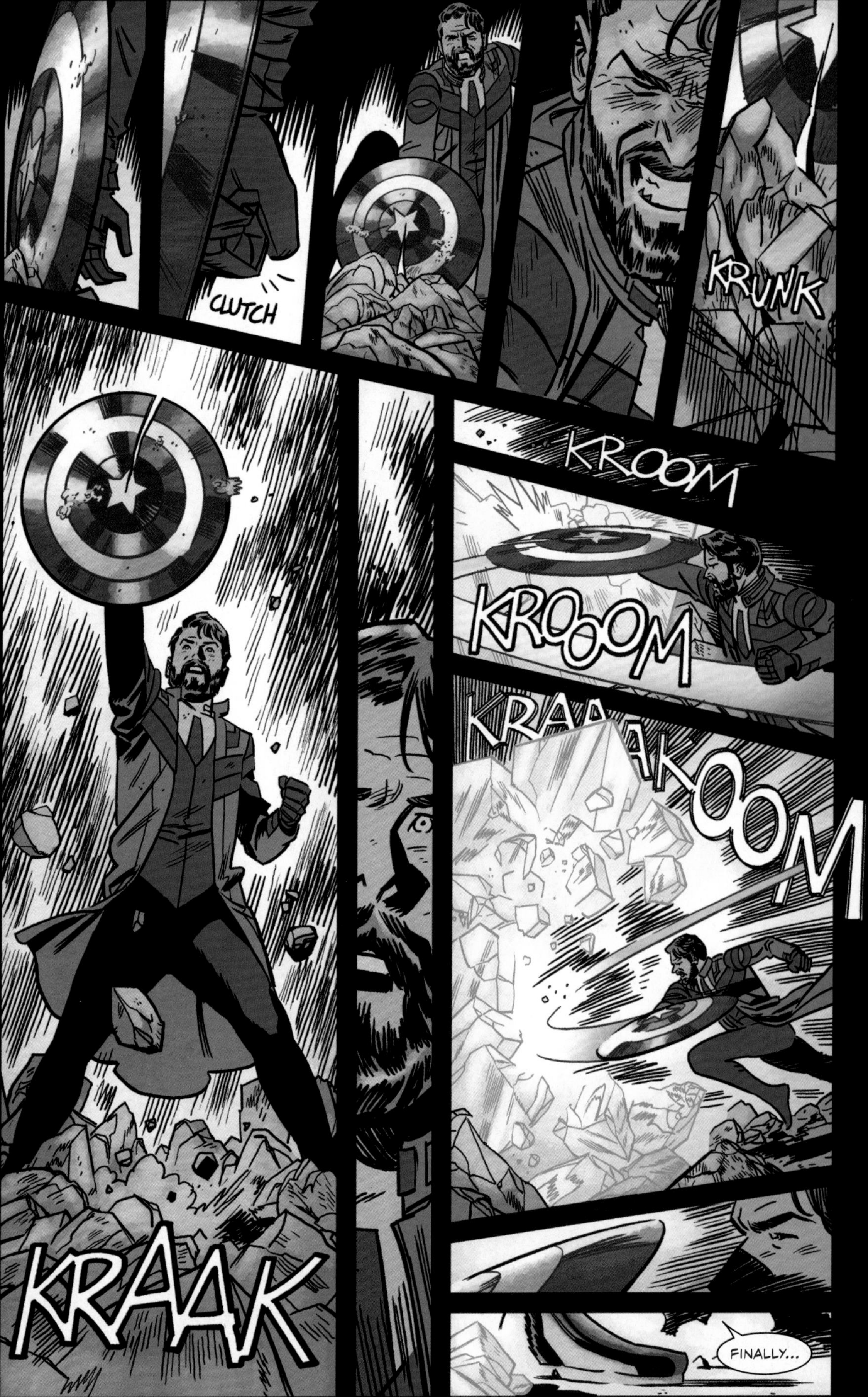
CLUTCH
KRUNK
KROOM
KROOOM
KRAAAKOOM
KRAAK
FINALLY...

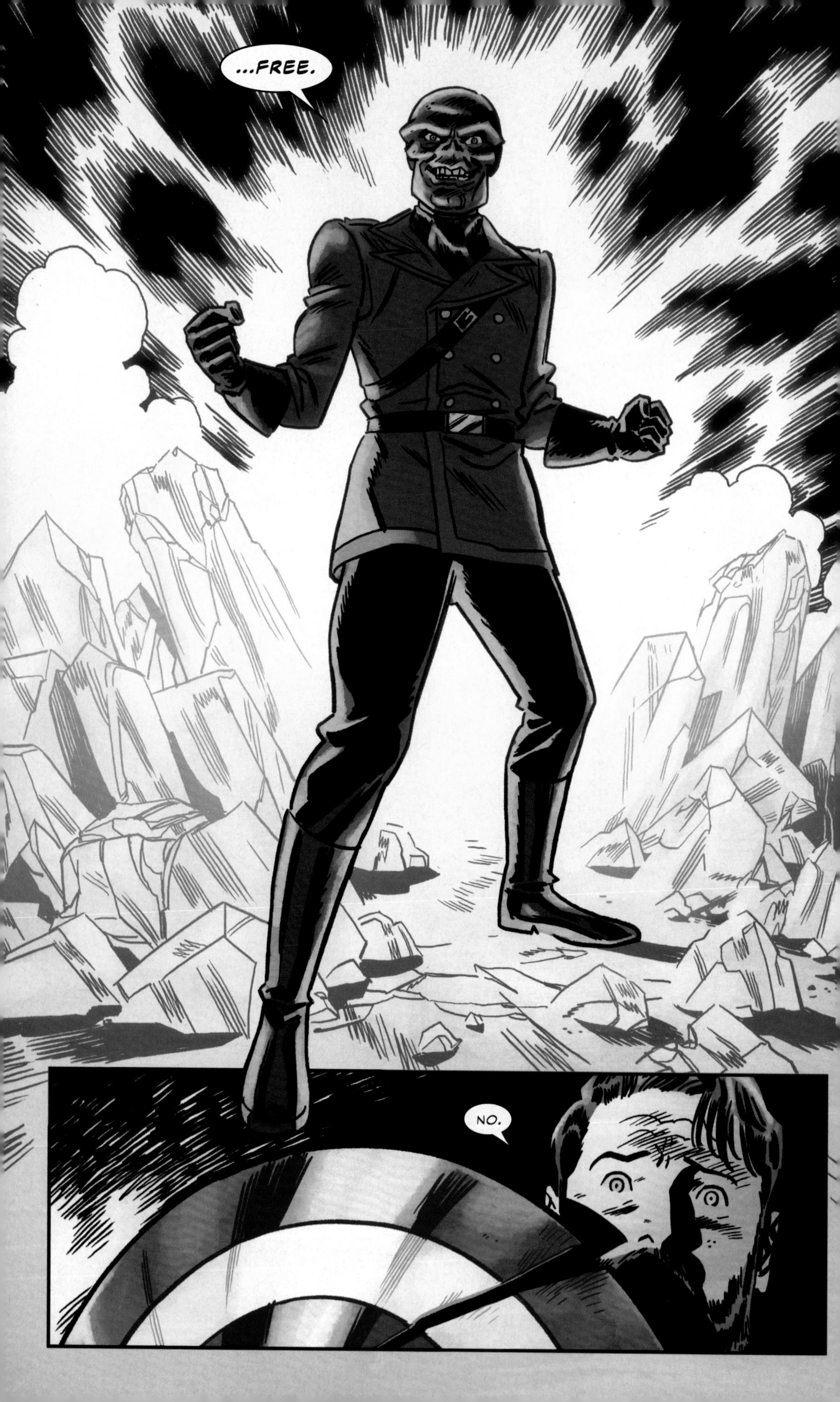
...FREE.
NO.

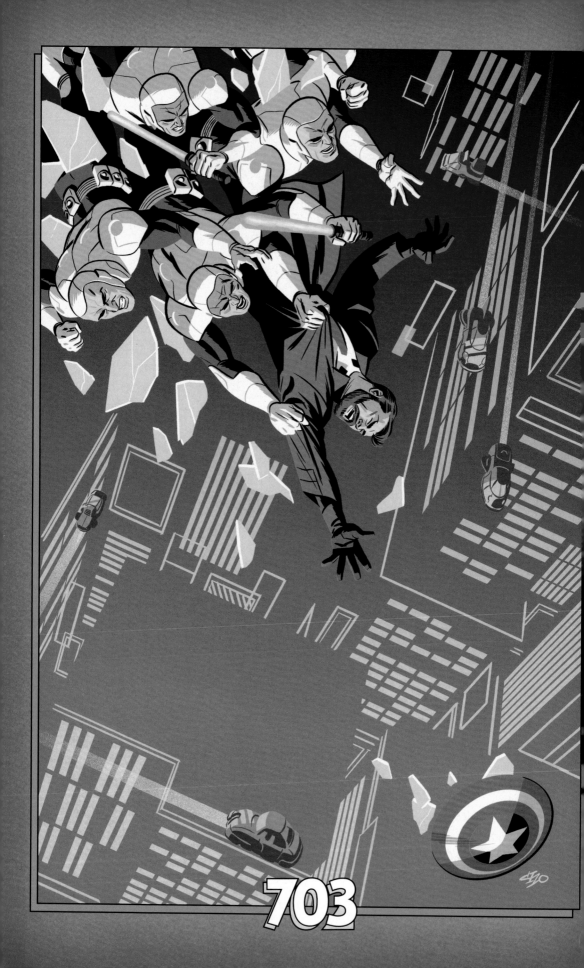

703

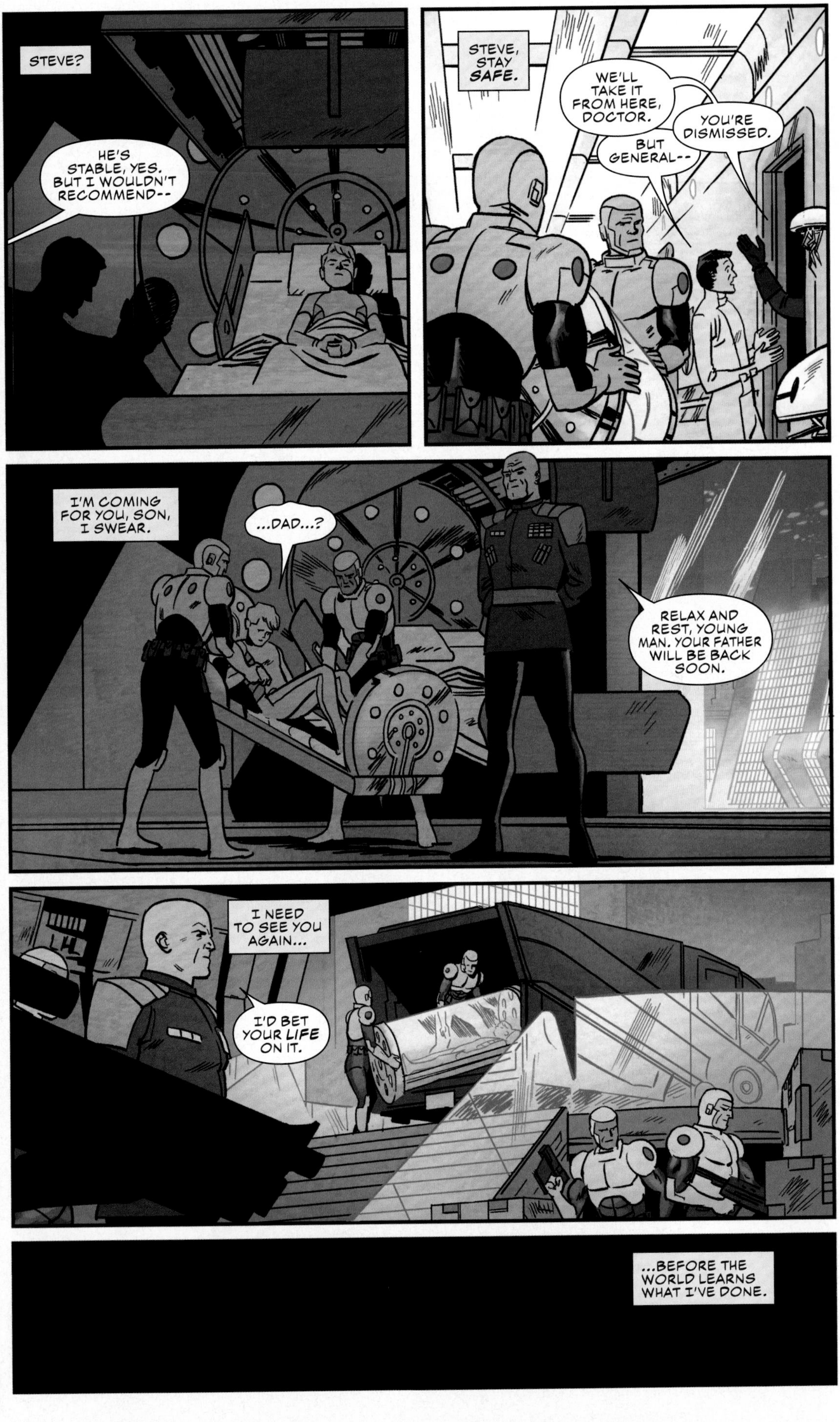
STEVE?
HE'S STABLE, YES. BUT I WOULDN'T RECOMMEND--
STEVE, STAY SAFE.
WE'LL TAKE IT FROM HERE, DOCTOR.
BUT GENERAL--
YOU'RE DISMISSED.
I'M COMING FOR YOU, SON, I SWEAR.
...DAD...?
RELAX AND REST, YOUNG MAN. YOUR FATHER WILL BE BACK SOON.
I NEED TO SEE YOU AGAIN...
I'D BET YOUR LIFE ON IT.
...BEFORE THE WORLD LEARNS WHAT I'VE DONE.

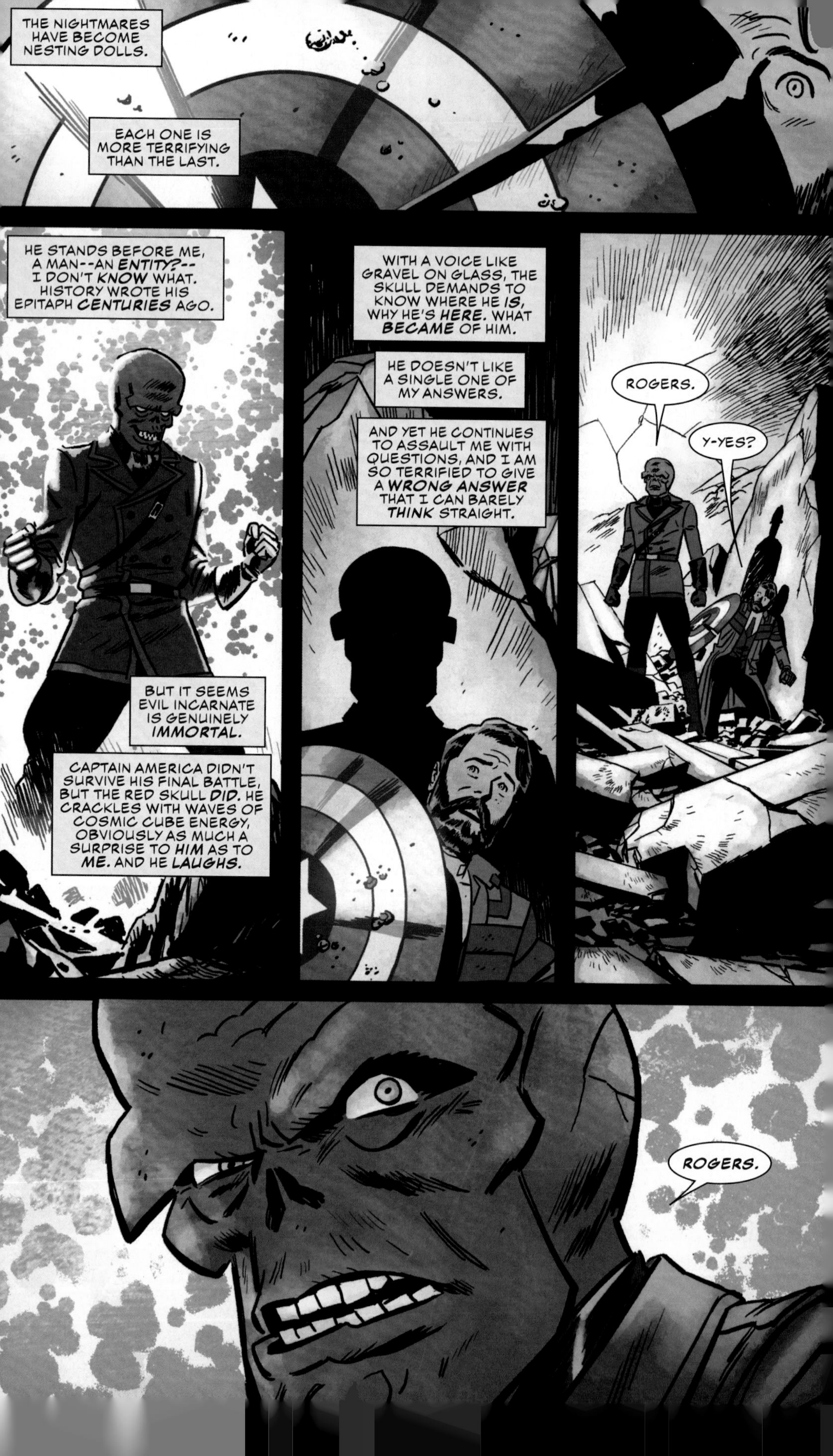
THE NIGHTMARES HAVE BECOME NESTING DOLLS.
EACH ONE IS MORE TERRIFYING THAN THE LAST.
HE STANDS BEFORE ME, A MAN--AN ENTITY?-- I DON'T KNOW WHAT. HISTORY WROTE HIS EPITAPH CENTURIES AGO.
BUT IT SEEMS EVIL INCARNATE IS GENUINELY IMMORTAL.
CAPTAIN AMERICA DIDN'T SURVIVE HIS FINAL BATTLE, BUT THE RED SKULL DID. HE CRACKLES WITH WAVES OF COSMIC CUBE ENERGY, OBVIOUSLY AS MUCH A SURPRISE TO HIM AS TO ME. AND HE LAUGHS.
WITH A VOICE LIKE GRAVEL ON GLASS, THE SKULL DEMANDS TO KNOW WHERE HE IS, WHY HE'S HERE. WHAT BECAME OF HIM.
HE DOESN'T LIKE A SINGLE ONE OF MY ANSWERS.
AND YET HE CONTINUES TO ASSAULT ME WITH QUESTIONS, AND I AM SO TERRIFIED TO GIVE A WRONG ANSWER THAT I CAN BARELY THINK STRAIGHT.
ROGERS.
Y-YES?
ROGERS.

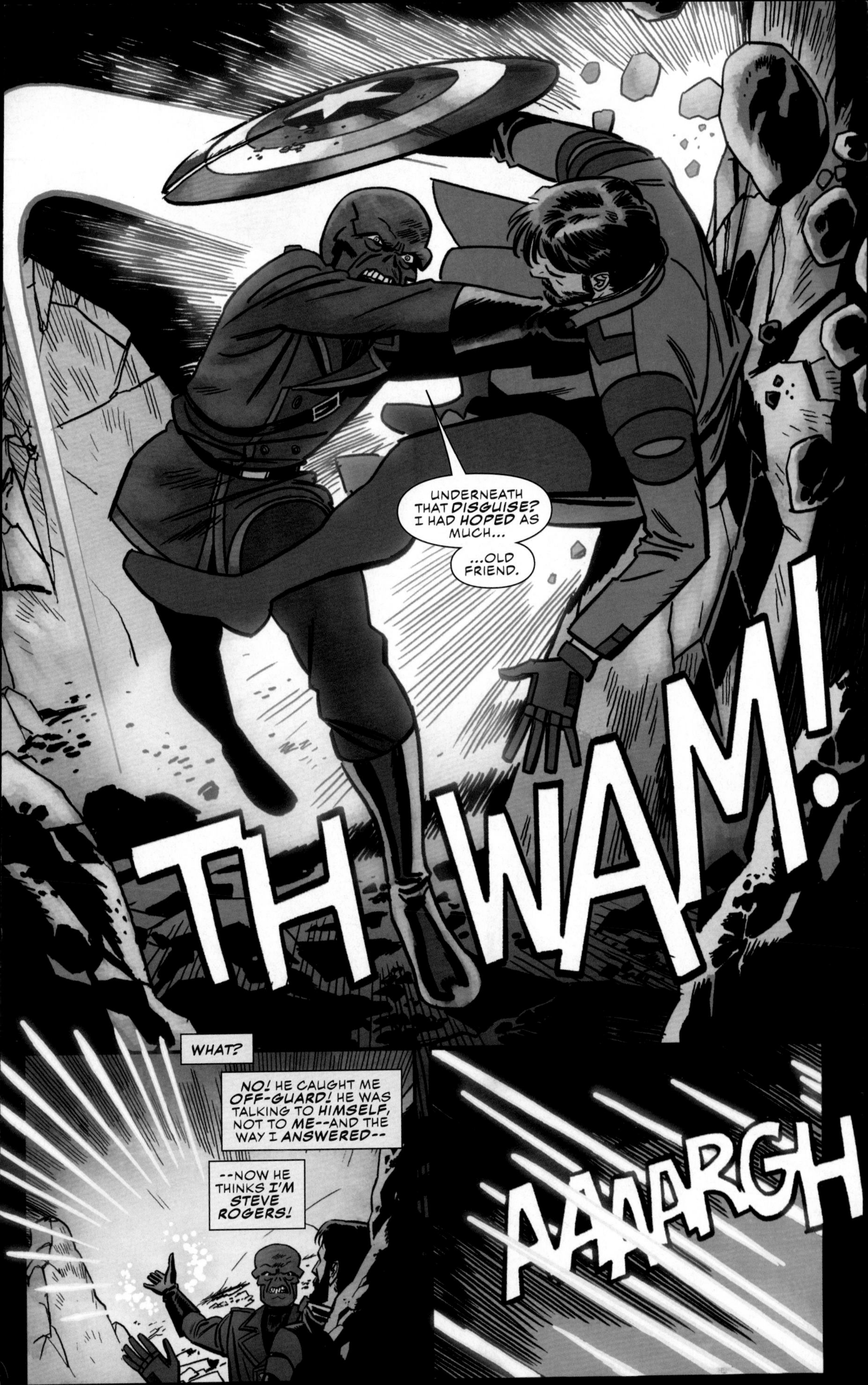
UNDERNEATH THAT DISGUISE? I HAD HOPED AS MUCH...
...OLD FRIEND.
THWAM!
WHAT?
NO! HE CAUGHT ME OFF-GUARD! HE WAS TALKING TO HIMSELF, NOT TO ME--AND THE WAY I ANSWERED--
--NOW HE THINKS I'M STEVE ROGERS!
AAAARGH

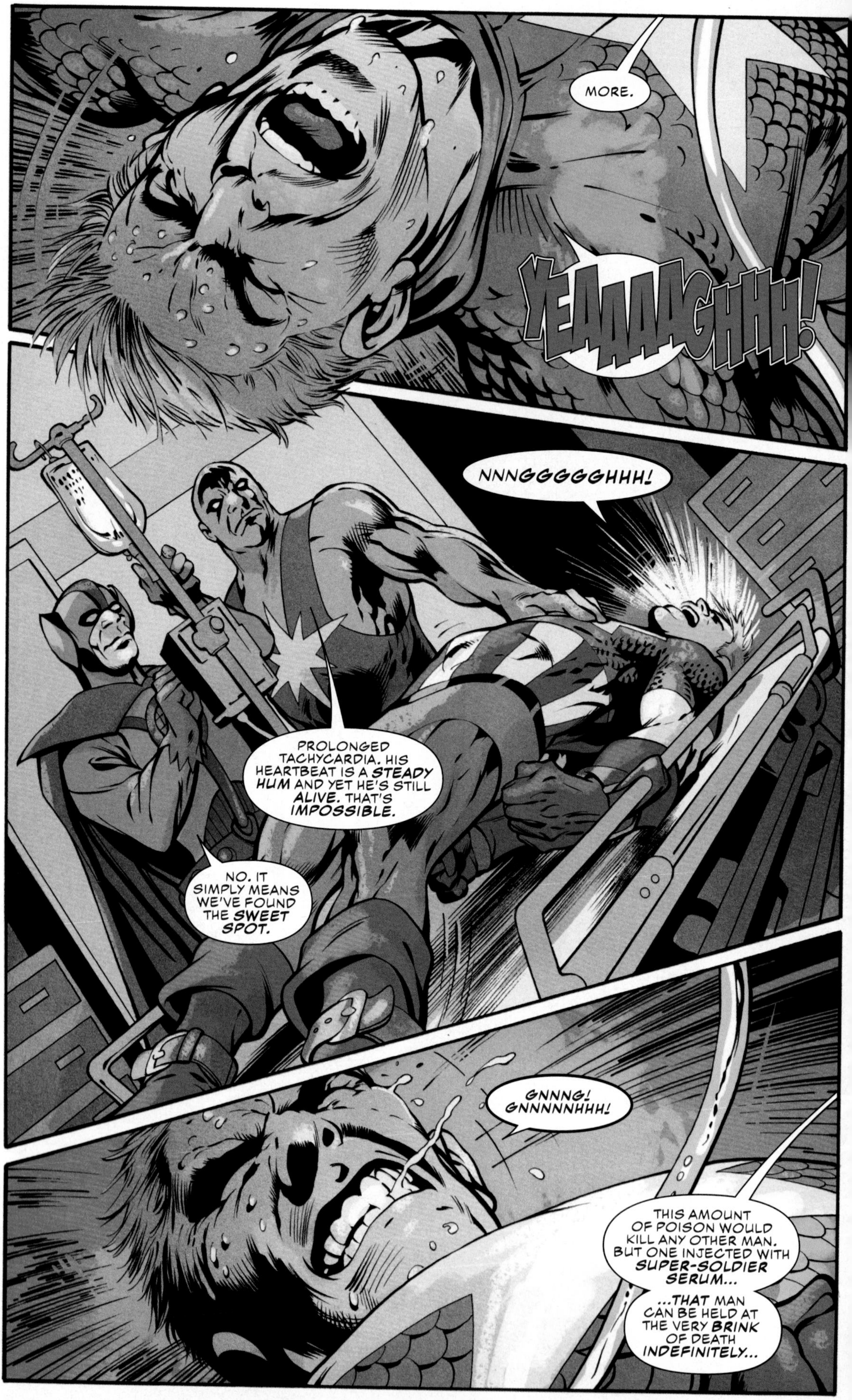
MORE.
YEAAAAGHHH!
NNNGGGGGHHH!
PROLONGED TACHYCARDIA. HIS HEARTBEAT IS A STEADY HUM AND YET HE'S STILL ALIVE. THAT'S IMPOSSIBLE.
NO. IT SIMPLY MEANS WE'VE FOUND THE SWEET SPOT.
GNNNG! GNNNNNHHH!
THIS AMOUNT OF POISON WOULD KILL ANY OTHER MAN. BUT ONE INJECTED WITH SUPER-SOLDIER SERUM...
...THAT MAN CAN BE HELD AT THE VERY BRINK OF DEATH INDEFINITELY...

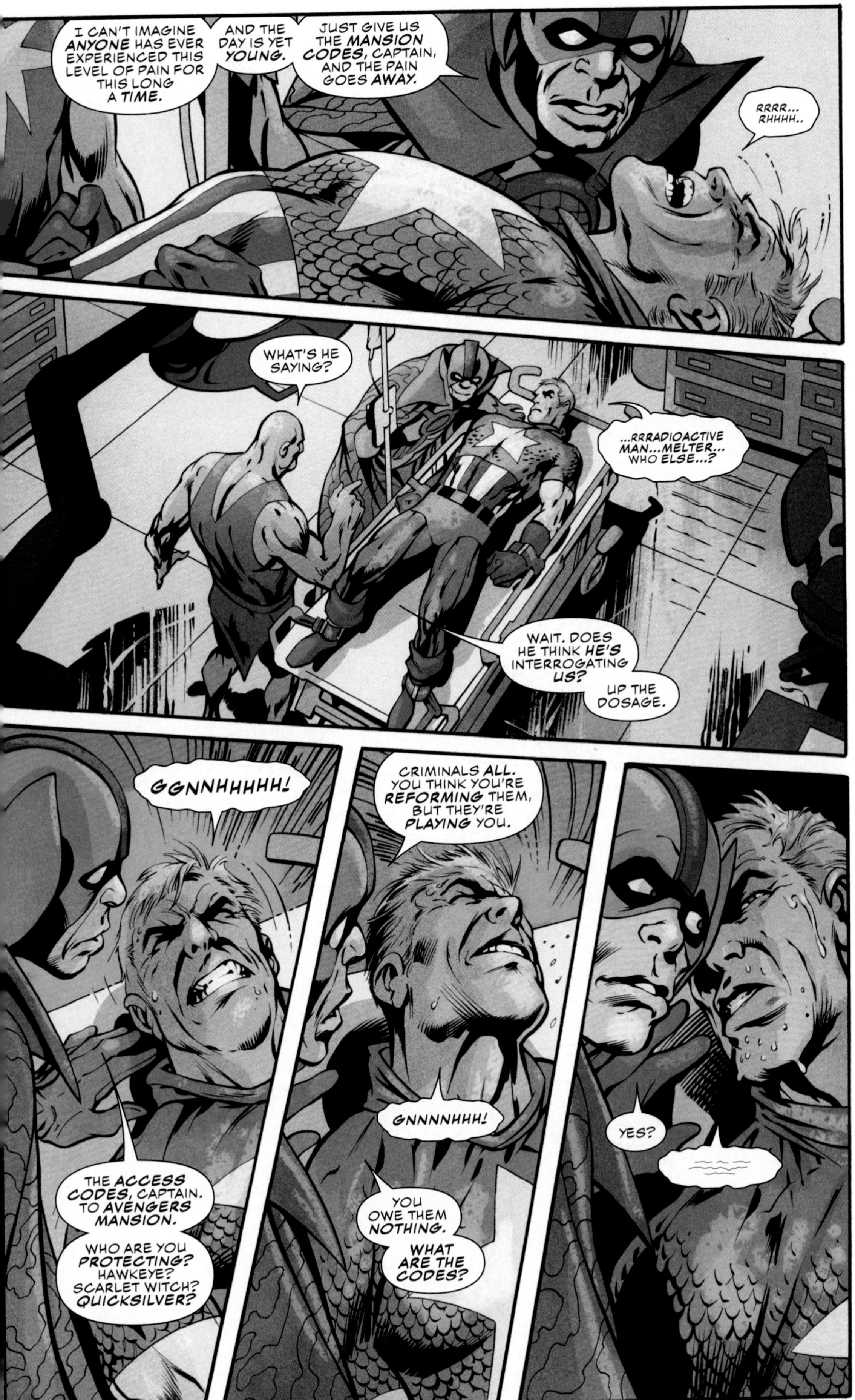

I CAN'T IMAGINE ANYONE HAS EVER EXPERIENCED THIS LEVEL OF PAIN FOR THIS LONG A TIME.
AND THE DAY IS YET YOUNG.
JUST GIVE US THE MANSION CODES, CAPTAIN, AND THE PAIN GOES AWAY.
RRRR... RHHHH..
WHAT'S HE SAYING?
...RRRADIOACTIVE MAN...MELTER... WHO ELSE...?
WAIT. DOES HE THINK HE'S INTERROGATING US?
UP THE DOSAGE.
GGNHHHHHH!
THE ACCESS CODES, CAPTAIN. TO AVENGERS MANSION.
WHO ARE YOU PROTECTING? HAWKEYE? SCARLET WITCH? QUICKSILVER?
CRIMINALS ALL. YOU THINK YOU'RE REFORMING THEM, BUT THEY'RE PLAYING YOU.
GNNNNHHH!
YOU OWE THEM NOTHING.
WHAT ARE THE CODES?
YES?

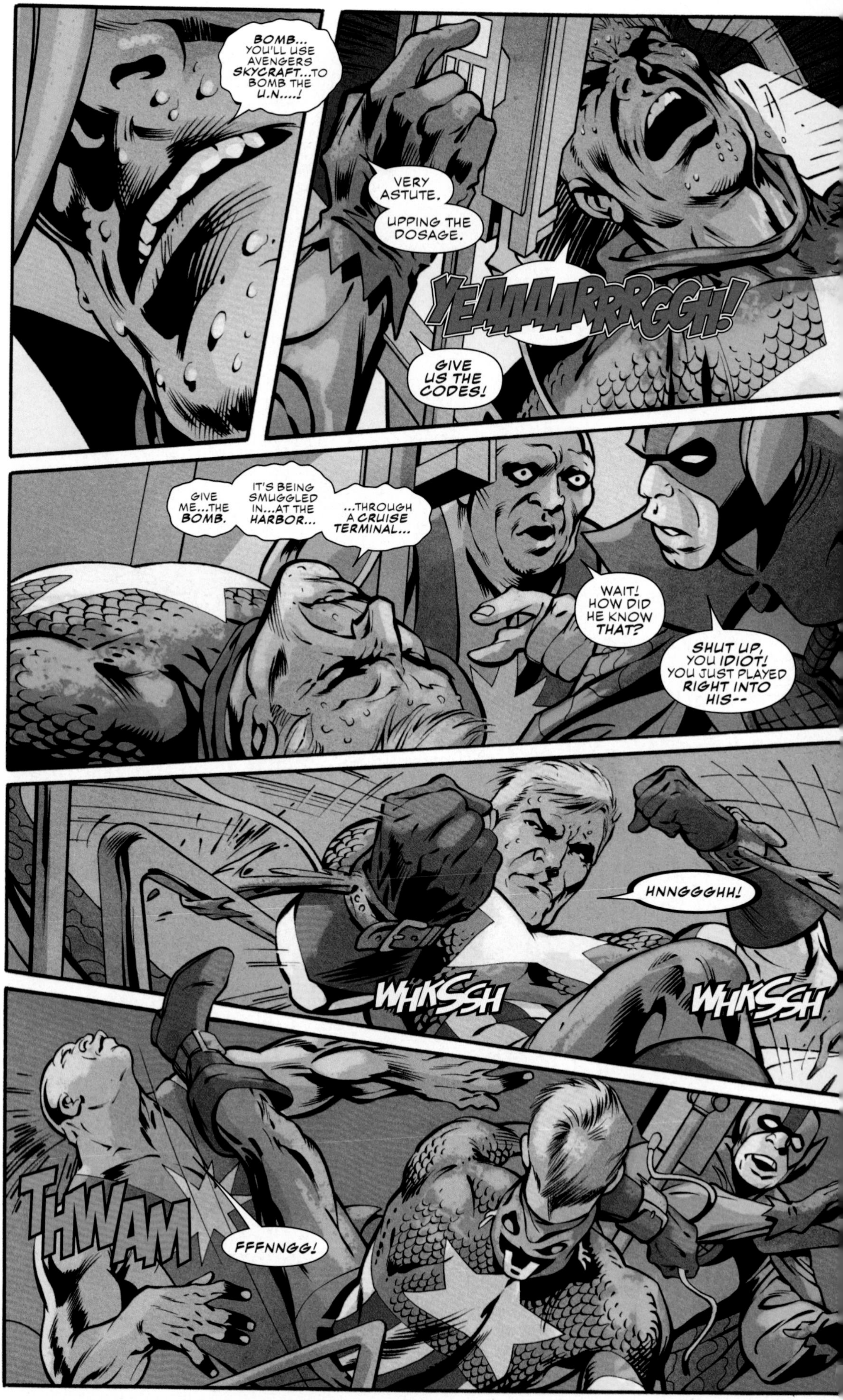

BOMB... YOU'LL USE AVENGERS SKYCRAFT...TO BOMB THE U.N....!
VERY ASTUTE.
UPPING THE DOSAGE.
YEAAAARRRGGH!
GIVE US THE CODES!
GIVE ME...THE BOMB.
IT'S BEING SMUGGLED IN...AT THE HARBOR...
...THROUGH A CRUISE TERMINAL...
WAIT! HOW DID HE KNOW THAT?
SHUT UP, YOU IDIOT! YOU JUST PLAYED RIGHT INTO HIS--
HNNGGGHH!
WHKSSH
WHKSSH
THWAM
FFFNNGG!

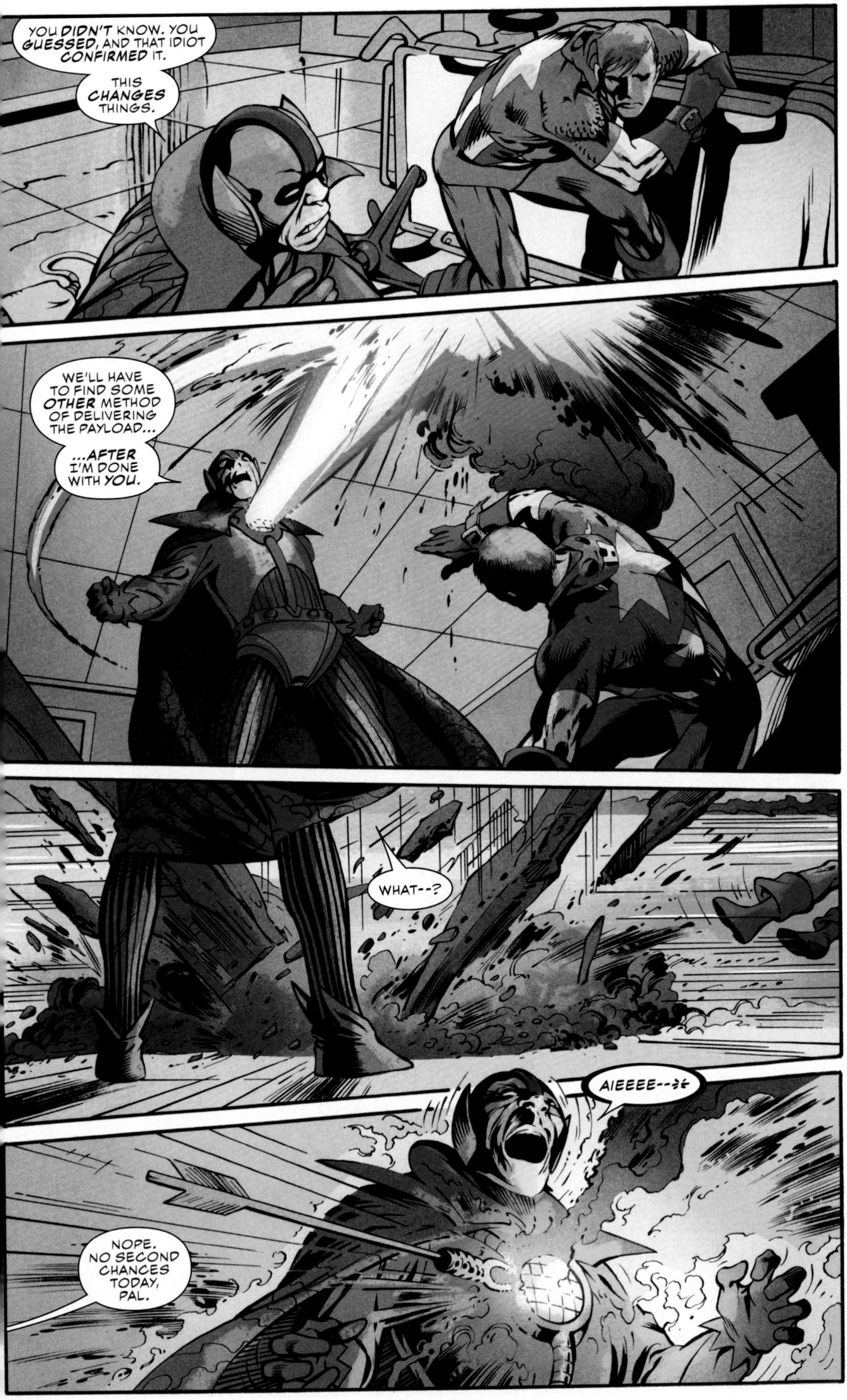
YOU DIDN'T KNOW. YOU GUESSED, AND THAT IDIOT CONFIRMED IT.
THIS CHANGES THINGS.
WE'LL HAVE TO FIND SOME OTHER METHOD OF DELIVERING THE PAYLOAD...
...AFTER I'M DONE WITH YOU.
WHAT--?
AIEEEE--
NOPE. NO SECOND CHANCES TODAY, PAL.

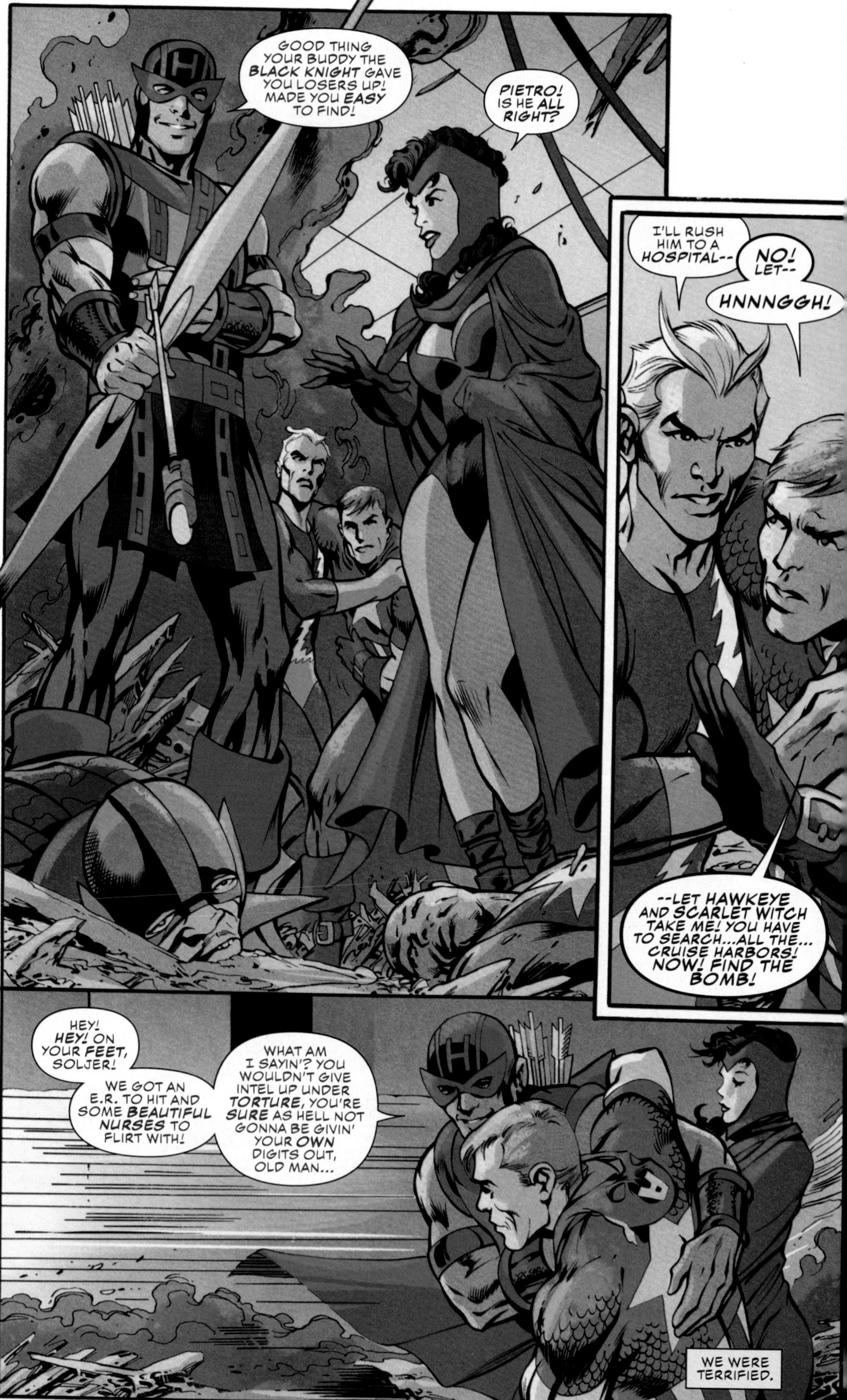
GOOD THING YOUR BUDDY THE BLACK KNIGHT GAVE YOU LOSERS UP! MADE YOU EASY TO FIND!
PIETRO! IS HE ALL RIGHT?
I'LL RUSH HIM TO A HOSPITAL--
NO! LET--
HNNNGGH!
--LET HAWKEYE AND SCARLET WITCH TAKE ME! YOU HAVE TO SEARCH...ALL THE... CRUISE HARBORS! NOW! FIND THE BOMB!
HEY! HEY! ON YOUR FEET, SOLJER!
WE GOT AN E.R. TO HIT AND SOME BEAUTIFUL NURSES TO FLIRT WITH!
WHAT AM I SAYIN'? YOU WOULDN'T GIVE INTEL UP UNDER TORTURE, YOU'RE SURE AS HELL NOT GONNA BE GIVIN' YOUR OWN DIGITS OUT, OLD MAN...
WE WERE TERRIFIED.

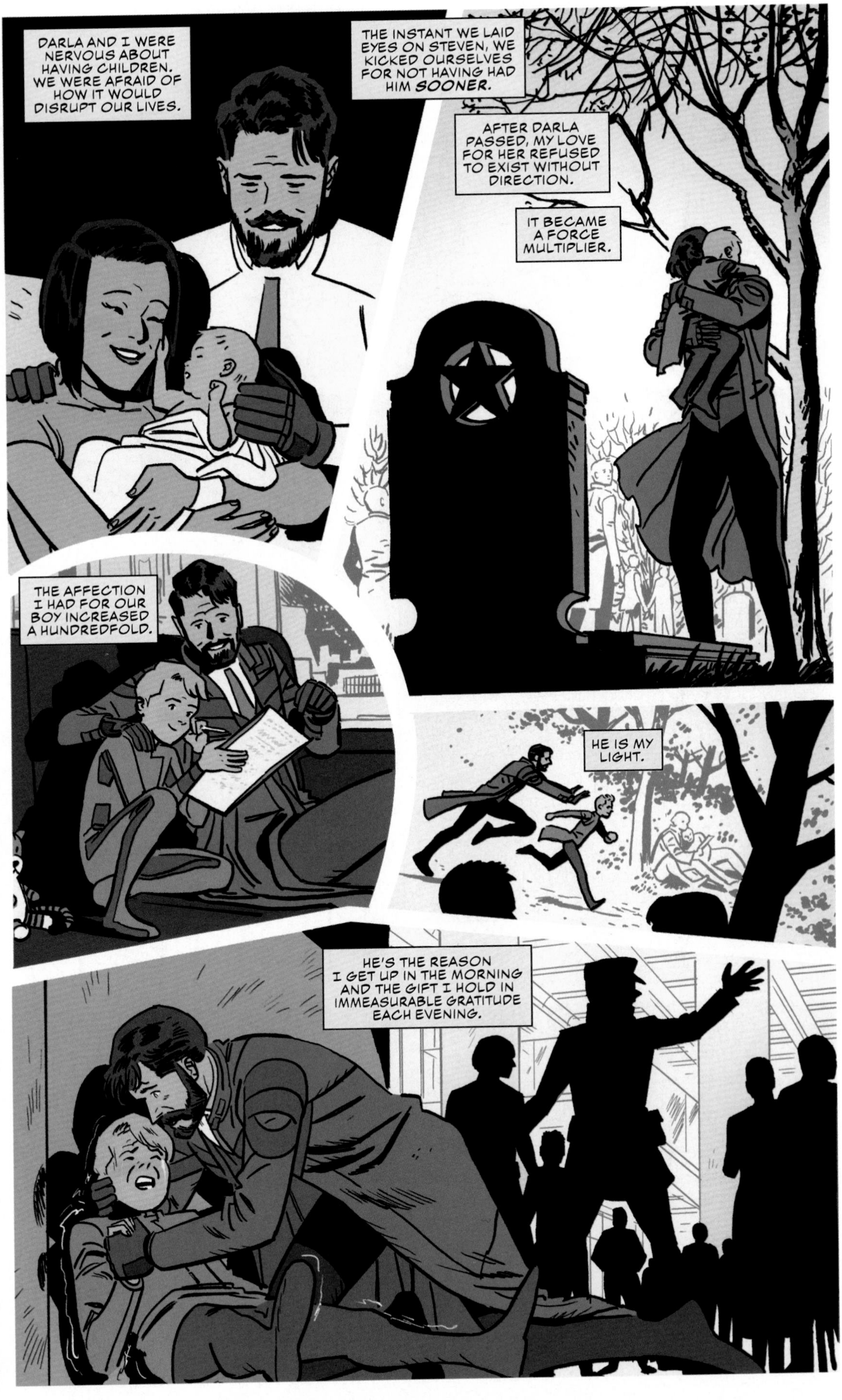
DARLA AND I WERE NERVOUS ABOUT HAVING CHILDREN. WE WERE AFRAID OF HOW IT WOULD DISRUPT OUR LIVES.
THE INSTANT WE LAID EYES ON STEVEN, WE KICKED OURSELVES FOR NOT HAVING HAD HIM SOONER.
AFTER DARLA PASSED, MY LOVE FOR HER REFUSED TO EXIST WITHOUT DIRECTION.
IT BECAME A FORCE MULTIPLIER.
THE AFFECTION I HAD FOR OUR BOY INCREASED A HUNDREDFOLD.
HE IS MY LIGHT.
HE'S THE REASON I GET UP IN THE MORNING AND THE GIFT I HOLD IN IMMEASURABLE GRATITUDE EACH EVENING.

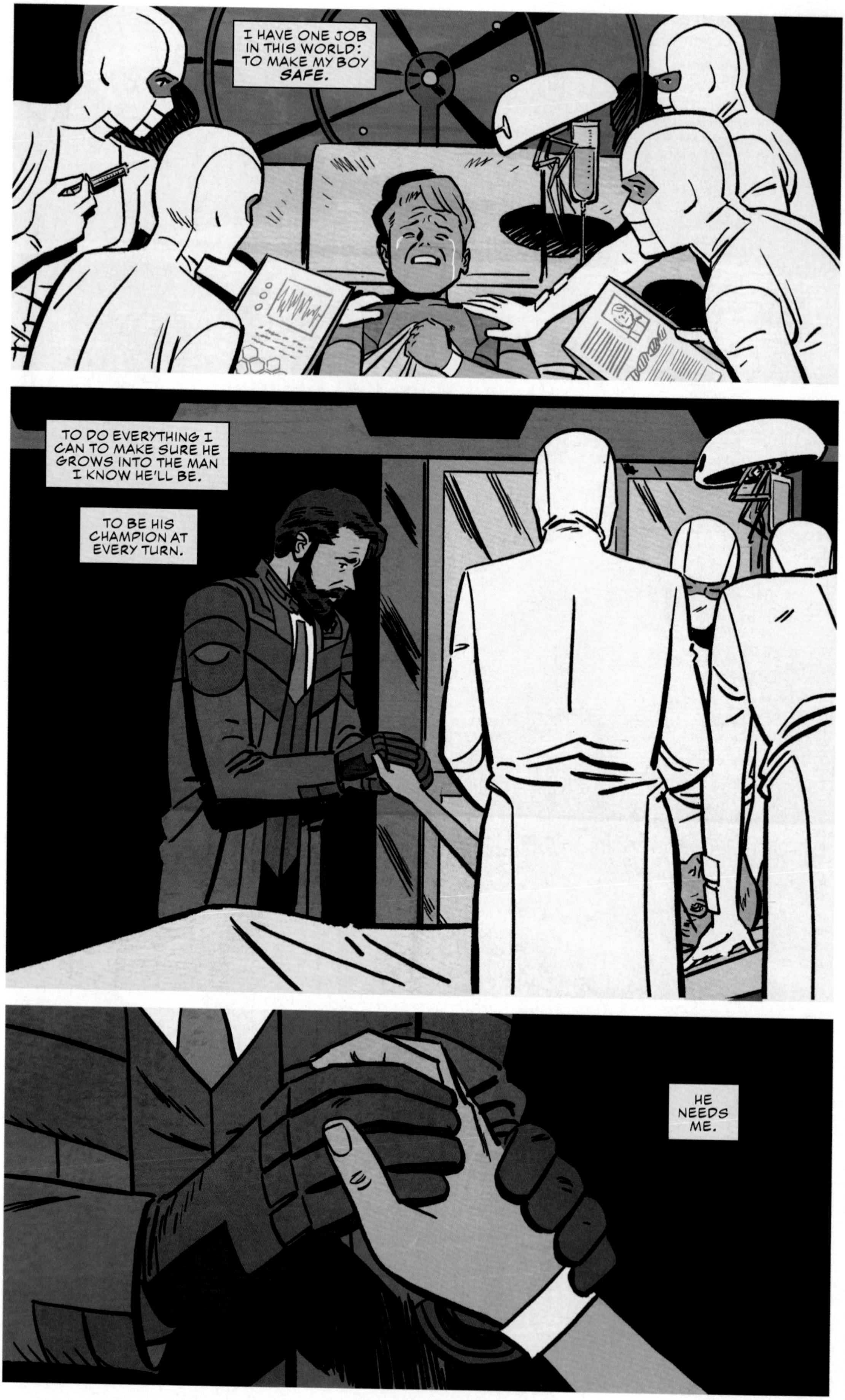
I HAVE ONE JOB IN THIS WORLD: TO MAKE MY BOY *SAFE.*
TO DO EVERYTHING I CAN TO MAKE SURE HE GROWS INTO THE MAN I KNOW HE'LL BE.
TO BE HIS CHAMPION AT EVERY TURN.
HE NEEDS ME.

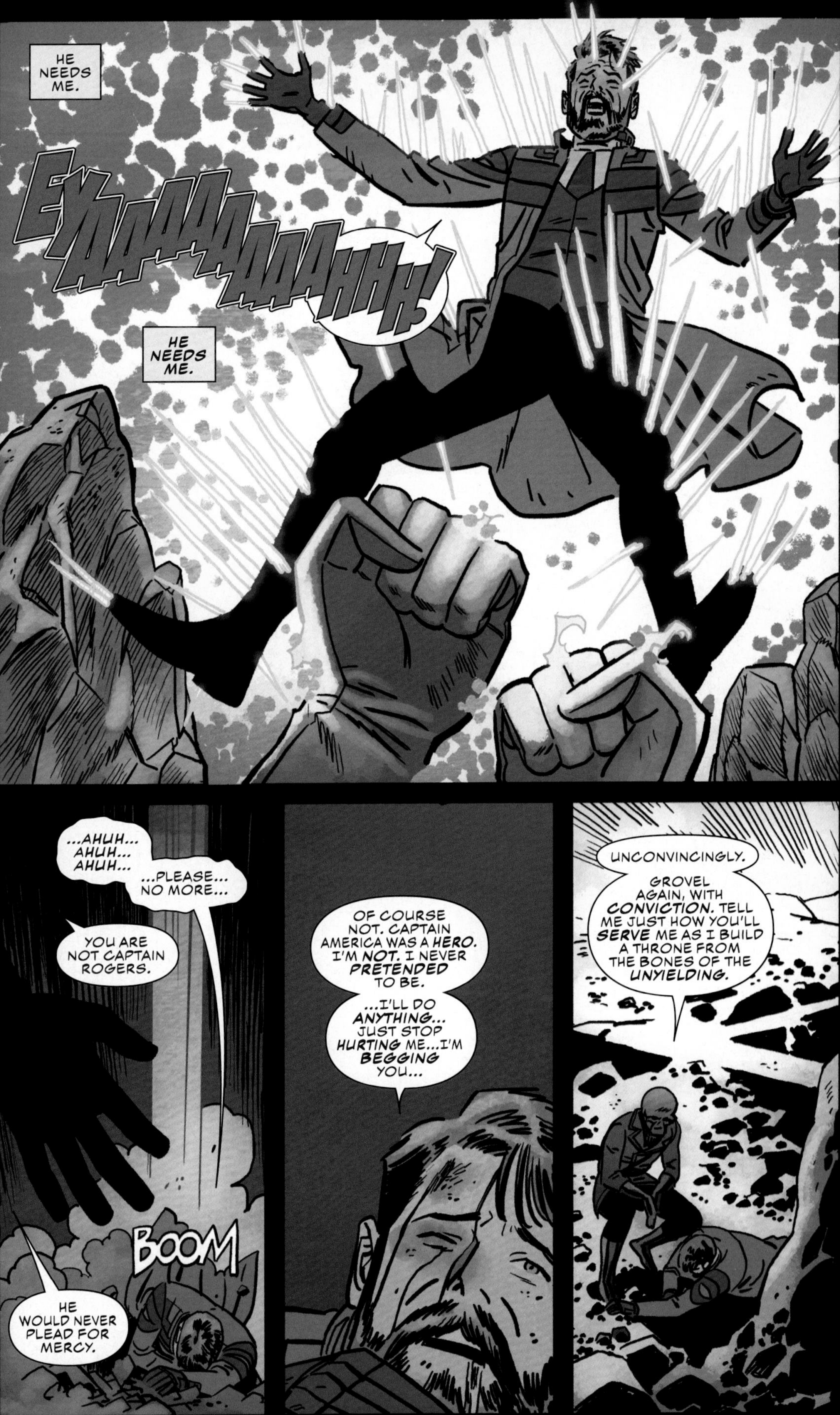
HE NEEDS ME.
EYAAAAAAAAAAAHHH!
HE NEEDS ME.
...AHUH... AHUH... AHUH...
...PLEASE... NO MORE...
YOU ARE NOT CAPTAIN ROGERS.
BOOM
HE WOULD NEVER PLEAD FOR MERCY.
OF COURSE NOT. CAPTAIN AMERICA WAS A HERO. I'M NOT. I NEVER PRETENDED TO BE.
...I'LL DO ANYTHING... JUST STOP HURTING ME...I'M BEGGING YOU...
UNCONVINCINGLY.
GROVEL AGAIN, WITH CONVICTION. TELL ME JUST HOW YOU'LL SERVE ME AS I BUILD A THRONE FROM THE BONES OF THE UNYIELDING.

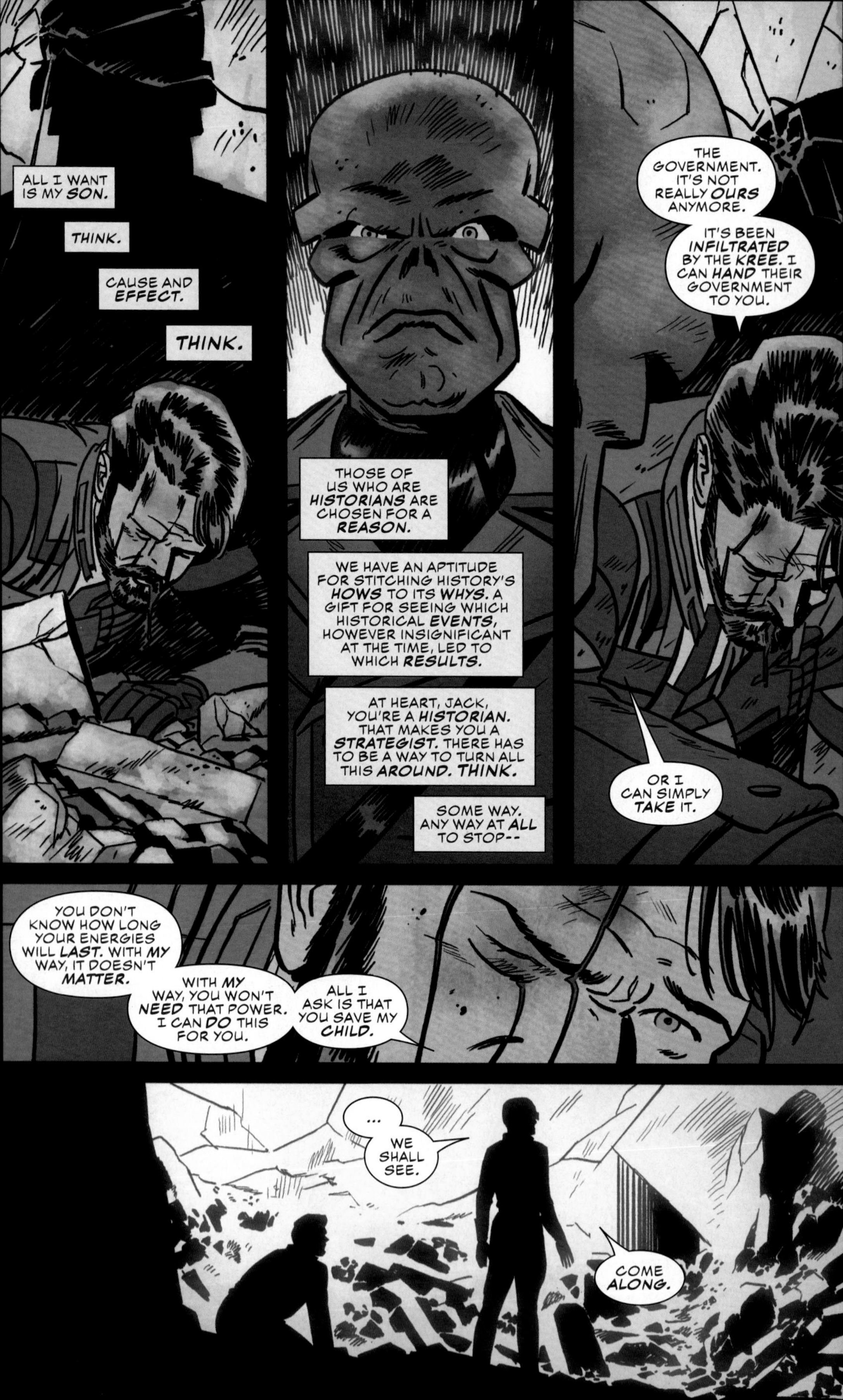

ALL I WANT IS MY SON.
THINK.
CAUSE AND EFFECT.
THINK.
THOSE OF US WHO ARE HISTORIANS ARE CHOSEN FOR A REASON.
WE HAVE AN APTITUDE FOR STITCHING HISTORY'S HOWS TO ITS WHYS. A GIFT FOR SEEING WHICH HISTORICAL EVENTS, HOWEVER INSIGNIFICANT AT THE TIME, LED TO WHICH RESULTS.
AT HEART, JACK, YOU'RE A HISTORIAN. THAT MAKES YOU A STRATEGIST. THERE HAS TO BE A WAY TO TURN ALL THIS AROUND. THINK.
SOME WAY. ANY WAY AT ALL TO STOP--
THE GOVERNMENT. IT'S NOT REALLY OURS ANYMORE.
IT'S BEEN INFILTRATED BY THE KREE. I CAN HAND THEIR GOVERNMENT TO YOU.
OR I CAN SIMPLY TAKE IT.
YOU DON'T KNOW HOW LONG YOUR ENERGIES WILL LAST. WITH MY WAY, IT DOESN'T MATTER.
WITH MY WAY, YOU WON'T NEED THAT POWER. I CAN DO THIS FOR YOU.
ALL I ASK IS THAT YOU SAVE MY CHILD.
... WE SHALL SEE.
COME ALONG.

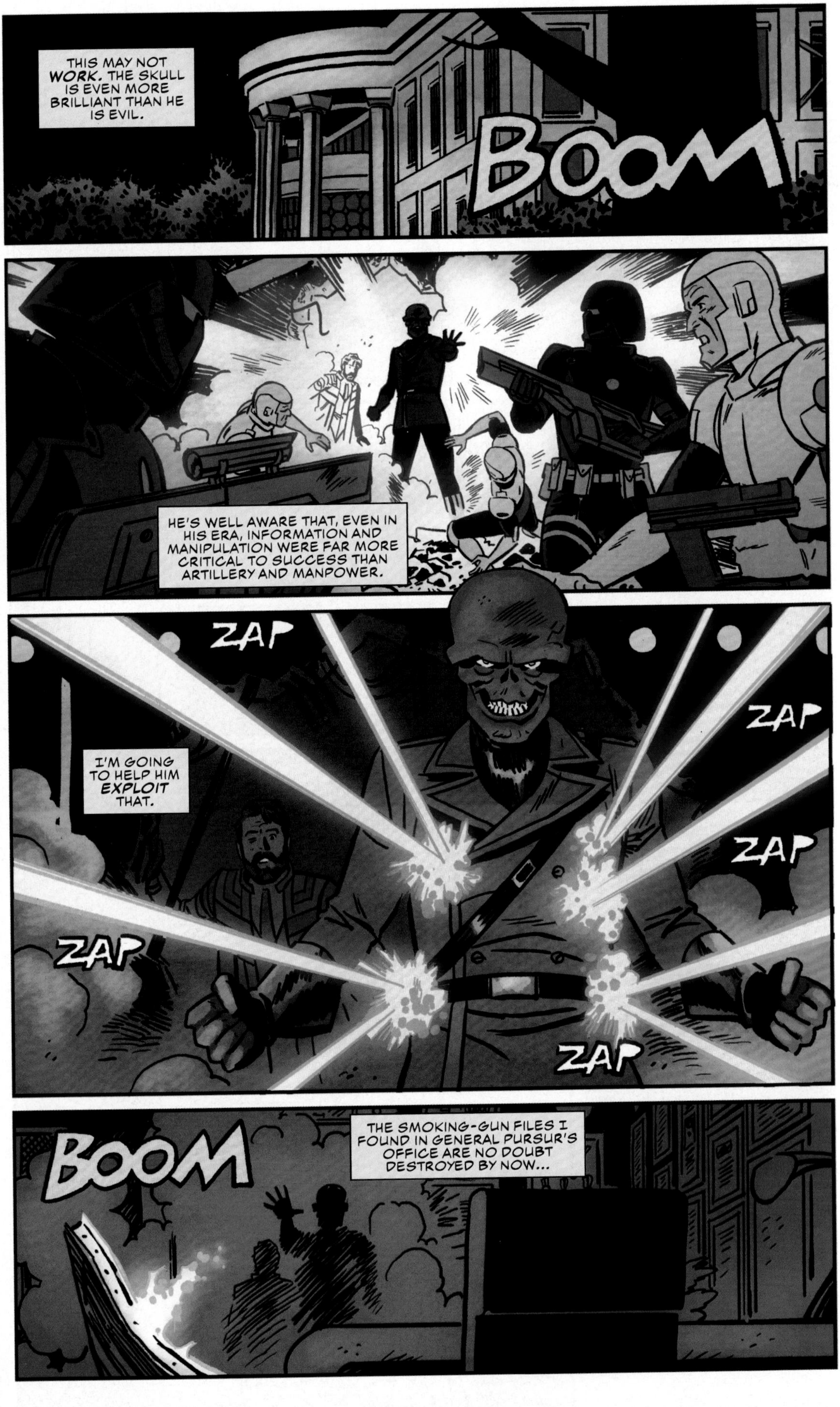
THIS MAY NOT WORK. THE SKULL IS EVEN MORE BRILLIANT THAN HE IS EVIL.
BOOM
HE'S WELL AWARE THAT, EVEN IN HIS ERA, INFORMATION AND MANIPULATION WERE FAR MORE CRITICAL TO SUCCESS THAN ARTILLERY AND MANPOWER.
ZAP
ZAP
I'M GOING TO HELP HIM EXPLOIT THAT.
ZAP
ZAP
ZAP
BOOM
THE SMOKING-GUN FILES I FOUND IN GENERAL PURSUR'S OFFICE ARE NO DOUBT DESTROYED BY NOW...

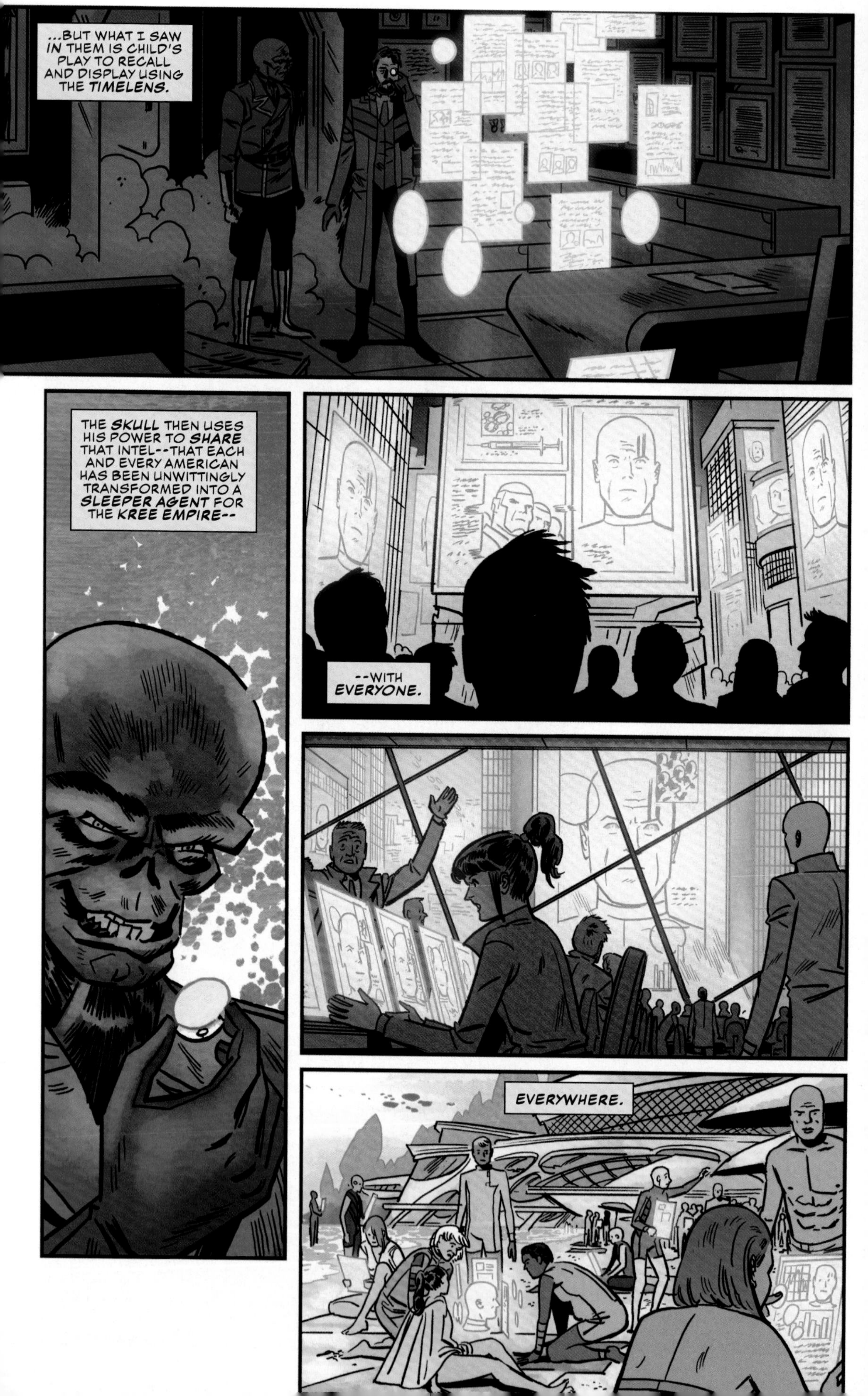
...BUT WHAT I SAW IN THEM IS CHILD'S PLAY TO RECALL AND DISPLAY USING THE TIMELENS.
THE SKULL THEN USES HIS POWER TO SHARE THAT INTEL--THAT EACH AND EVERY AMERICAN HAS BEEN UNWITTINGLY TRANSFORMED INTO A SLEEPER AGENT FOR THE KREE EMPIRE--
--WITH EVERYONE.
EVERYWHERE.

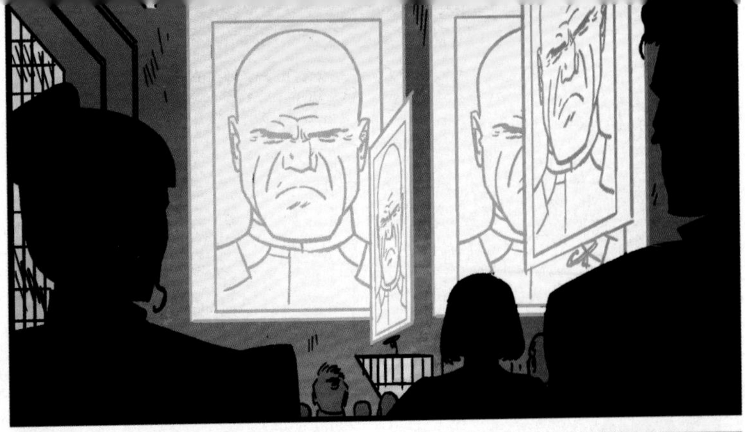

IN A MATTER OF *MINUTES*, THE ENTIRE KREE CONSPIRACY GOES *PUBLIC*. AMERICAN CITIZENS HAVE JUST AWAKENED TO THE TRUTH THAT THEY'VE BEEN BRED AS *CANNON FODDER*.

THE KREE CONSPIRATORS WILL BE LOSING THEIR *MINDS* AND SEEKING *RETRIBUTION* AGAINST THE SKULL AND ME.

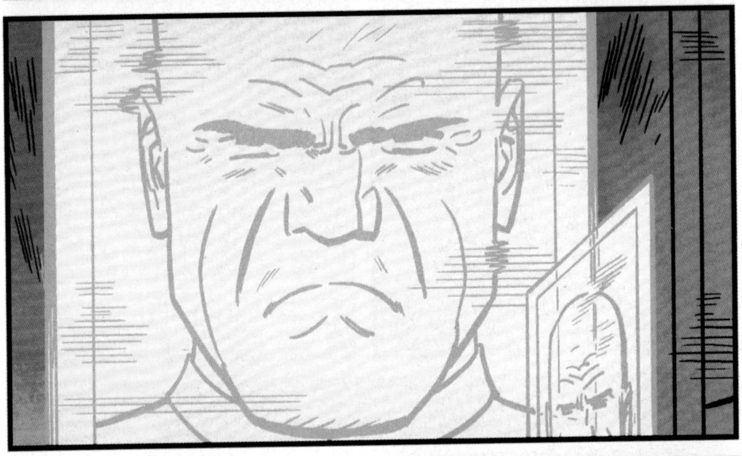

IN 1948, THE CHINESE COMMUNIST PARTY AND THE NATIONALIST PARTY OF KUOMINTANG WENT TO WAR IN PART THANKS TO RUSSIAN MANIPULATION.

THE "LET'S YOU AND HIM FIGHT SO I CAN ADVANCE" DOCTRINE.

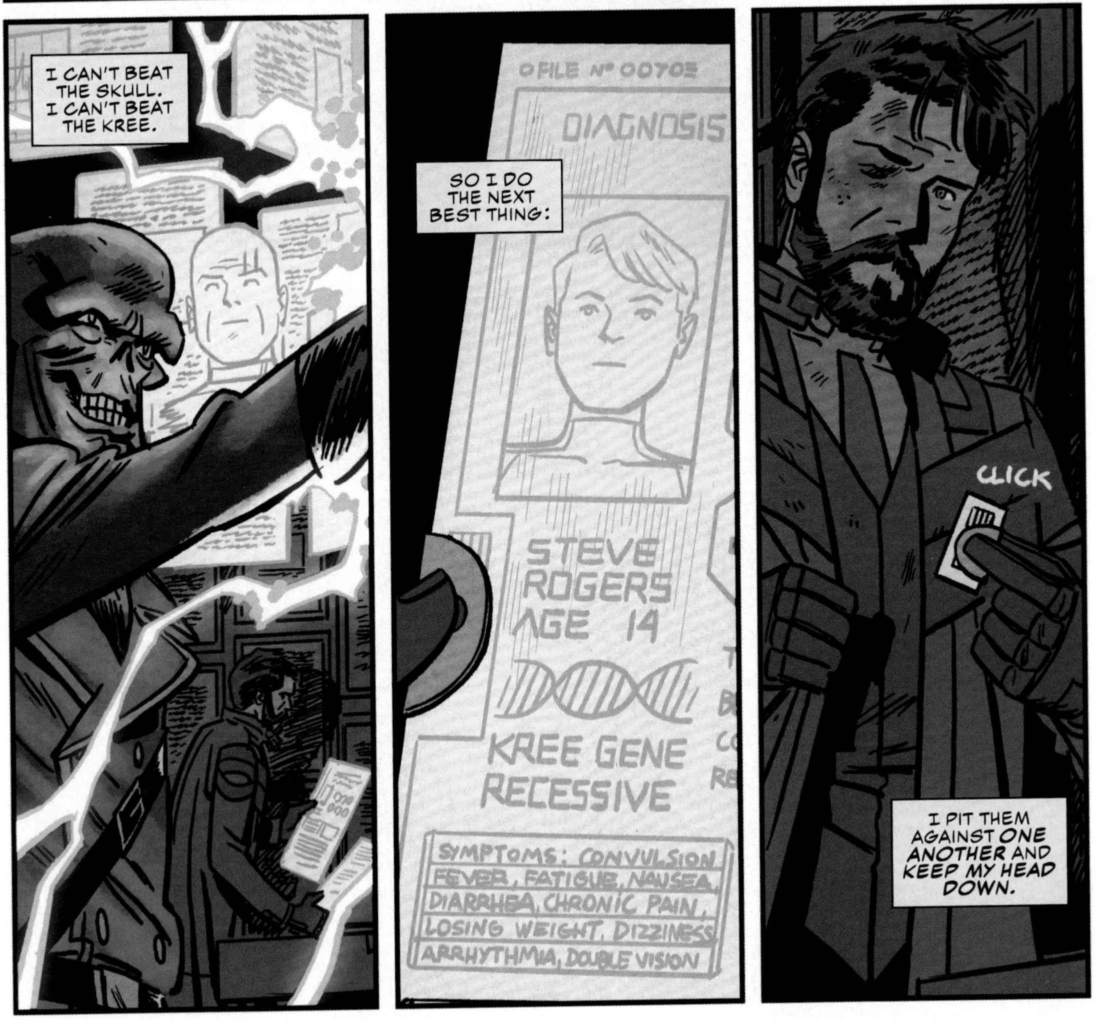
I CAN'T BEAT THE SKULL. I CAN'T BEAT THE KREE.
SO I DO THE NEXT BEST THING:
DIAGNOSIS
STEVE ROGERS
AGE 14
KREE GENE RECESSIVE
SYMPTOMS: CONVULSION
FEVER, FATIGUE, NAUSEA,
DIARRHEA, CHRONIC PAIN,
LOSING WEIGHT, DIZZINESS
ARRHYTHMIA, DOUBLE VISION
CLICK
I PIT THEM AGAINST *ONE ANOTHER* AND *KEEP MY HEAD DOWN.*

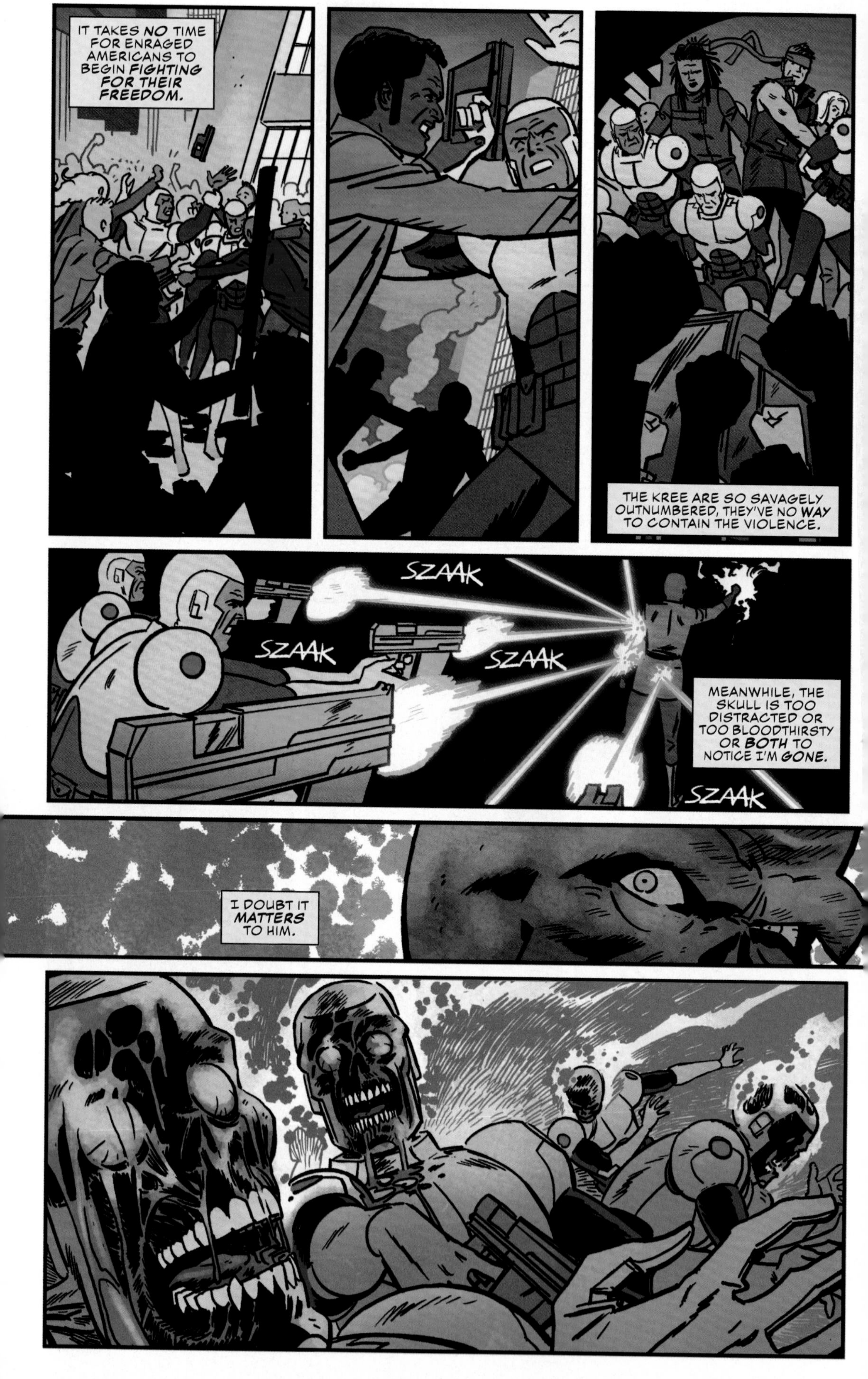
IT TAKES NO TIME FOR ENRAGED AMERICANS TO BEGIN FIGHTING FOR THEIR FREEDOM.
THE KREE ARE SO SAVAGELY OUTNUMBERED, THEY'VE NO WAY TO CONTAIN THE VIOLENCE.
SZAAK
SZAAK
SZAAK
MEANWHILE, THE SKULL IS TOO DISTRACTED OR TOO BLOODTHIRSTY OR BOTH TO NOTICE I'M GONE.
SZAAK
I DOUBT IT MATTERS TO HIM.

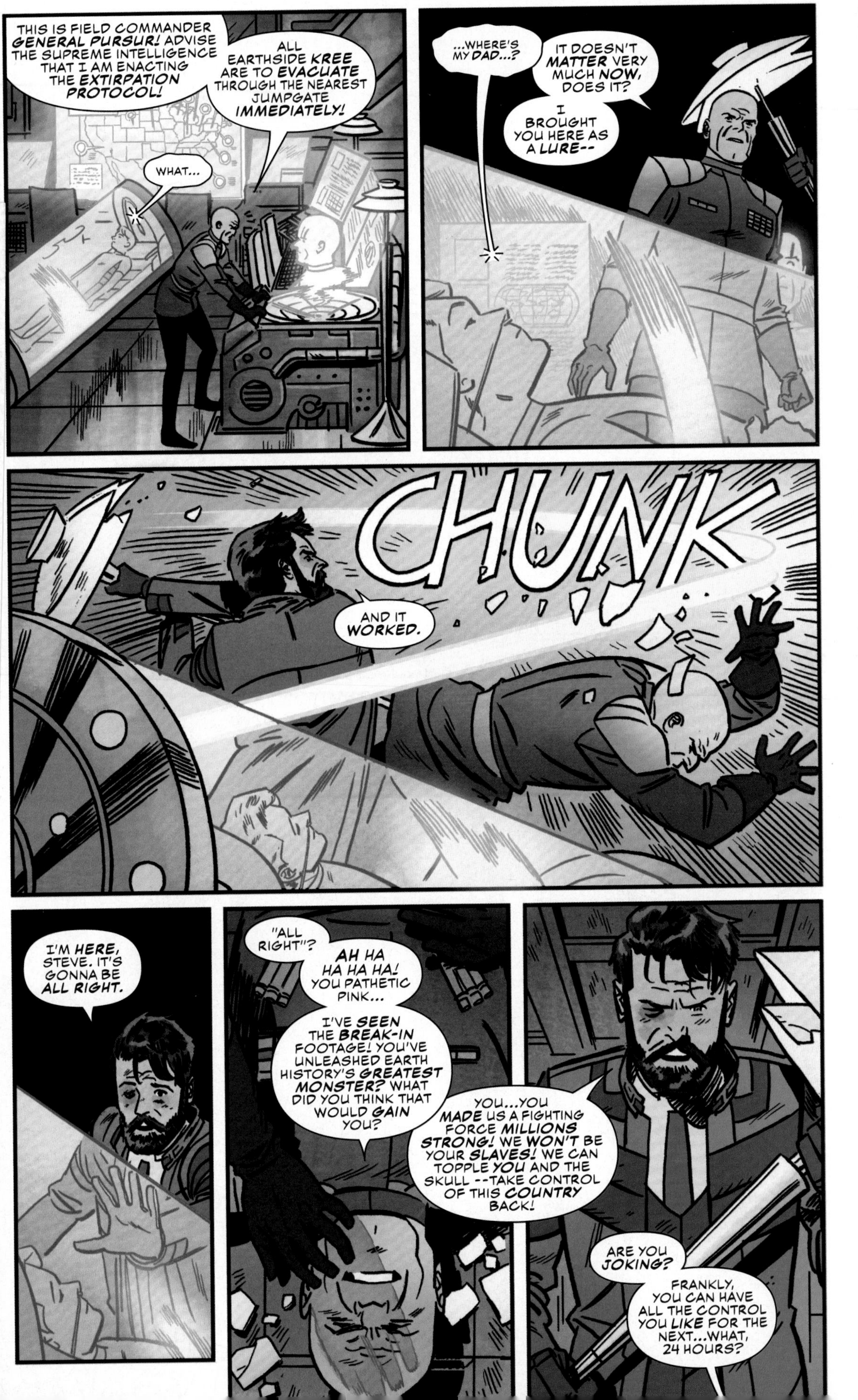
THIS IS FIELD COMMANDER GENERAL PURSUR! ADVISE THE SUPREME INTELLIGENCE THAT I AM ENACTING THE EXTIRPATION PROTOCOL!
ALL EARTHSIDE KREE ARE TO EVACUATE THROUGH THE NEAREST JUMPGATE IMMEDIATELY!
WHAT...
...WHERE'S MY DAD...?
IT DOESN'T MATTER VERY MUCH NOW, DOES IT?
I BROUGHT YOU HERE AS A LURE--
CHUNK
AND IT WORKED.
I'M HERE, STEVE. IT'S GONNA BE ALL RIGHT.
"ALL RIGHT"?
AH HA HA HA HA! YOU PATHETIC PINK...
I'VE SEEN THE BREAK-IN FOOTAGE! YOU'VE UNLEASHED EARTH HISTORY'S GREATEST MONSTER? WHAT DID YOU THINK THAT WOULD GAIN YOU?
YOU...YOU MADE US A FIGHTING FORCE MILLIONS STRONG! WE WON'T BE YOUR SLAVES! WE CAN TOPPLE YOU AND THE SKULL --TAKE CONTROL OF THIS COUNTRY BACK!
ARE YOU JOKING?
FRANKLY, YOU CAN HAVE ALL THE CONTROL YOU LIKE FOR THE NEXT...WHAT, 24 HOURS?

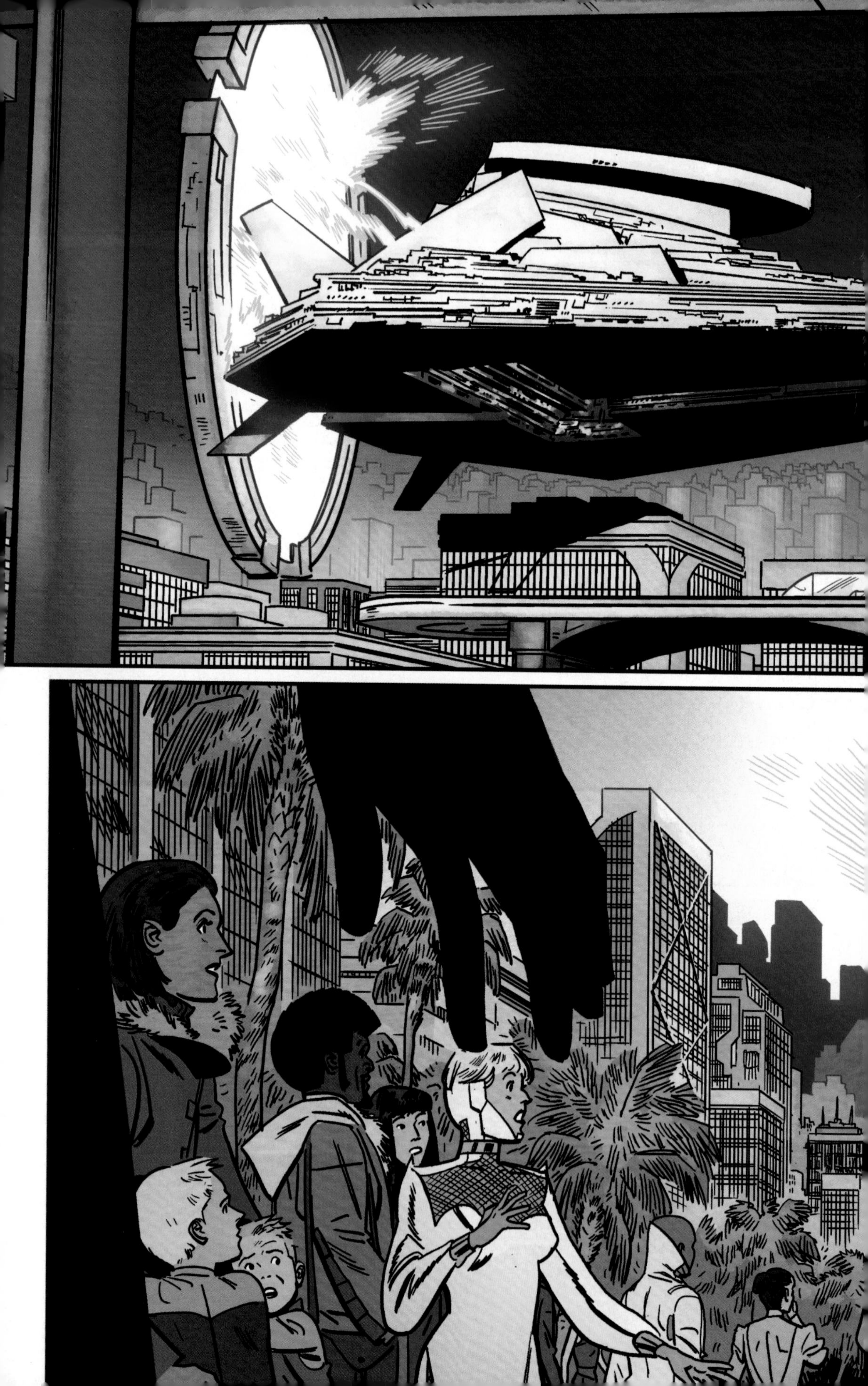

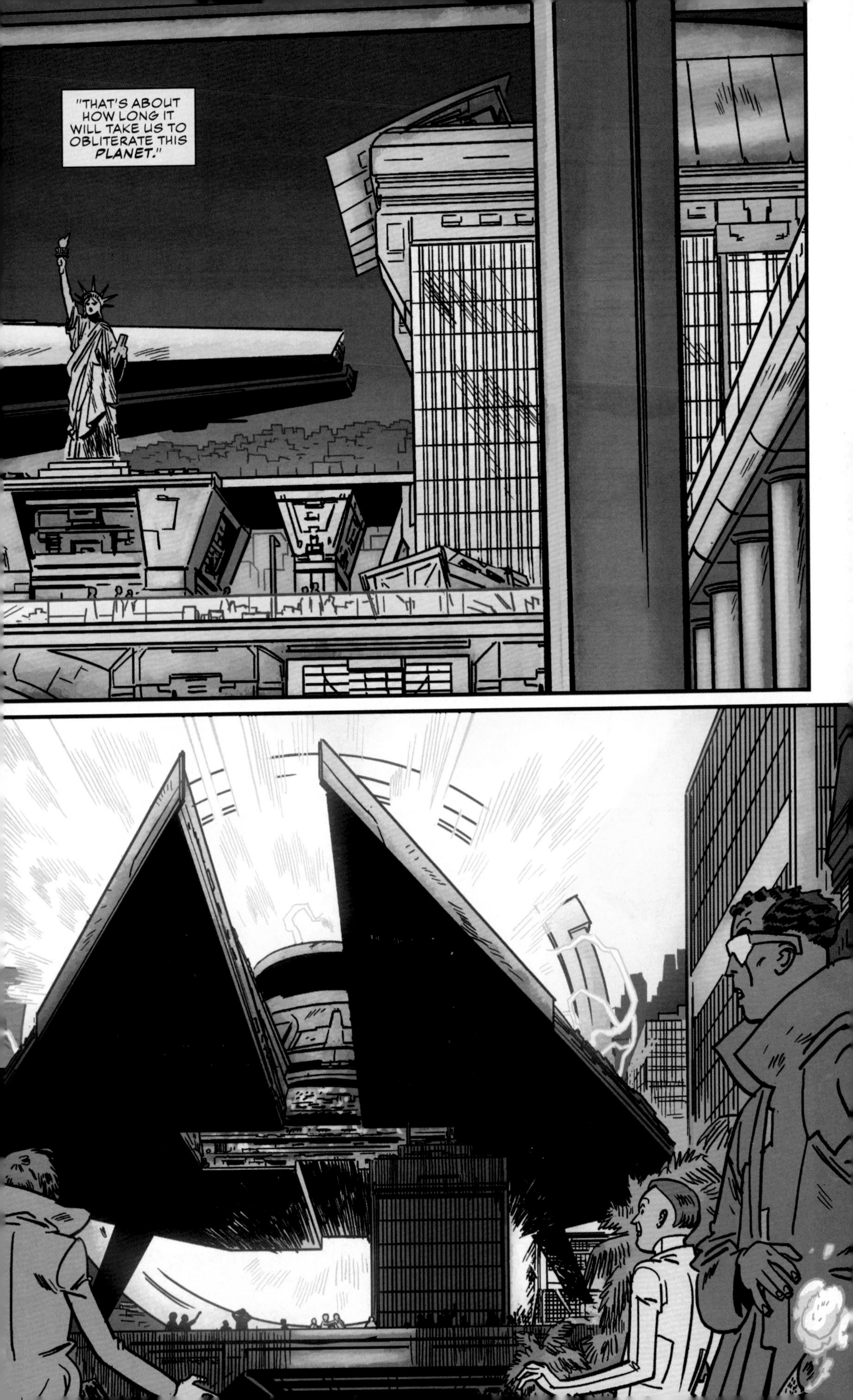
"THAT'S ABOUT HOW LONG IT WILL TAKE US TO OBLITERATE THIS PLANET."

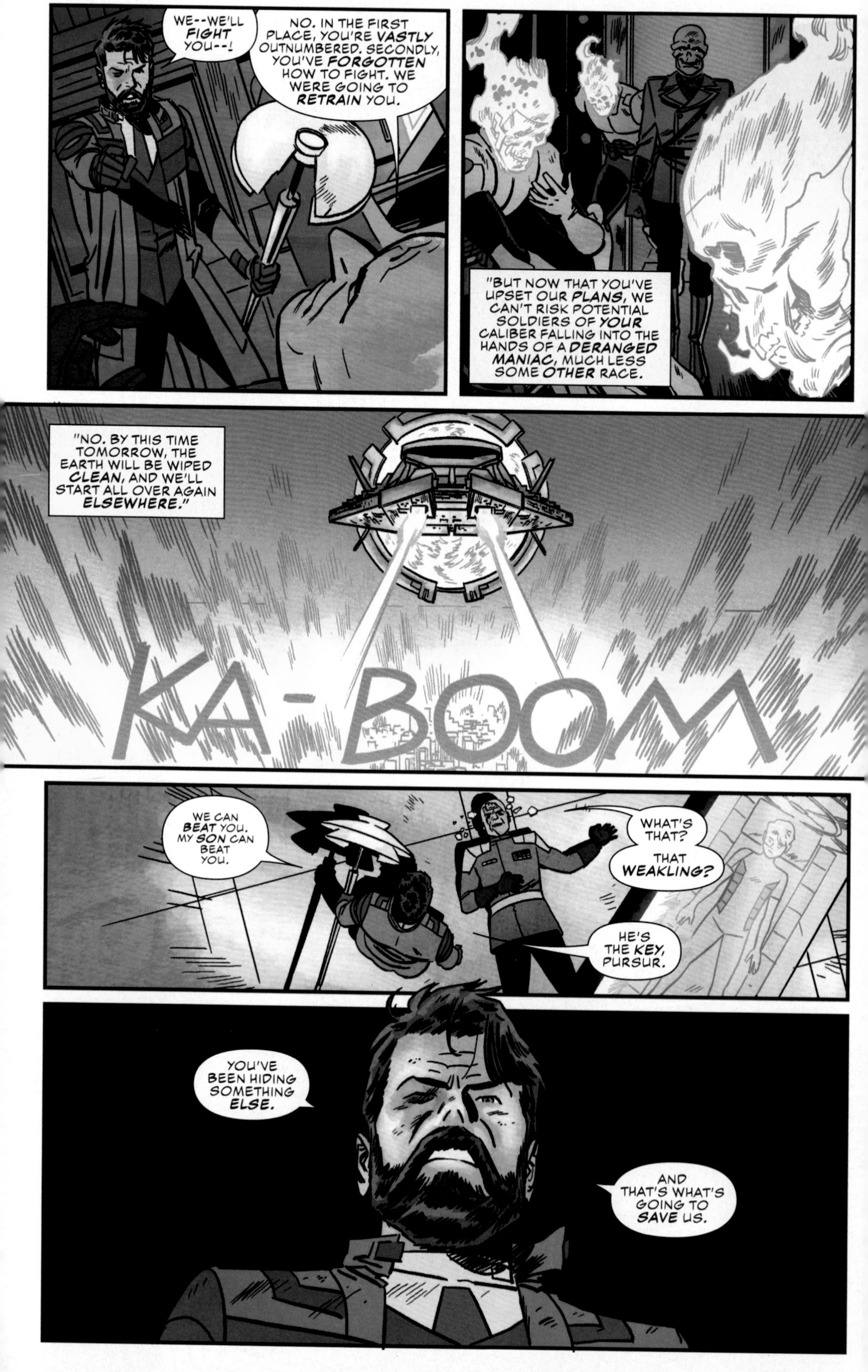

WE--WE'LL FIGHT YOU--!
NO. IN THE FIRST PLACE, YOU'RE VASTLY OUTNUMBERED. SECONDLY, YOU'VE FORGOTTEN HOW TO FIGHT. WE WERE GOING TO RETRAIN YOU.
"BUT NOW THAT YOU'VE UPSET OUR PLANS, WE CAN'T RISK POTENTIAL SOLDIERS OF YOUR CALIBER FALLING INTO THE HANDS OF A DERANGED MANIAC, MUCH LESS SOME OTHER RACE.
"NO. BY THIS TIME TOMORROW, THE EARTH WILL BE WIPED CLEAN, AND WE'LL START ALL OVER AGAIN ELSEWHERE."
KA-BOOM
WE CAN BEAT YOU. MY SON CAN BEAT YOU.
WHAT'S THAT?
THAT WEAKLING?
HE'S THE KEY, PURSUR.
YOU'VE BEEN HIDING SOMETHING ELSE.
AND THAT'S WHAT'S GOING TO SAVE US.

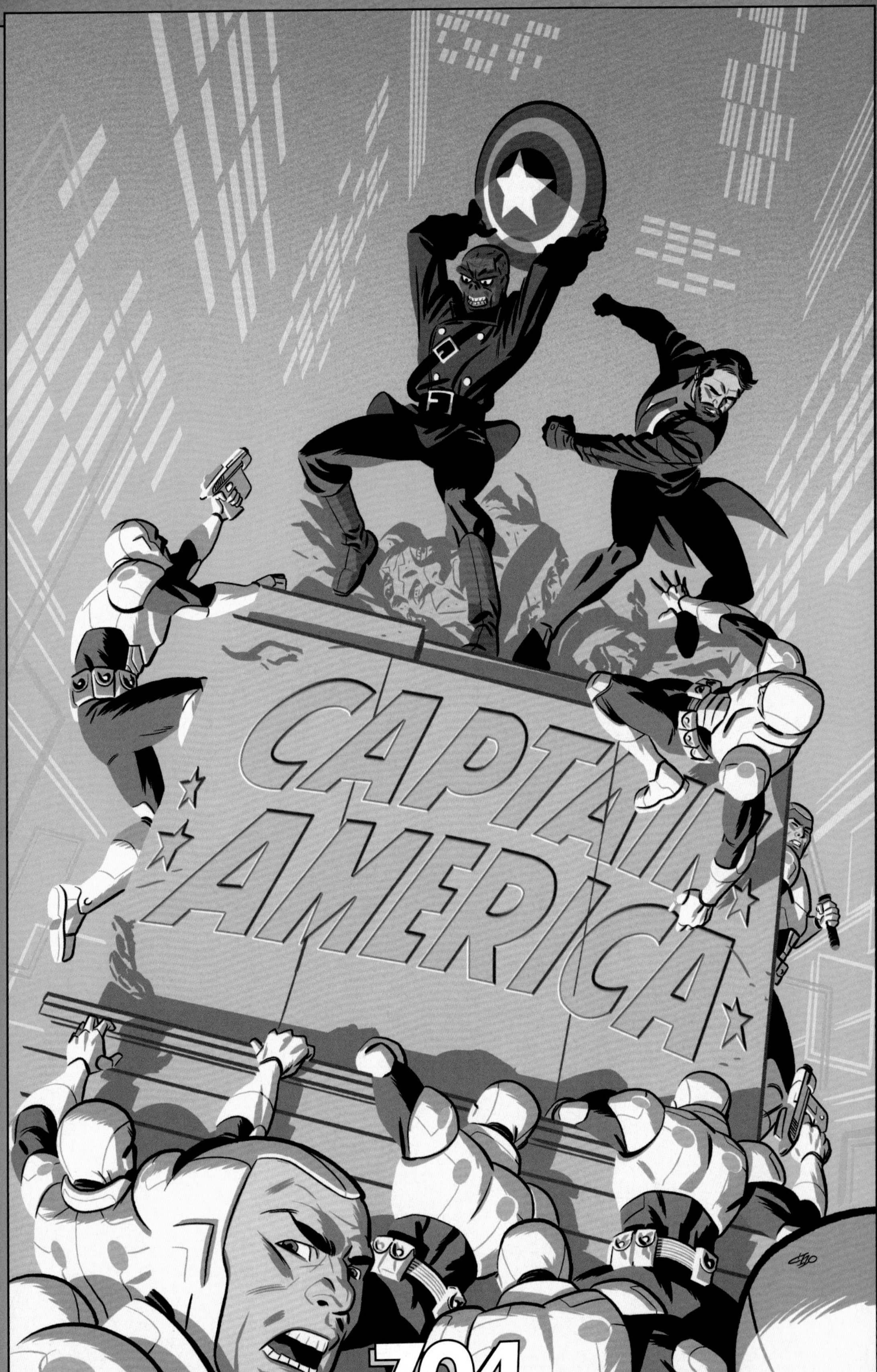
CAPTAIN AMERICA
704

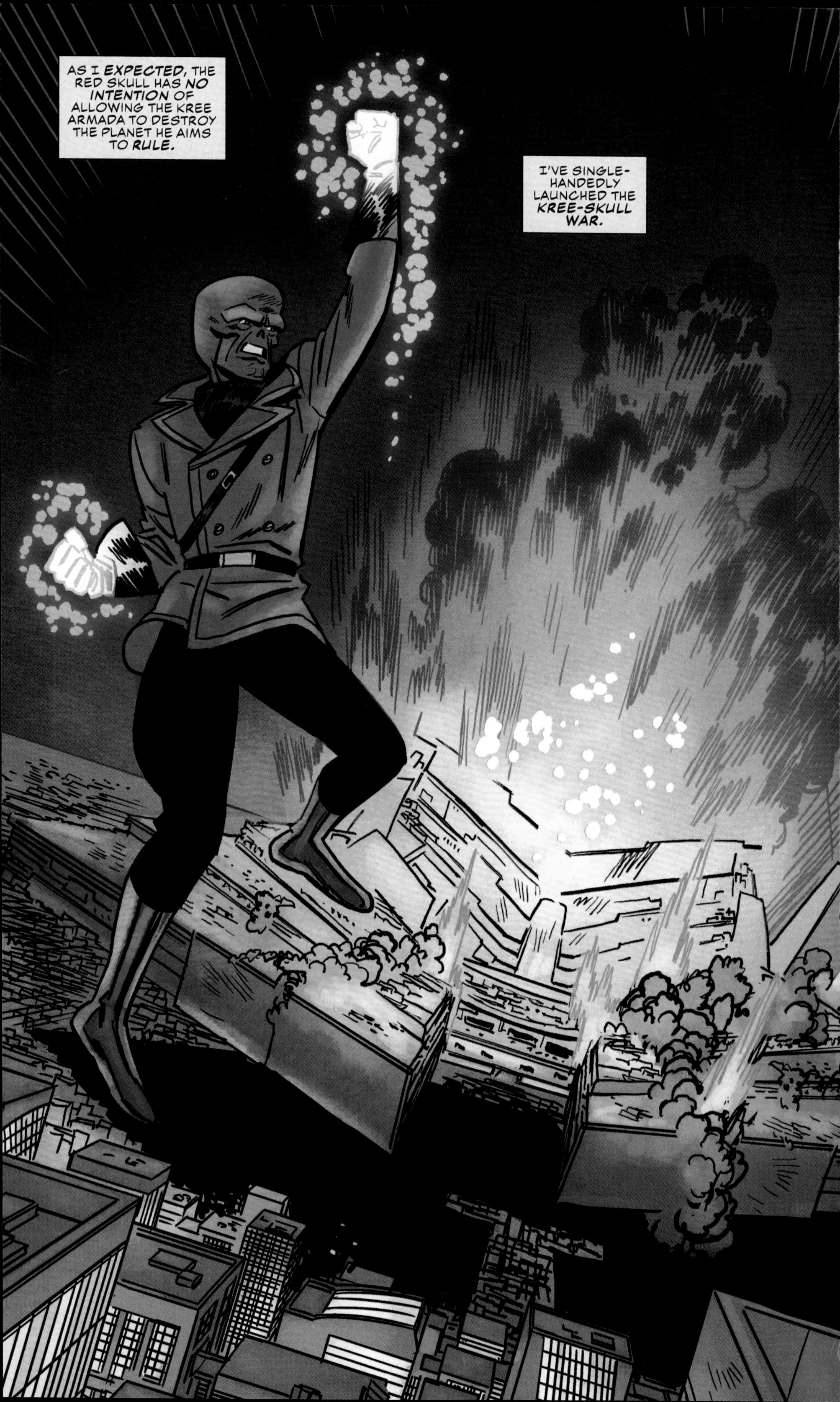

AS I EXPECTED, THE RED SKULL HAS NO INTENTION OF ALLOWING THE KREE ARMADA TO DESTROY THE PLANET HE AIMS TO RULE.
I'VE SINGLE-HANDEDLY LAUNCHED THE KREE-SKULL WAR.

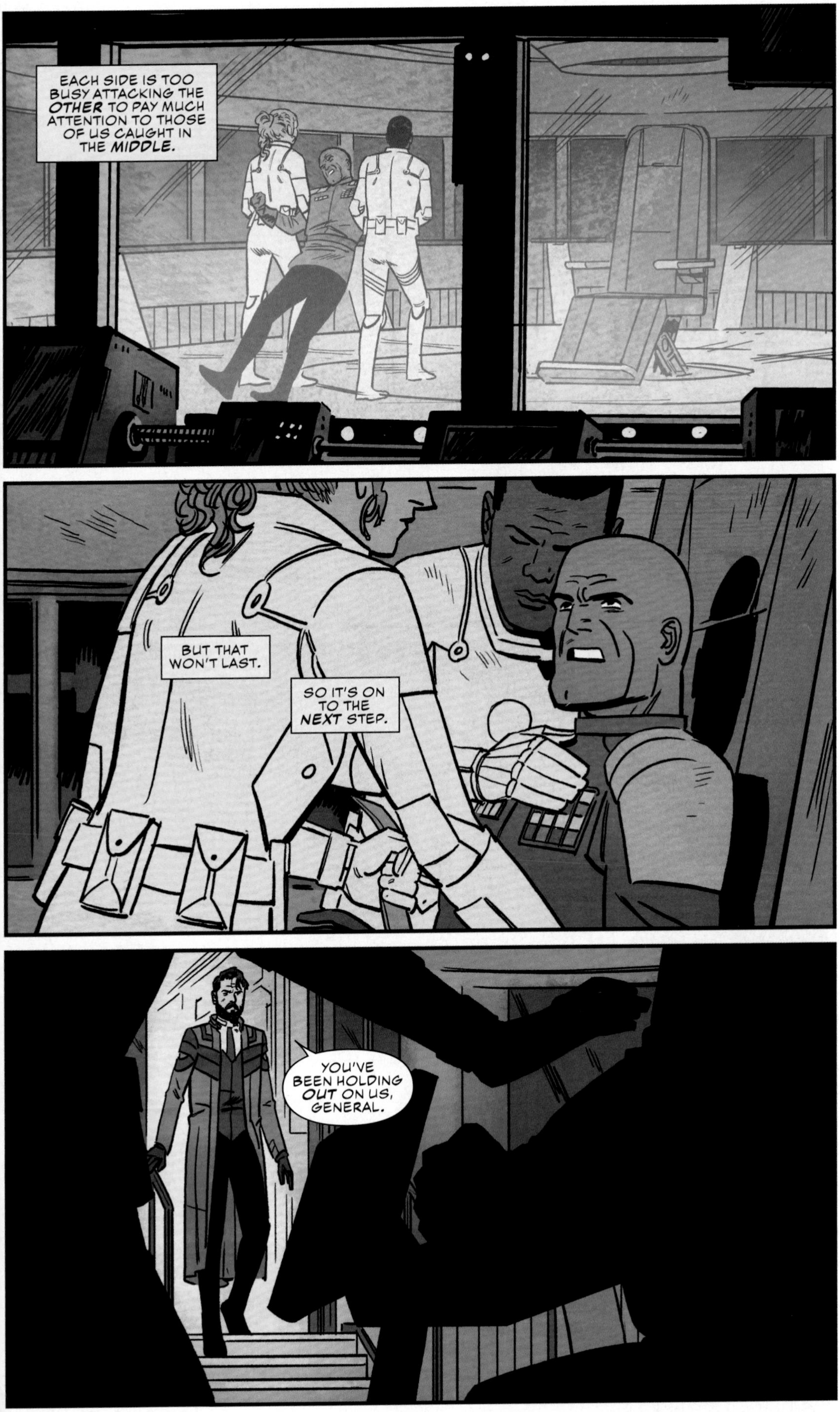
EACH SIDE IS TOO BUSY ATTACKING THE OTHER TO PAY MUCH ATTENTION TO THOSE OF US CAUGHT IN THE MIDDLE.
BUT THAT WON'T LAST.
SO IT'S ON TO THE NEXT STEP.
YOU'VE BEEN HOLDING OUT ON US, GENERAL.

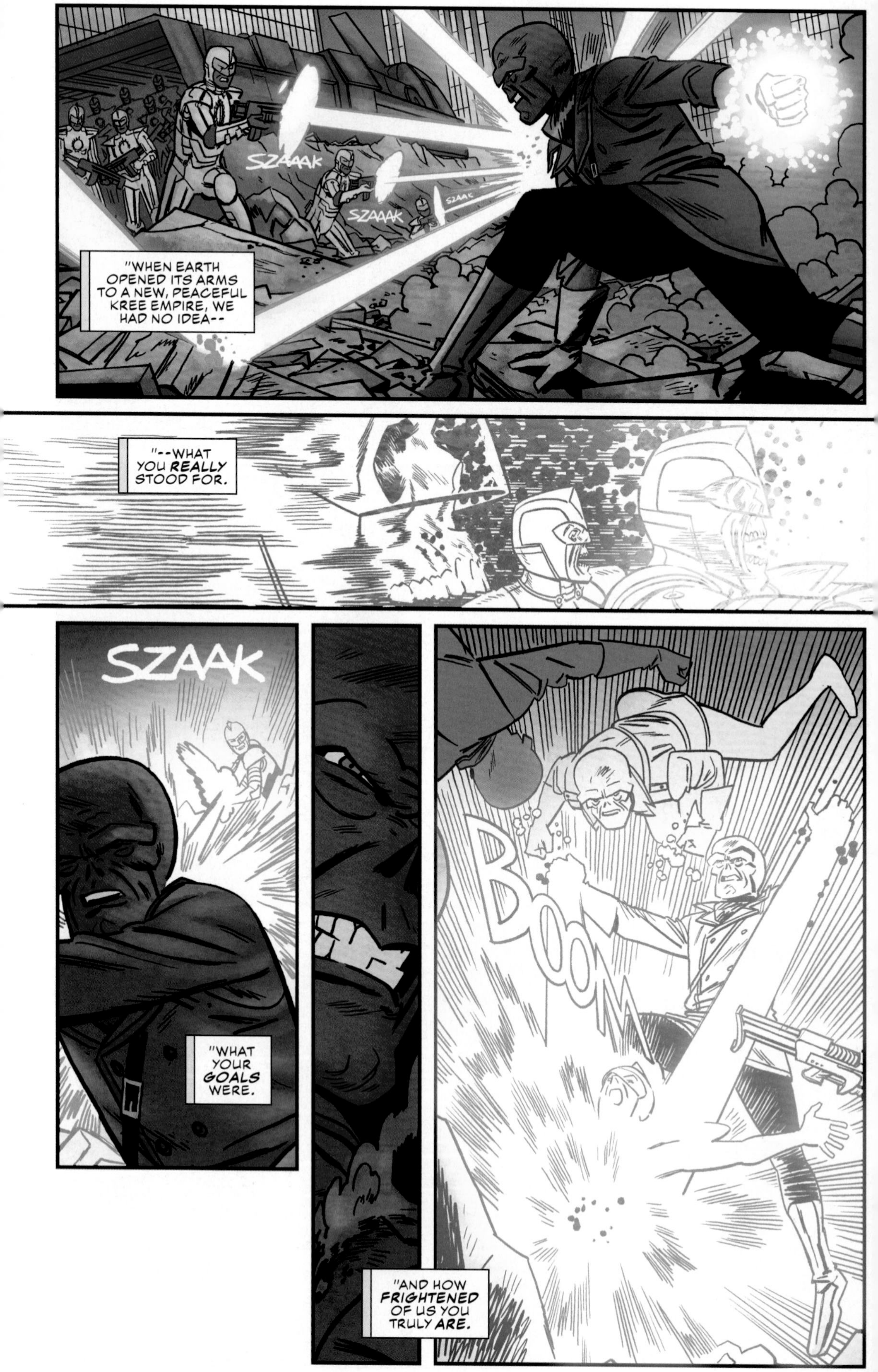
SZAAAK
SZAAAK
SZAAAK
"WHEN EARTH OPENED ITS ARMS TO A NEW, PEACEFUL KREE EMPIRE, WE HAD NO IDEA--
"--WHAT YOU REALLY STOOD FOR.
SZAAK
"WHAT YOUR GOALS WERE.
BOOOM
"AND HOW FRIGHTENED OF US YOU TRULY ARE.

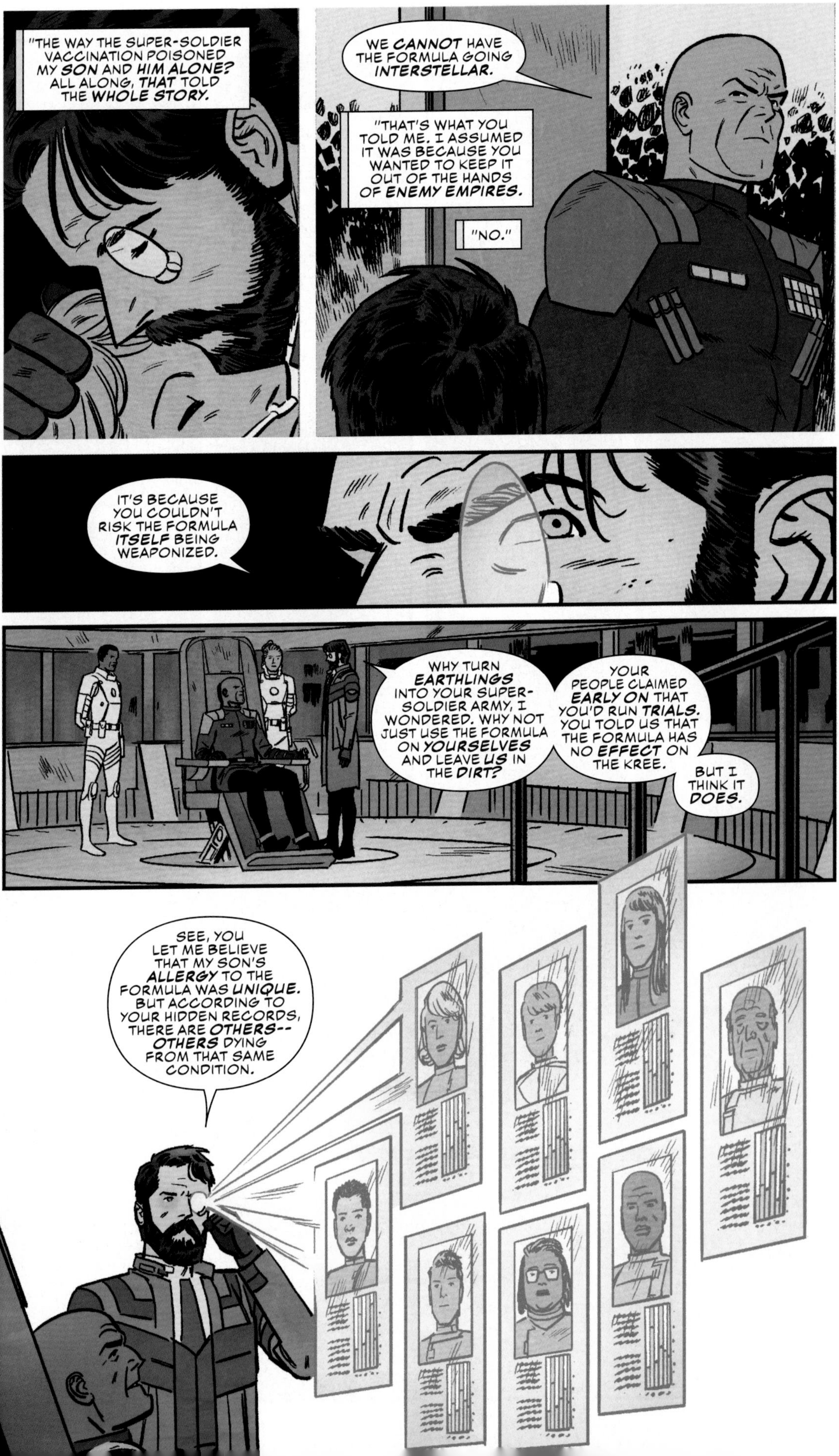
"THE WAY THE SUPER-SOLDIER VACCINATION POISONED MY SON AND HIM ALONE? ALL ALONG, THAT TOLD THE WHOLE STORY.
WE CANNOT HAVE THE FORMULA GOING INTERSTELLAR.
"THAT'S WHAT YOU TOLD ME. I ASSUMED IT WAS BECAUSE YOU WANTED TO KEEP IT OUT OF THE HANDS OF ENEMY EMPIRES.
"NO."
IT'S BECAUSE YOU COULDN'T RISK THE FORMULA ITSELF BEING WEAPONIZED.
WHY TURN EARTHLINGS INTO YOUR SUPER-SOLDIER ARMY, I WONDERED. WHY NOT JUST USE THE FORMULA ON YOURSELVES AND LEAVE US IN THE DIRT?
YOUR PEOPLE CLAIMED EARLY ON THAT YOU'D RUN TRIALS. YOU TOLD US THAT THE FORMULA HAS NO EFFECT ON THE KREE.
BUT I THINK IT DOES.
SEE, YOU LET ME BELIEVE THAT MY SON'S ALLERGY TO THE FORMULA WAS UNIQUE. BUT ACCORDING TO YOUR HIDDEN RECORDS, THERE ARE OTHERS-- OTHERS DYING FROM THAT SAME CONDITION.

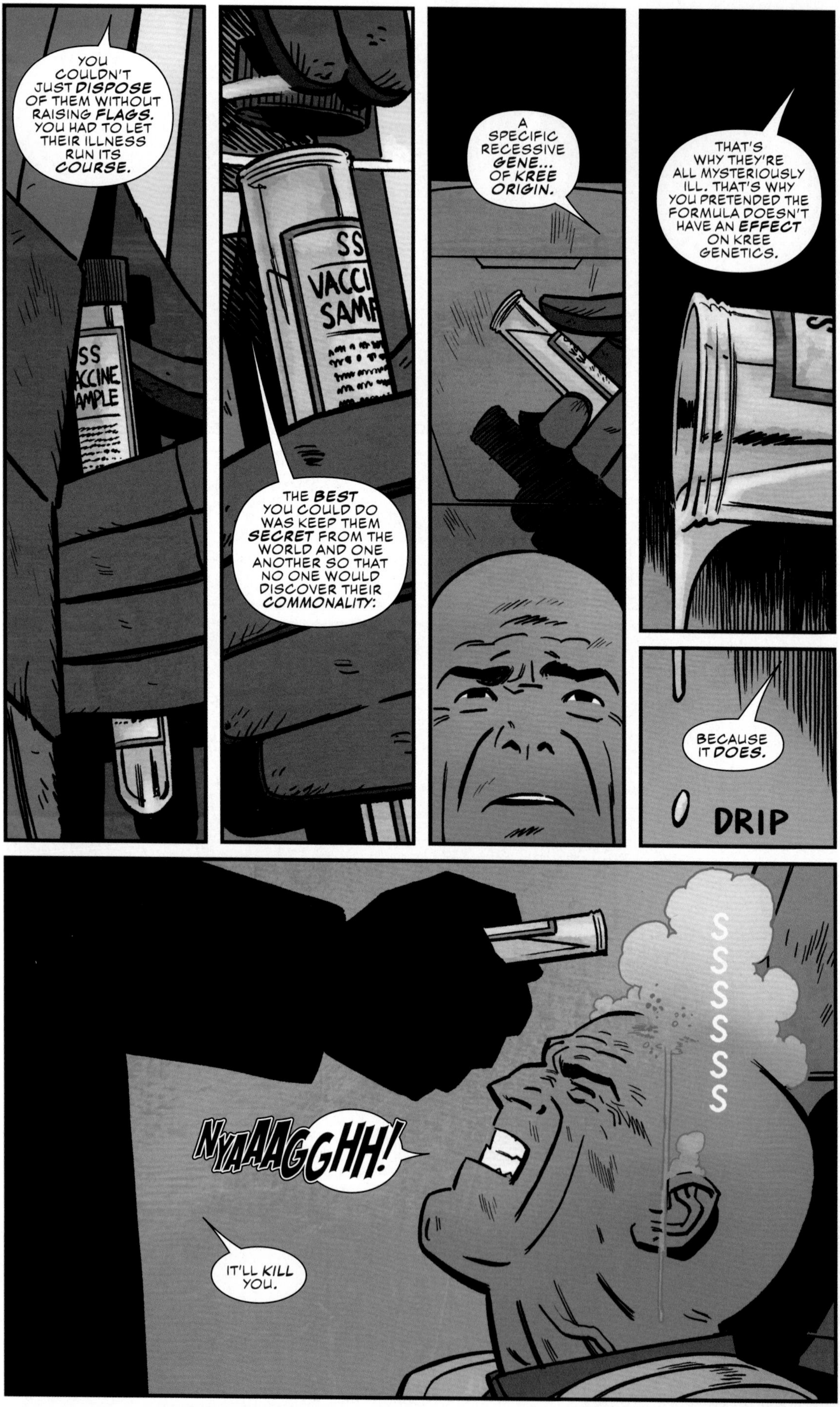
YOU COULDN'T JUST DISPOSE OF THEM WITHOUT RAISING FLAGS. YOU HAD TO LET THEIR ILLNESS RUN ITS COURSE.
SS VACCINE SAMPLE
SS VACCINE SAMPLE
THE BEST YOU COULD DO WAS KEEP THEM SECRET FROM THE WORLD AND ONE ANOTHER SO THAT NO ONE WOULD DISCOVER THEIR COMMONALITY:
A SPECIFIC RECESSIVE GENE... OF KREE ORIGIN.
THAT'S WHY THEY'RE ALL MYSTERIOUSLY ILL. THAT'S WHY YOU PRETENDED THE FORMULA DOESN'T HAVE AN EFFECT ON KREE GENETICS.
BECAUSE IT DOES.
DRIP
SSSSSS
NYAAAGGHH!
IT'LL KILL YOU.

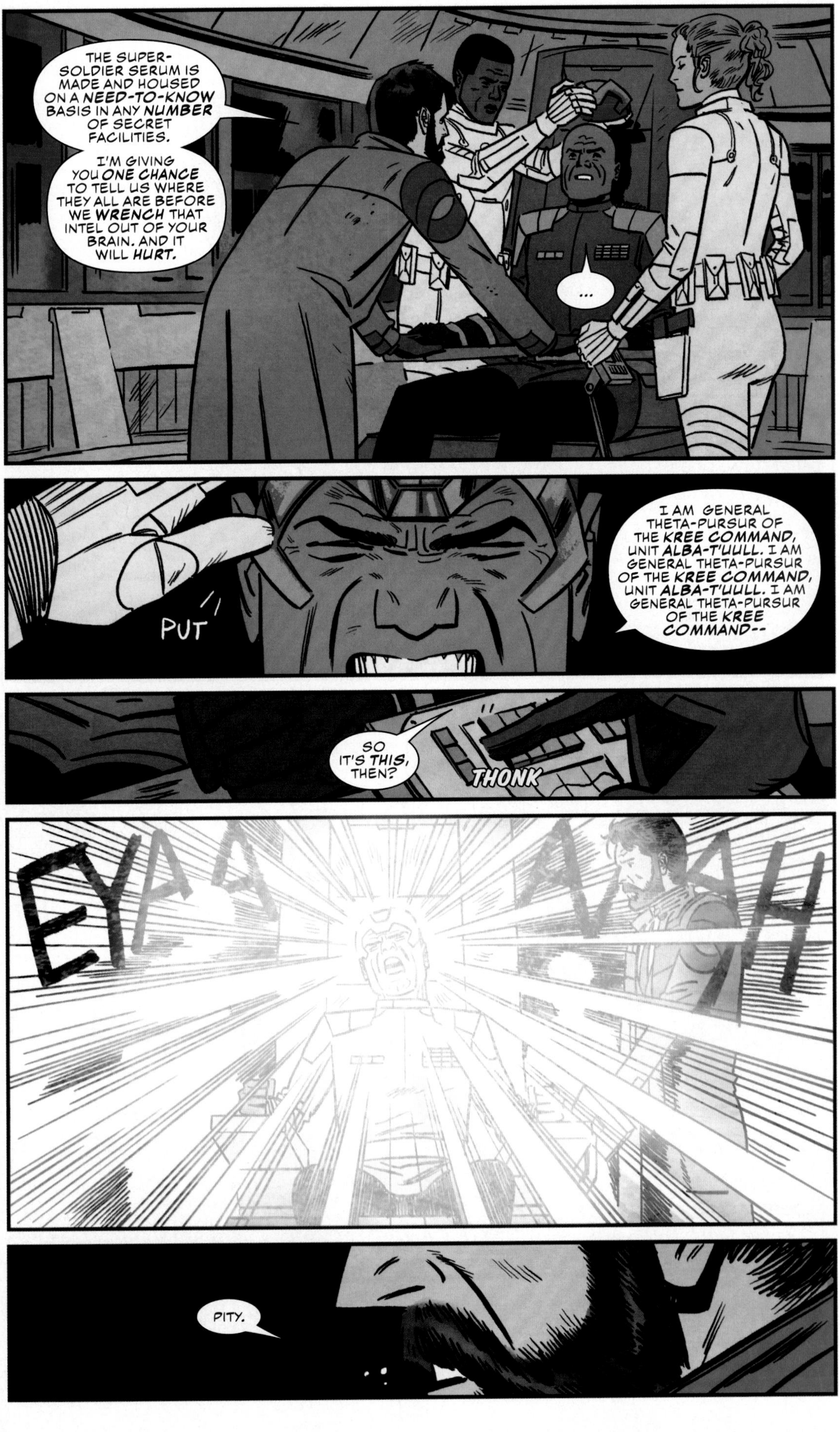
THE SUPER-SOLDIER SERUM IS MADE AND HOUSED ON A NEED-TO-KNOW BASIS IN ANY NUMBER OF SECRET FACILITIES.
I'M GIVING YOU ONE CHANCE TO TELL US WHERE THEY ALL ARE BEFORE WE WRENCH THAT INTEL OUT OF YOUR BRAIN. AND IT WILL HURT.
...
PUT
I AM GENERAL THETA-PURSUR OF THE KREE COMMAND, UNIT ALBA-T'UULL. I AM GENERAL THETA-PURSUR OF THE KREE COMMAND, UNIT ALBA-T'UULL. I AM GENERAL THETA-PURSUR OF THE KREE COMMAND--
SO IT'S THIS, THEN?
THONK
EYAAAAH
PITY.

WITHIN MINUTES, WE HAVE ACCESS TO ALL THE PERTINENT INFORMATION ABOUT THE SERUM.

THE LOCATIONS OF THE STORAGE FACILITIES.

CRASH!

THE HOLDING TANKS.

BATCH 1678665

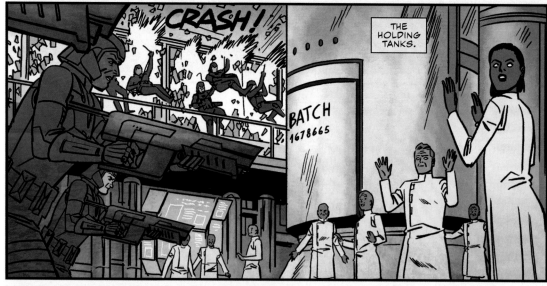

THE LABORATORIES. THE PIPELINES.

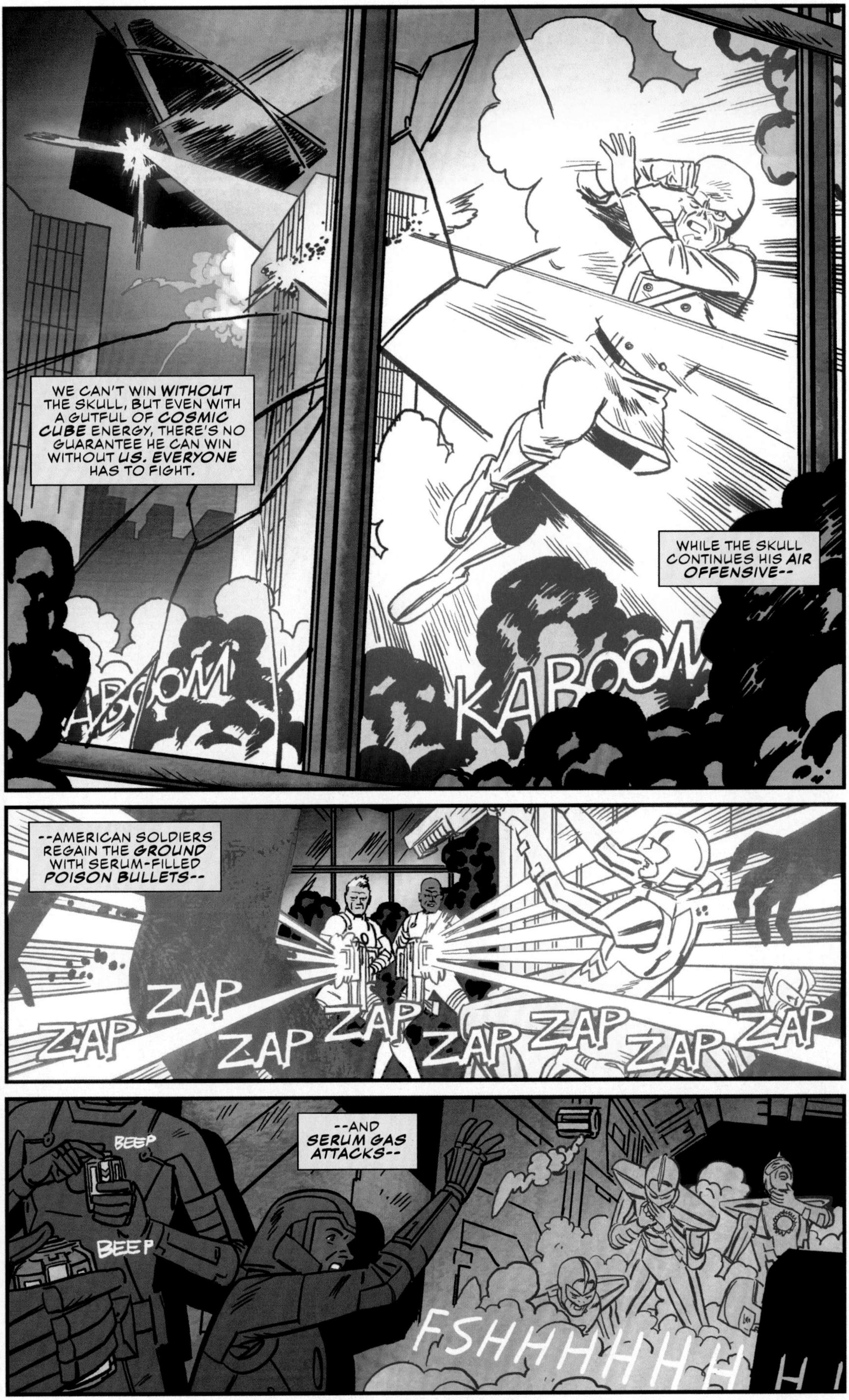
WE CAN'T WIN WITHOUT THE SKULL, BUT EVEN WITH A GUTFUL OF COSMIC CUBE ENERGY, THERE'S NO GUARANTEE HE CAN WIN WITHOUT US. EVERYONE HAS TO FIGHT.
WHILE THE SKULL CONTINUES HIS AIR OFFENSIVE--
KABOOM
KABOOM
--AMERICAN SOLDIERS REGAIN THE GROUND WITH SERUM-FILLED POISON BULLETS--
ZAP ZAP ZAP ZAP ZAP ZAP ZAP ZAP
--AND SERUM GAS ATTACKS--
BEEP
BEEP
FSHHHHHHHH

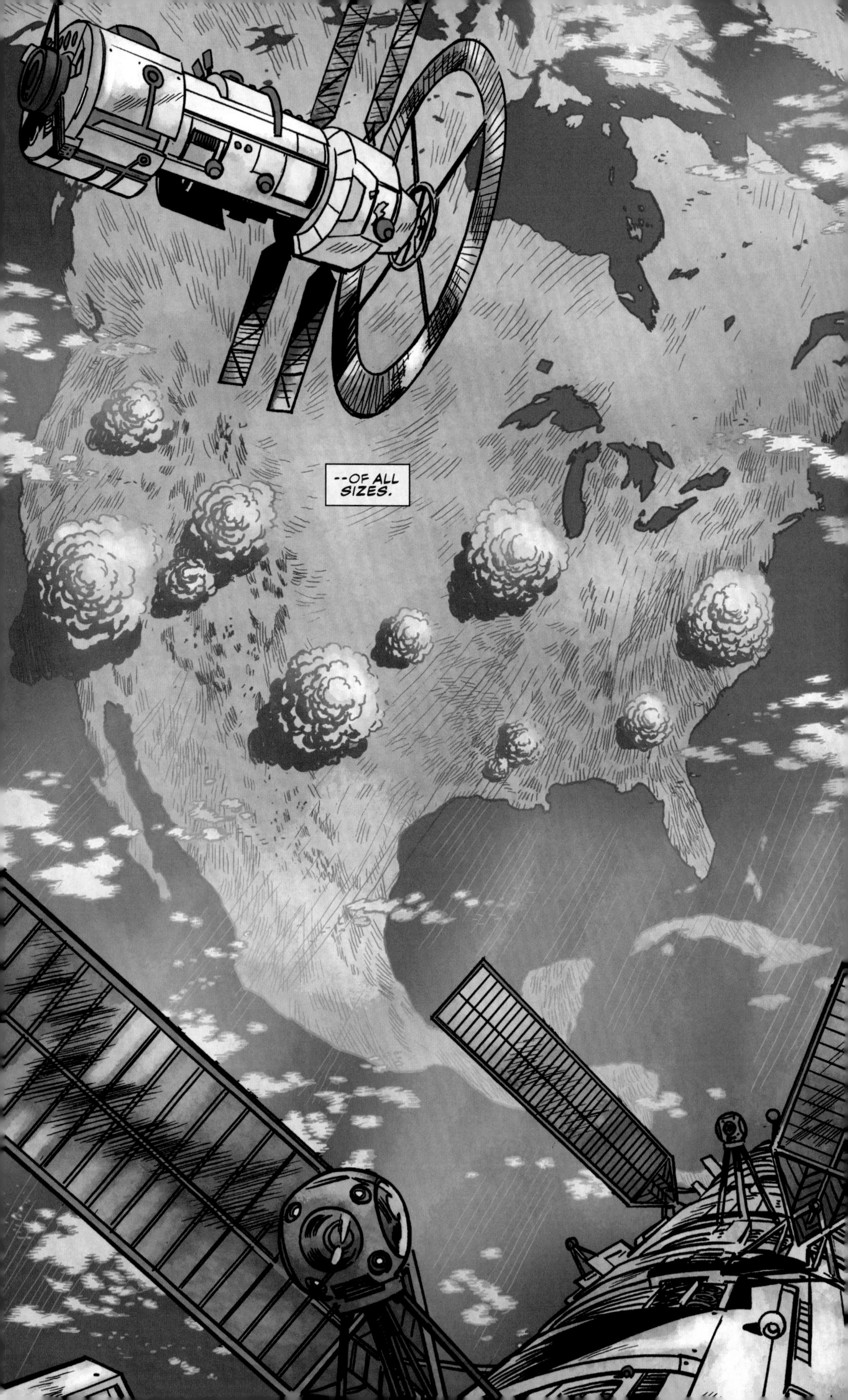
--OF ALL SIZES.

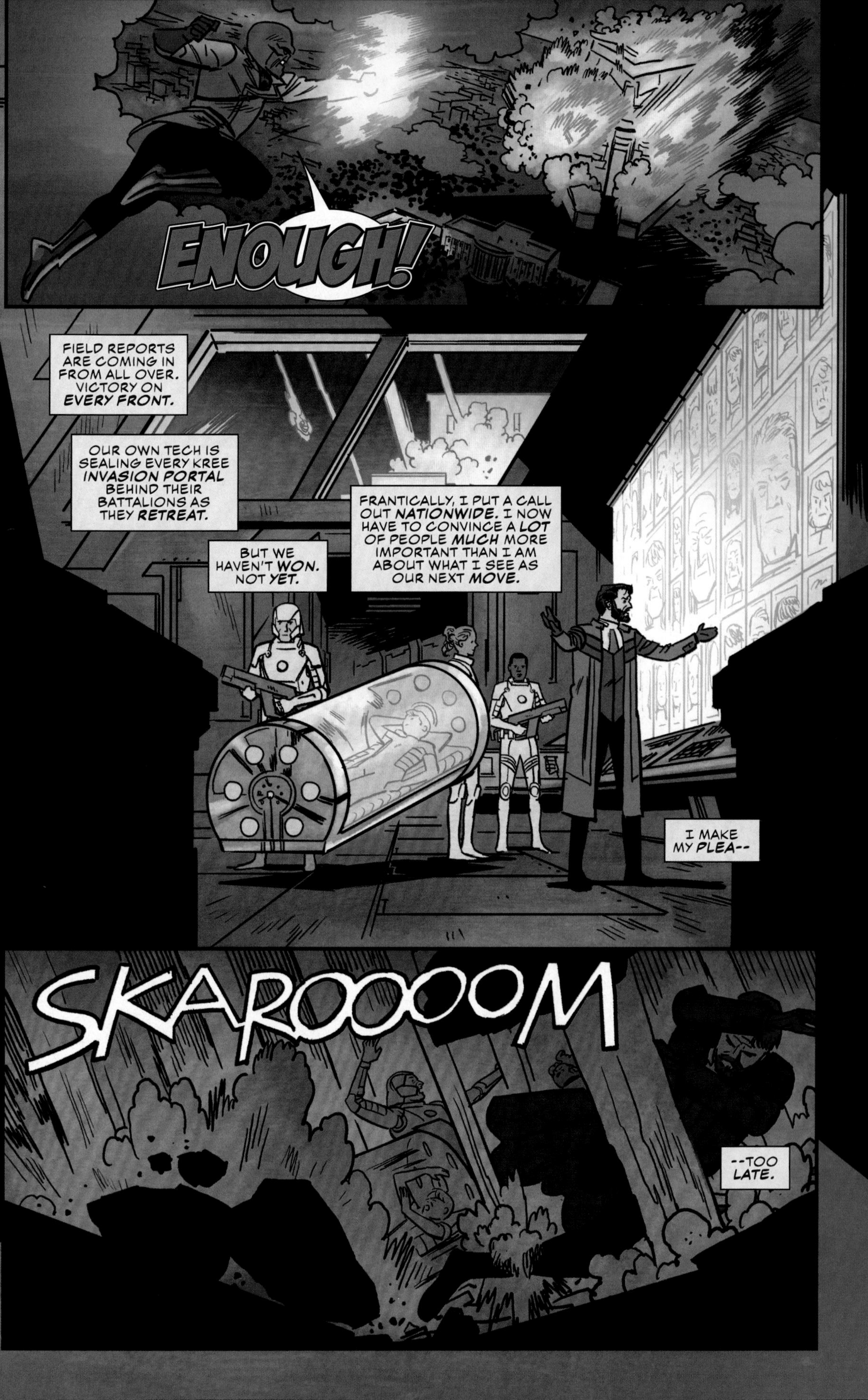
ENOUGH!
FIELD REPORTS ARE COMING IN FROM ALL OVER. VICTORY ON EVERY FRONT.
OUR OWN TECH IS SEALING EVERY KREE INVASION PORTAL BEHIND THEIR BATTALIONS AS THEY RETREAT.
BUT WE HAVEN'T WON. NOT YET.
FRANTICALLY, I PUT A CALL OUT NATIONWIDE. I NOW HAVE TO CONVINCE A LOT OF PEOPLE MUCH MORE IMPORTANT THAN I AM ABOUT WHAT I SEE AS OUR NEXT MOVE.
I MAKE MY PLEA--
SKAROOOOM
--TOO LATE.

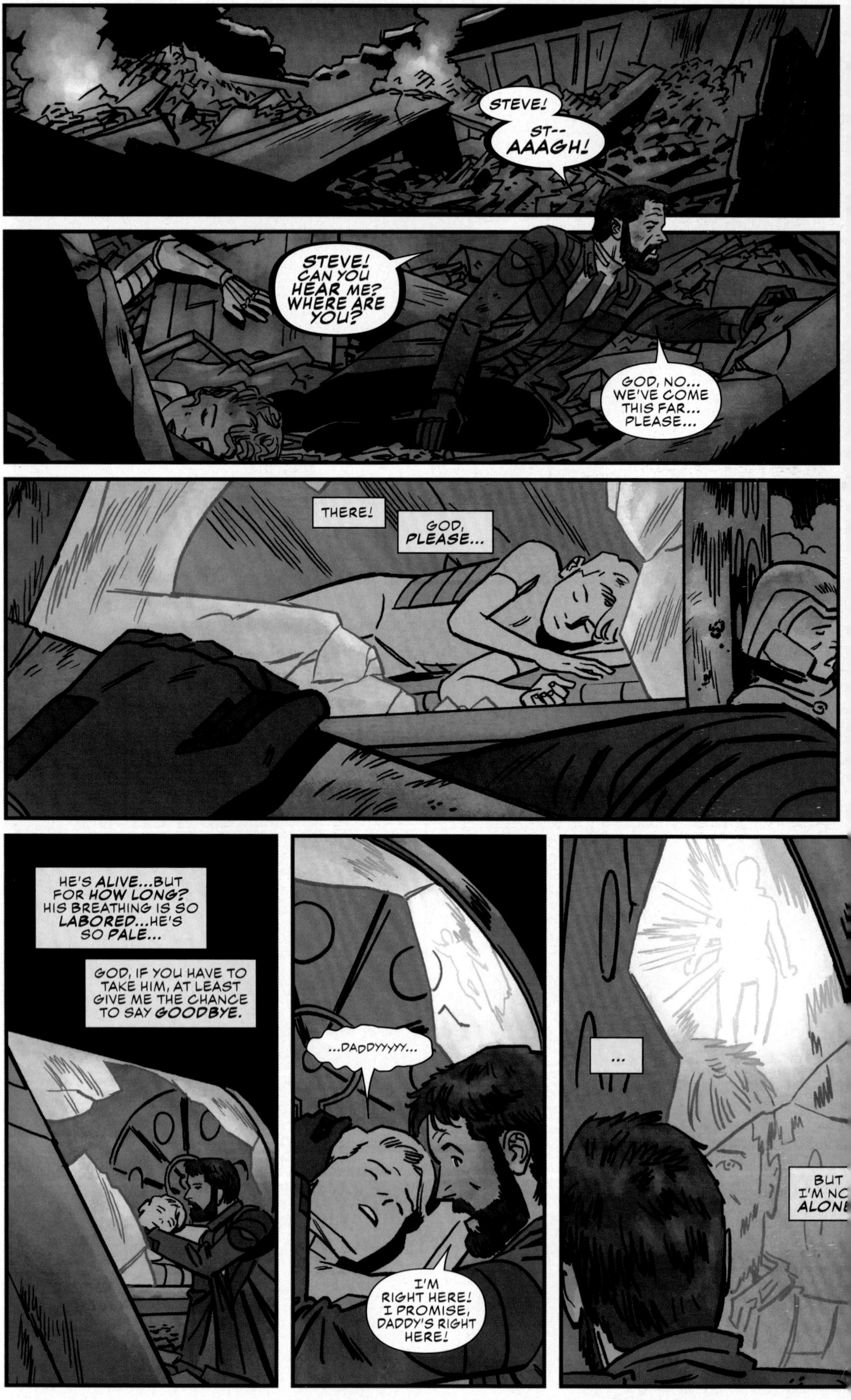
STEVE!
ST-- AAAGH!
STEVE! CAN YOU HEAR ME? WHERE ARE YOU?
GOD, NO... WE'VE COME THIS FAR... PLEASE...
THERE!
GOD, PLEASE...
HE'S ALIVE...BUT FOR HOW LONG? HIS BREATHING IS SO LABORED...HE'S SO PALE...
GOD, IF YOU HAVE TO TAKE HIM, AT LEAST GIVE ME THE CHANCE TO SAY GOODBYE.
...DADDYYYYY...
I'M RIGHT HERE! I PROMISE, DADDY'S RIGHT HERE!
...

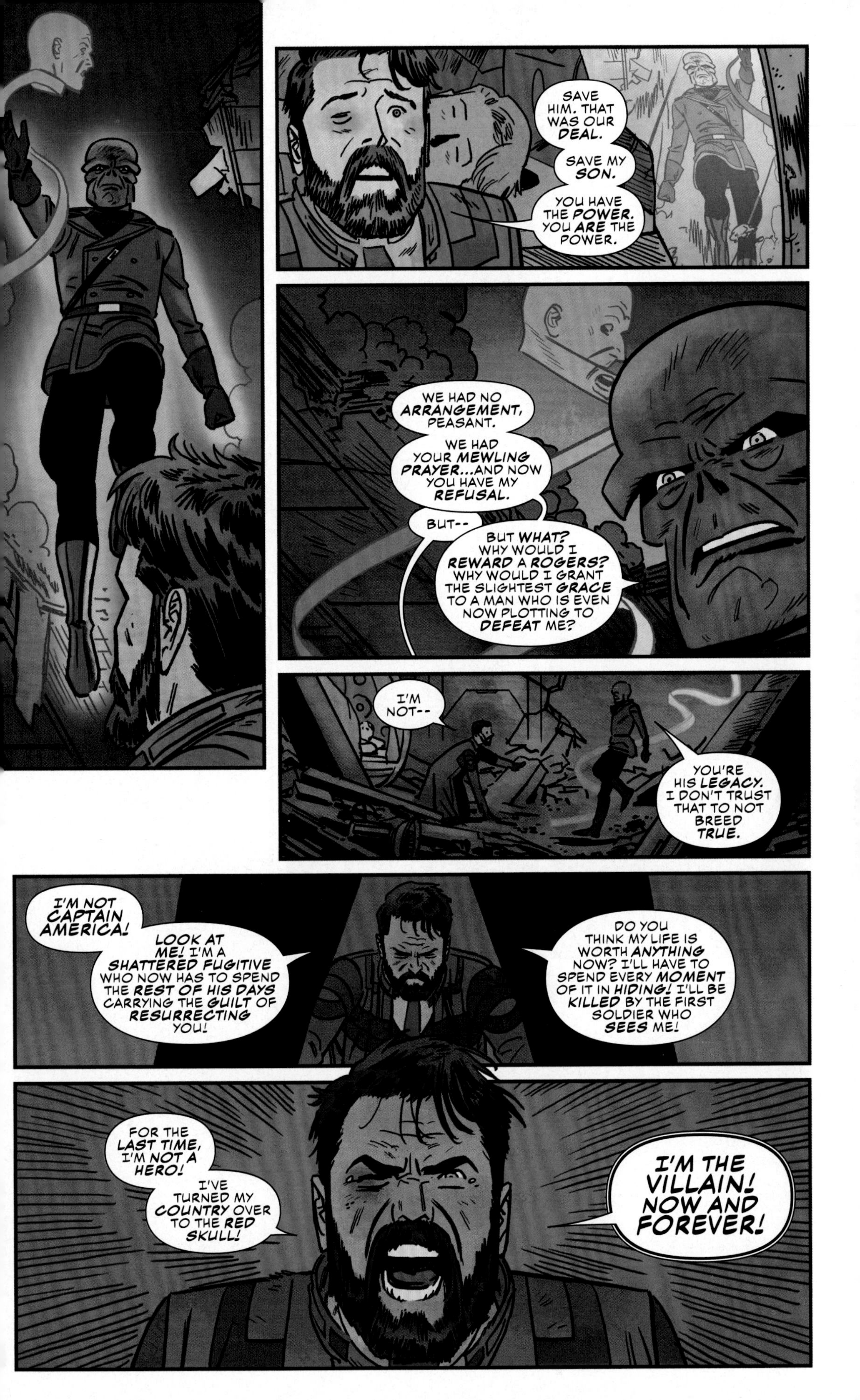
SAVE HIM. THAT WAS OUR DEAL.
SAVE MY SON.
YOU HAVE THE POWER. YOU ARE THE POWER.
WE HAD NO ARRANGEMENT, PEASANT.
WE HAD YOUR MEWLING PRAYER...AND NOW YOU HAVE MY REFUSAL.
BUT--
BUT WHAT? WHY WOULD I REWARD A ROGERS? WHY WOULD I GRANT THE SLIGHTEST GRACE TO A MAN WHO IS EVEN NOW PLOTTING TO DEFEAT ME?
I'M NOT--
YOU'RE HIS LEGACY. I DON'T TRUST THAT TO NOT BREED TRUE.
I'M NOT CAPTAIN AMERICA!
LOOK AT ME! I'M A SHATTERED FUGITIVE WHO NOW HAS TO SPEND THE REST OF HIS DAYS CARRYING THE GUILT OF RESURRECTING YOU!
DO YOU THINK MY LIFE IS WORTH ANYTHING NOW? I'LL HAVE TO SPEND EVERY MOMENT OF IT IN HIDING! I'LL BE KILLED BY THE FIRST SOLDIER WHO SEES ME!
FOR THE LAST TIME, I'M NOT A HERO!
I'VE TURNED MY COUNTRY OVER TO THE RED SKULL!
I'M THE VILLAIN! NOW AND FOREVER!

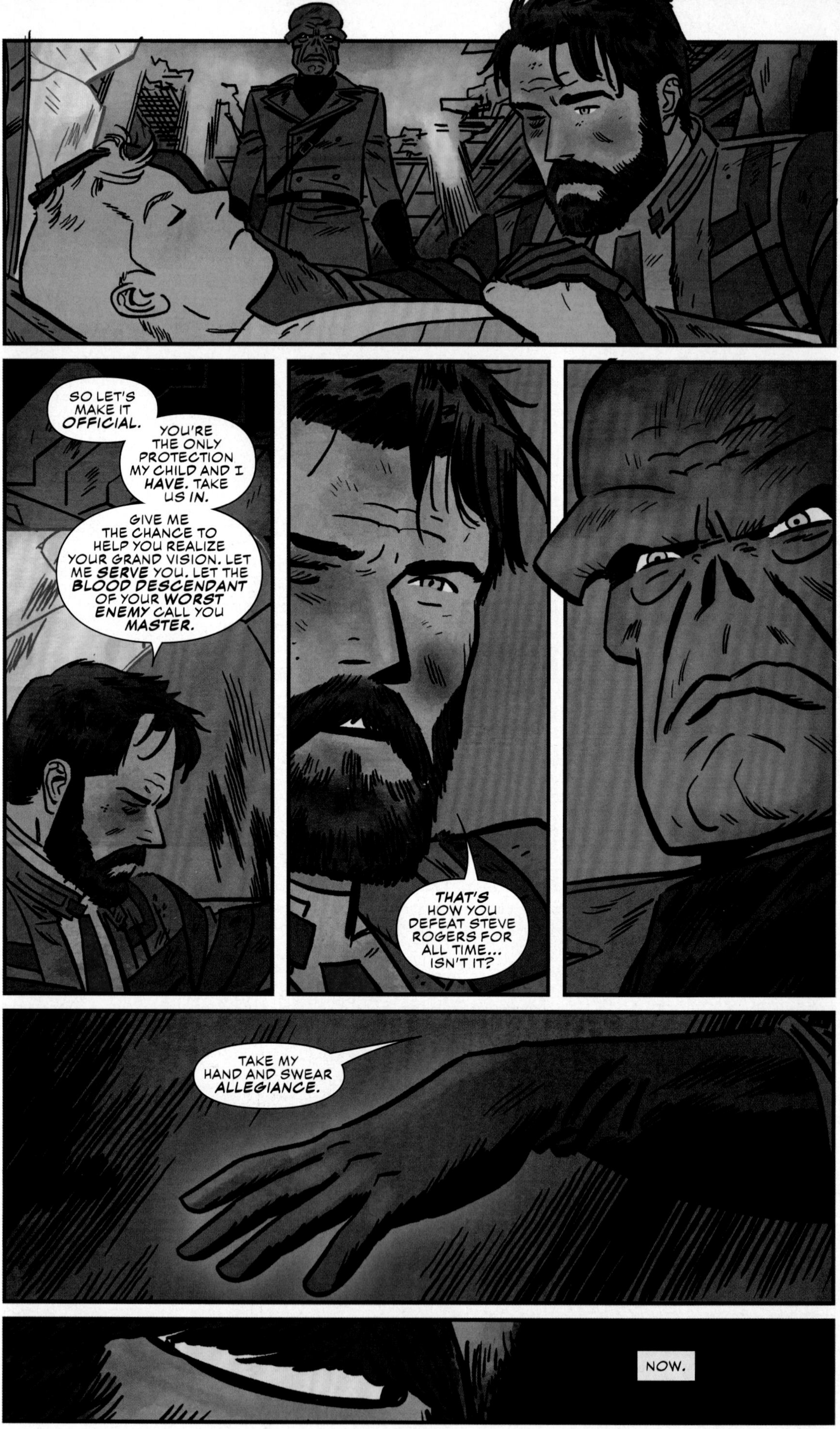
SO LET'S MAKE IT OFFICIAL.
YOU'RE THE ONLY PROTECTION MY CHILD AND I HAVE. TAKE US IN.
GIVE ME THE CHANCE TO HELP YOU REALIZE YOUR GRAND VISION. LET ME SERVE YOU. LET THE BLOOD DESCENDANT OF YOUR WORST ENEMY CALL YOU MASTER.
THAT'S HOW YOU DEFEAT STEVE ROGERS FOR ALL TIME... ISN'T IT?
TAKE MY HAND AND SWEAR ALLEGIANCE.
NOW.

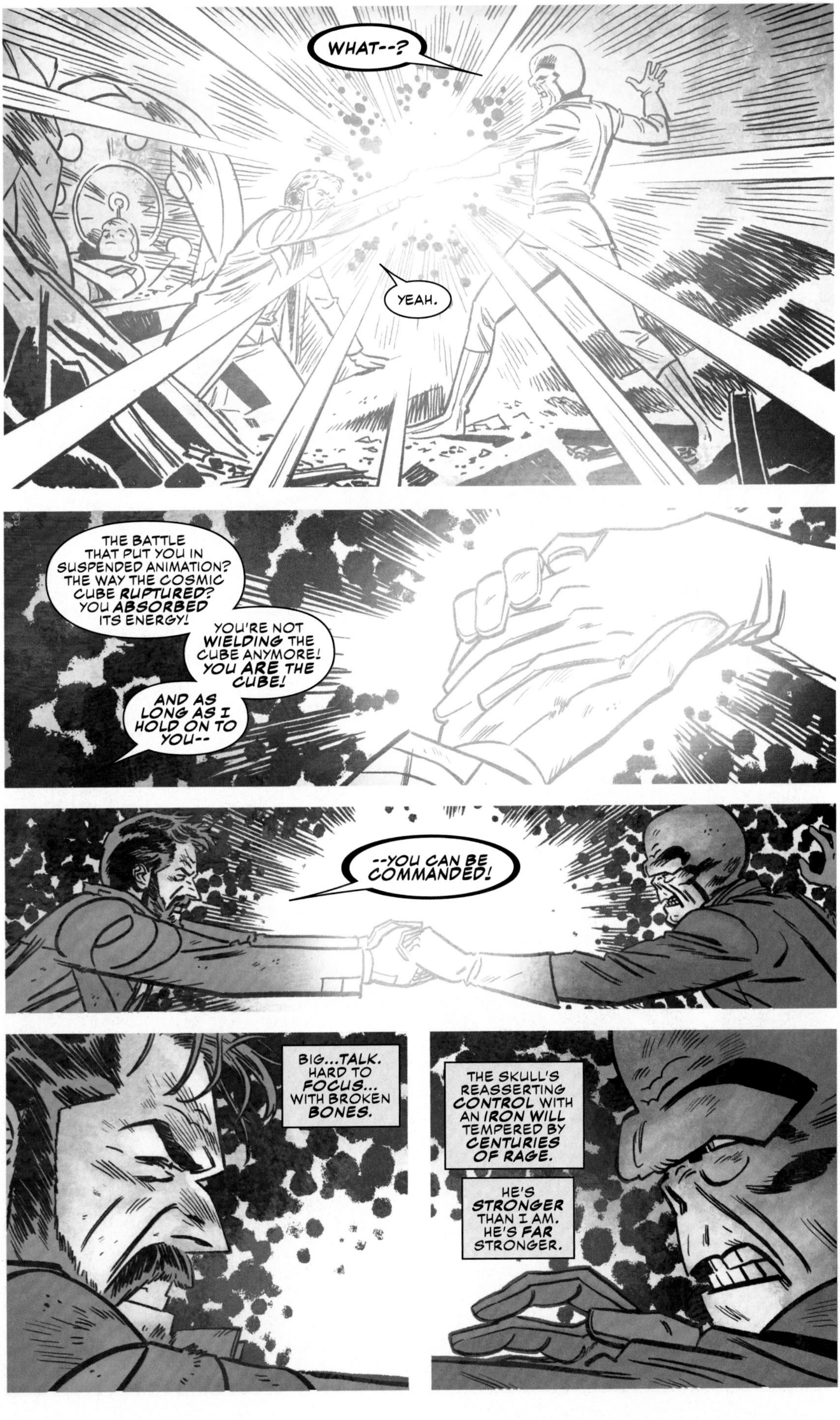
WHAT--?
YEAH.
THE BATTLE THAT PUT YOU IN SUSPENDED ANIMATION? THE WAY THE COSMIC CUBE RUPTURED? YOU ABSORBED ITS ENERGY!
YOU'RE NOT WIELDING THE CUBE ANYMORE! YOU ARE THE CUBE!
AND AS LONG AS I HOLD ON TO YOU--
--YOU CAN BE COMMANDED!
BIG...TALK. HARD TO FOCUS... WITH BROKEN BONES.
THE SKULL'S REASSERTING CONTROL WITH AN IRON WILL TEMPERED BY CENTURIES OF RAGE.
HE'S STRONGER THAN I AM. HE'S FAR STRONGER.

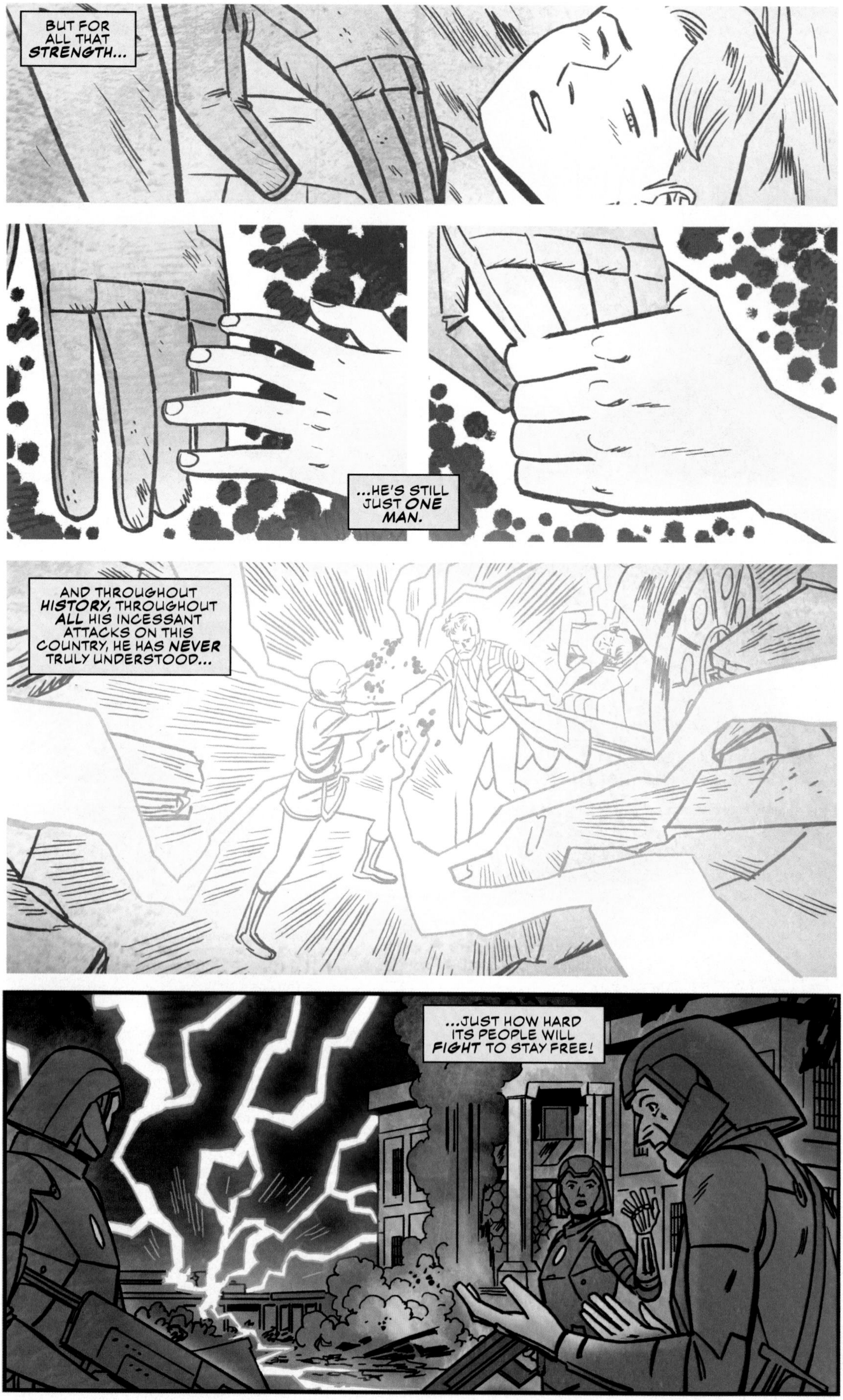
BUT FOR ALL THAT STRENGTH...
...HE'S STILL JUST ONE MAN.
AND THROUGHOUT HISTORY, THROUGHOUT ALL HIS INCESSANT ATTACKS ON THIS COUNTRY, HE HAS NEVER TRULY UNDERSTOOD...
...JUST HOW HARD ITS PEOPLE WILL FIGHT TO STAY FREE!

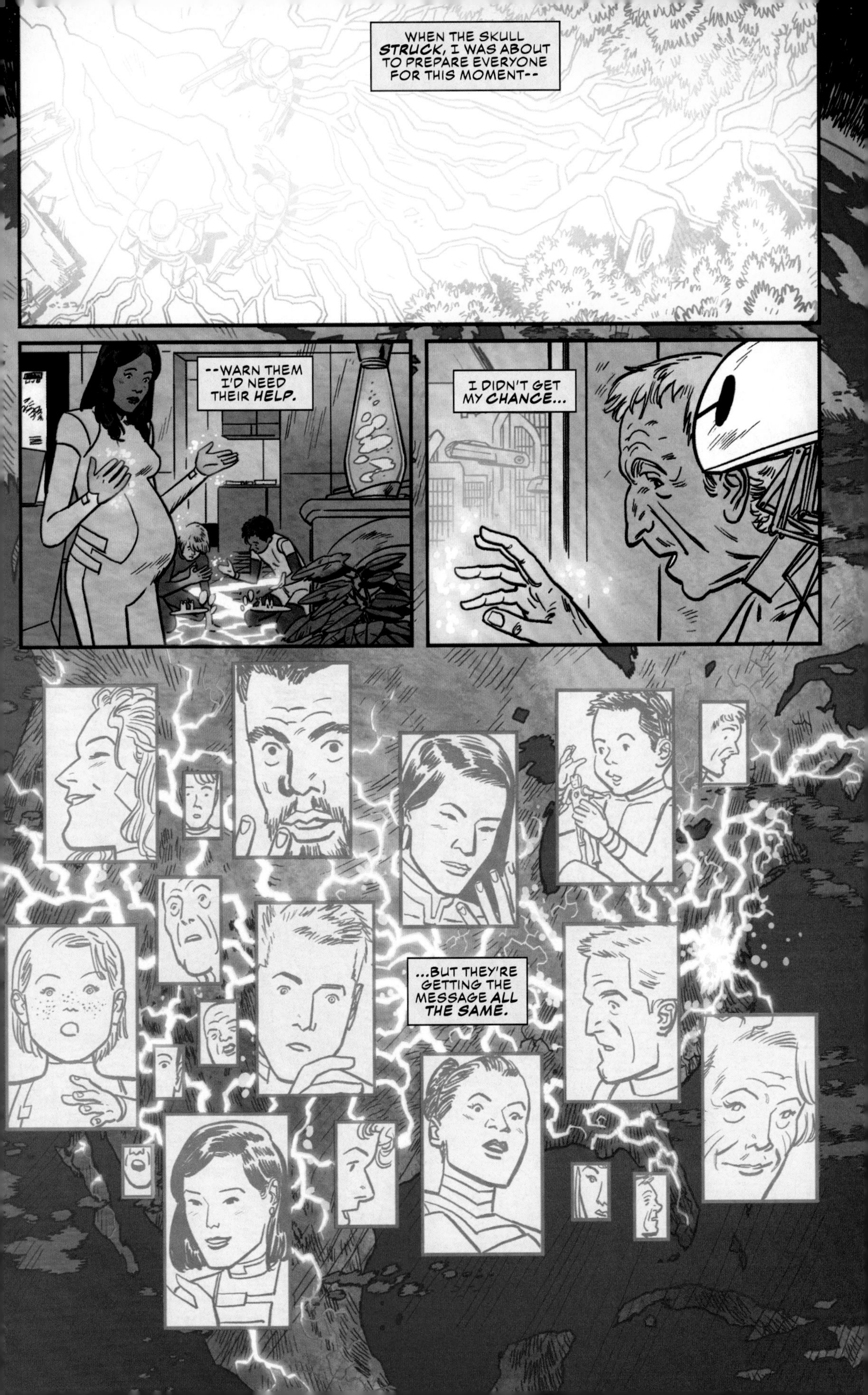
WHEN THE SKULL STRUCK, I WAS ABOUT TO PREPARE EVERYONE FOR THIS MOMENT--
--WARN THEM I'D NEED THEIR HELP.
I DIDN'T GET MY CHANCE...
...BUT THEY'RE GETTING THE MESSAGE ALL THE SAME.

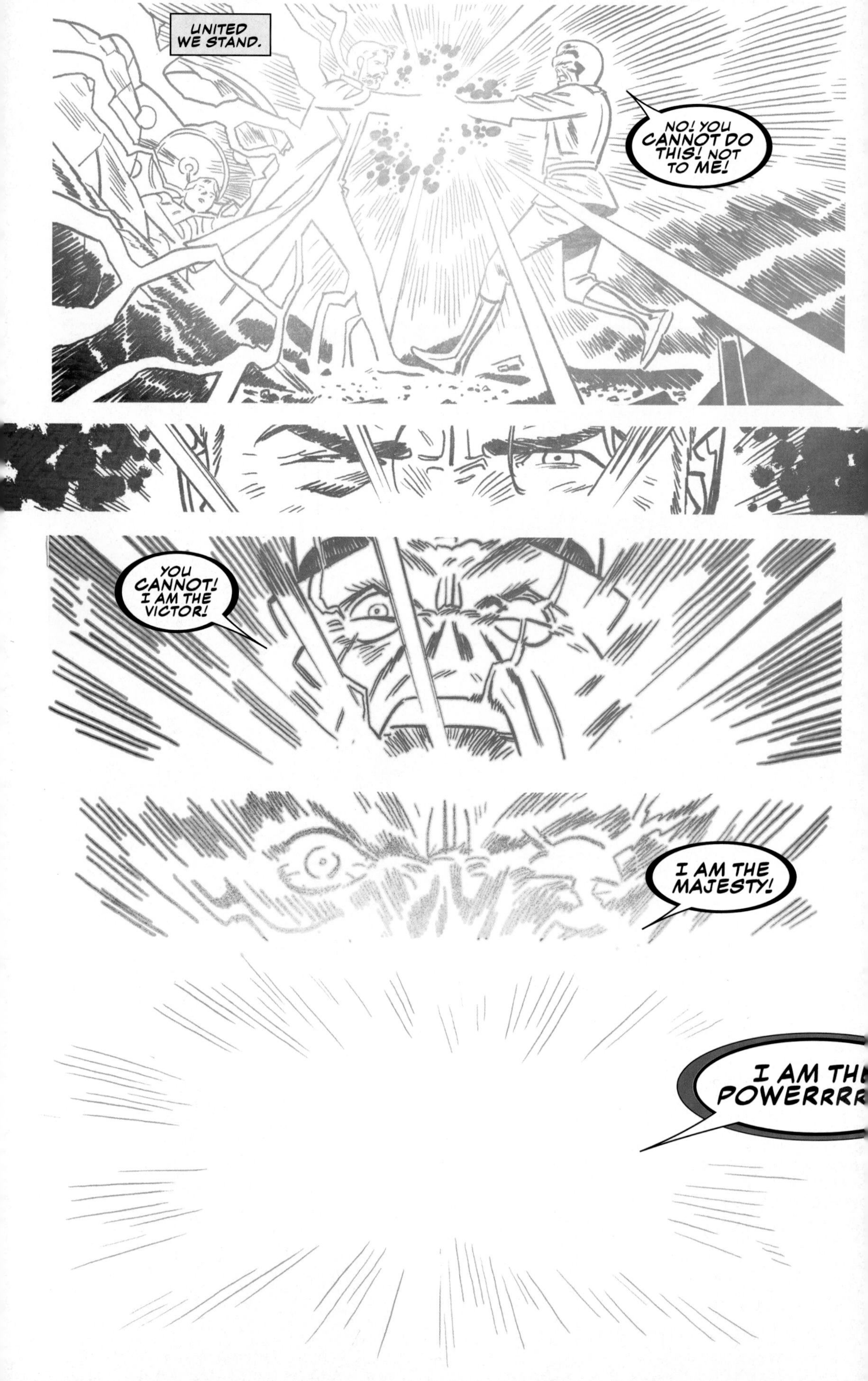
UNITED WE STAND.
NO! YOU CANNOT DO THIS! NOT TO ME!
YOU CANNOT! I AM THE VICTOR!
I AM THE MAJESTY!
I AM THE POWERRRR

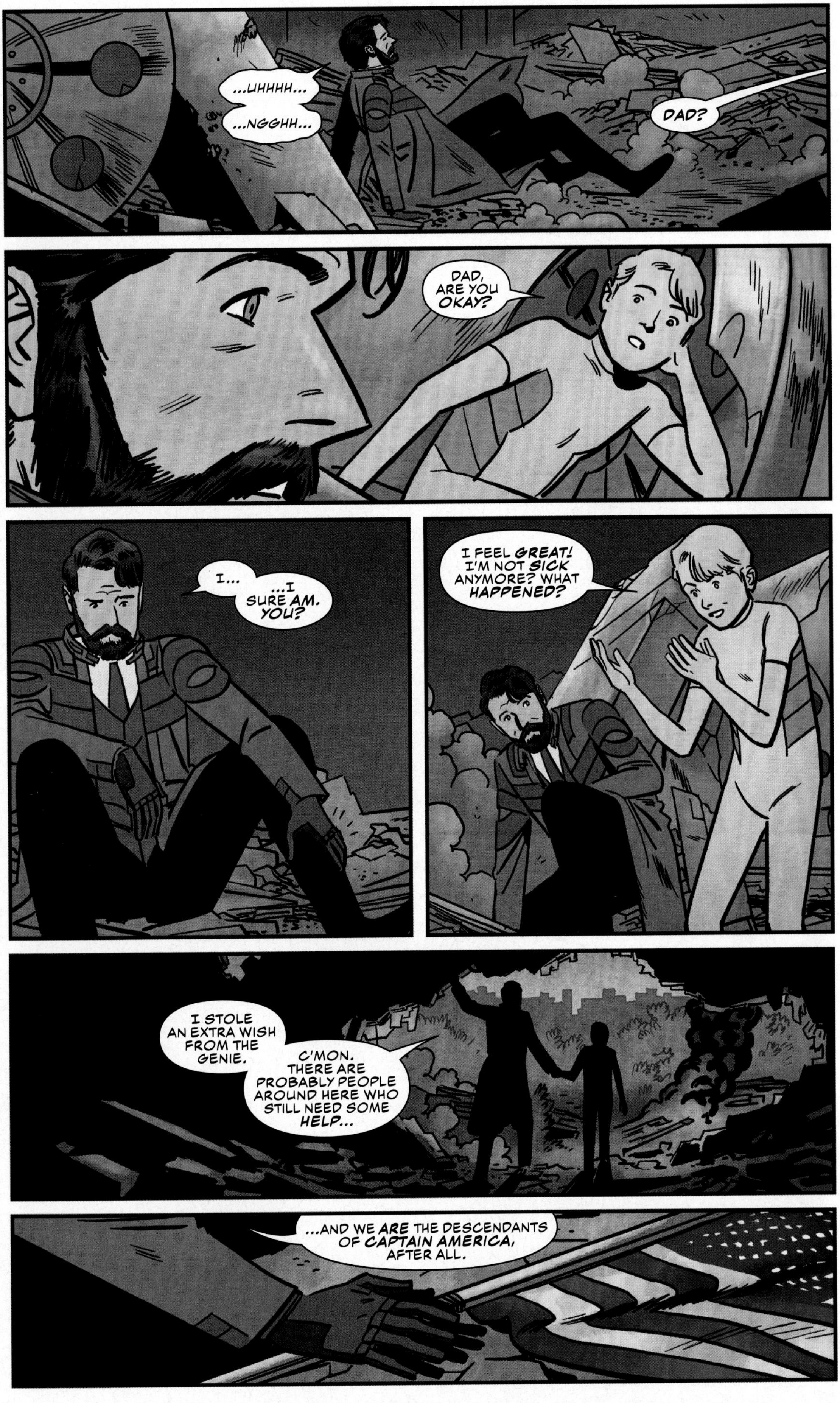
...UHHHH...
...NGGHH...
DAD?
DAD, ARE YOU OKAY?
I...
...I SURE AM. YOU?
I FEEL GREAT! I'M NOT SICK ANYMORE? WHAT HAPPENED?
I STOLE AN EXTRA WISH FROM THE GENIE.
C'MON. THERE ARE PROBABLY PEOPLE AROUND HERE WHO STILL NEED SOME HELP...
...AND WE ARE THE DESCENDANTS OF CAPTAIN AMERICA, AFTER ALL.

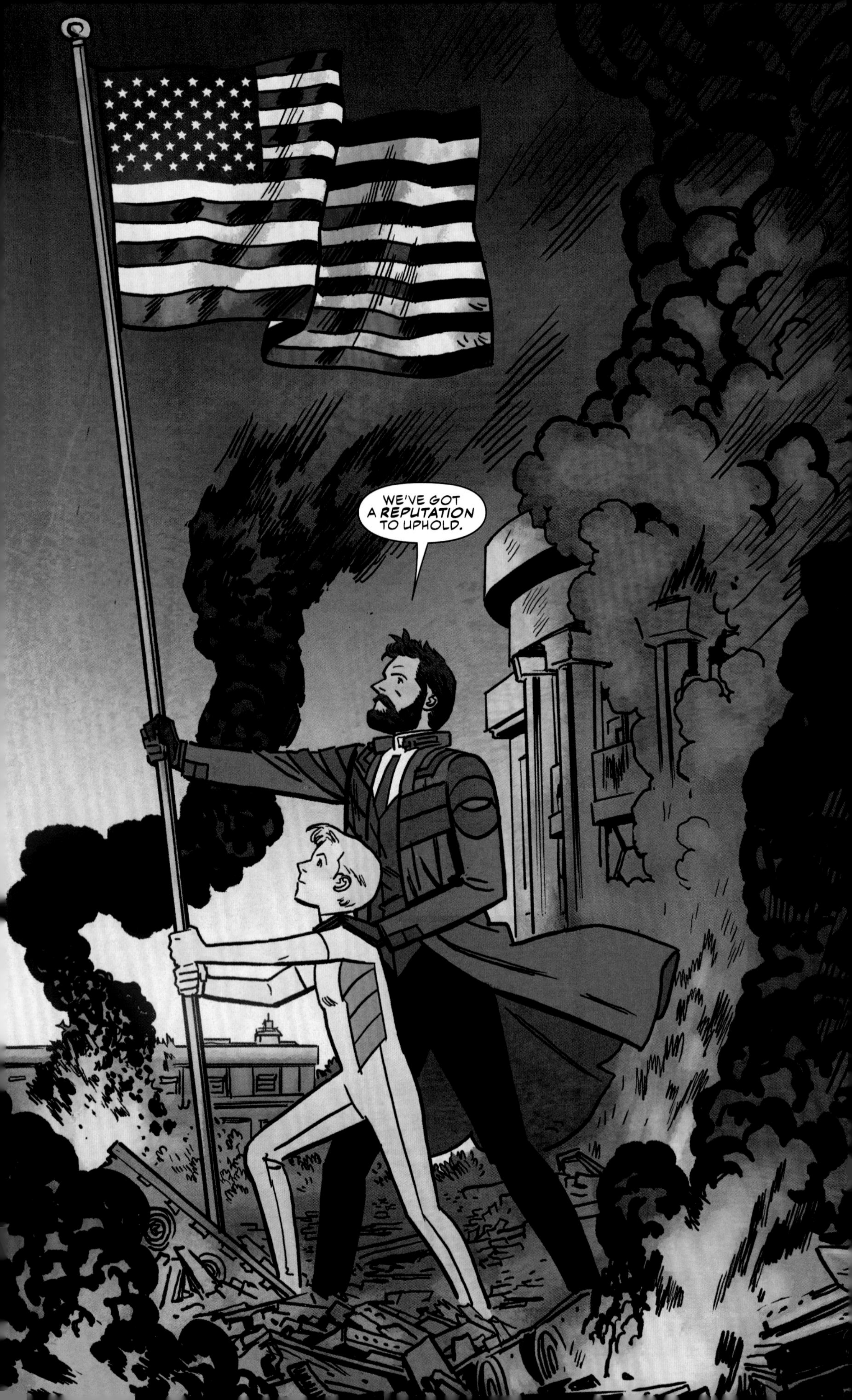
WE'VE GOT A REPUTATION TO UPHOLD.

EPILOGUE.

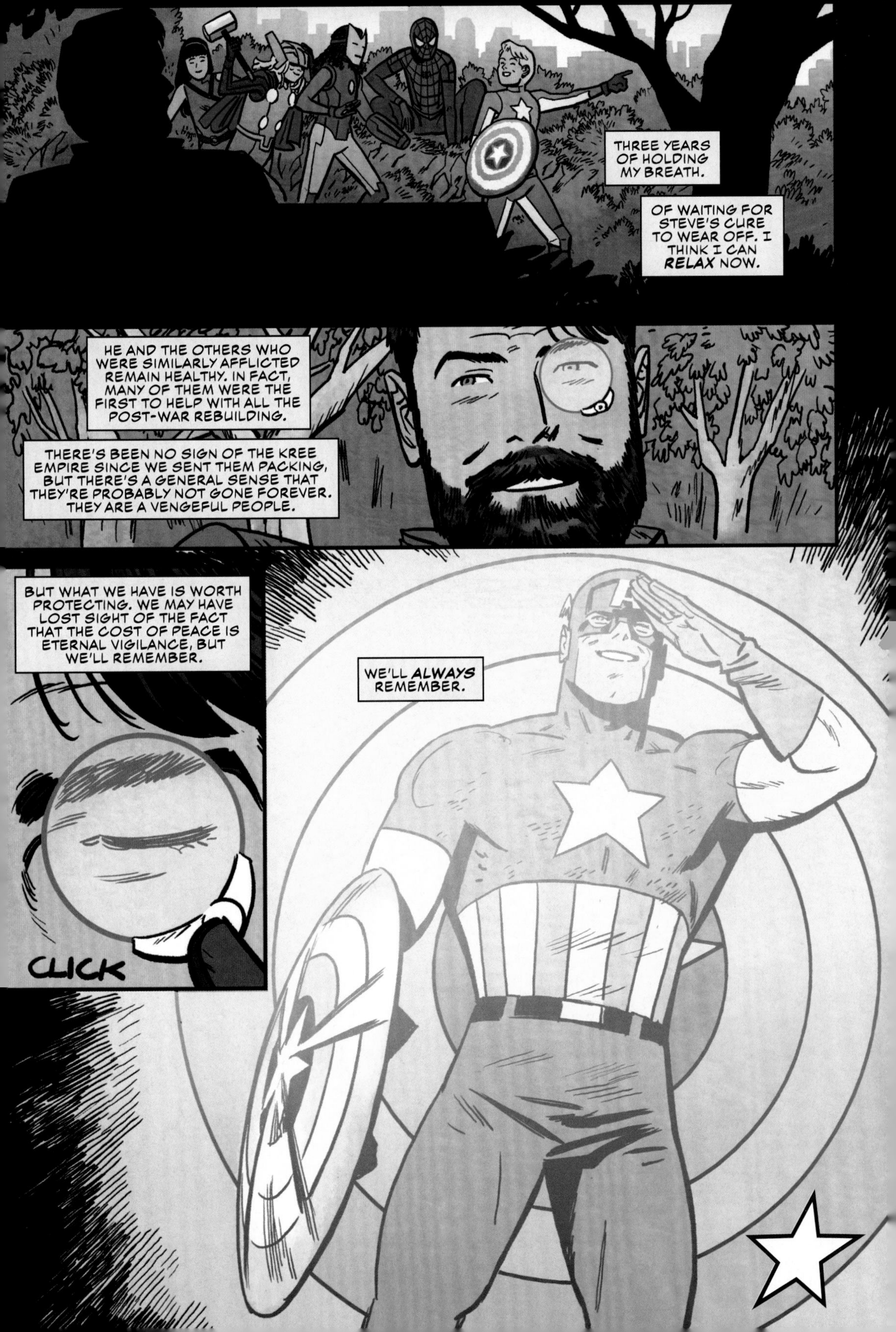
THREE YEARS OF HOLDING MY BREATH.
OF WAITING FOR STEVE'S CURE TO WEAR OFF. I THINK I CAN **RELAX** NOW.
HE AND THE OTHERS WHO WERE SIMILARLY AFFLICTED REMAIN HEALTHY. IN FACT, MANY OF THEM WERE THE FIRST TO HELP WITH ALL THE POST-WAR REBUILDING.
THERE'S BEEN NO SIGN OF THE KREE EMPIRE SINCE WE SENT THEM PACKING, BUT THERE'S A GENERAL SENSE THAT THEY'RE PROBABLY NOT GONE FOREVER. THEY ARE A VENGEFUL PEOPLE.
BUT WHAT WE HAVE IS WORTH PROTECTING. WE MAY HAVE LOST SIGHT OF THE FACT THAT THE COST OF PEACE IS ETERNAL VIGILANCE, BUT WE'LL REMEMBER.
CLICK
WE'LL ***ALWAYS*** REMEMBER.

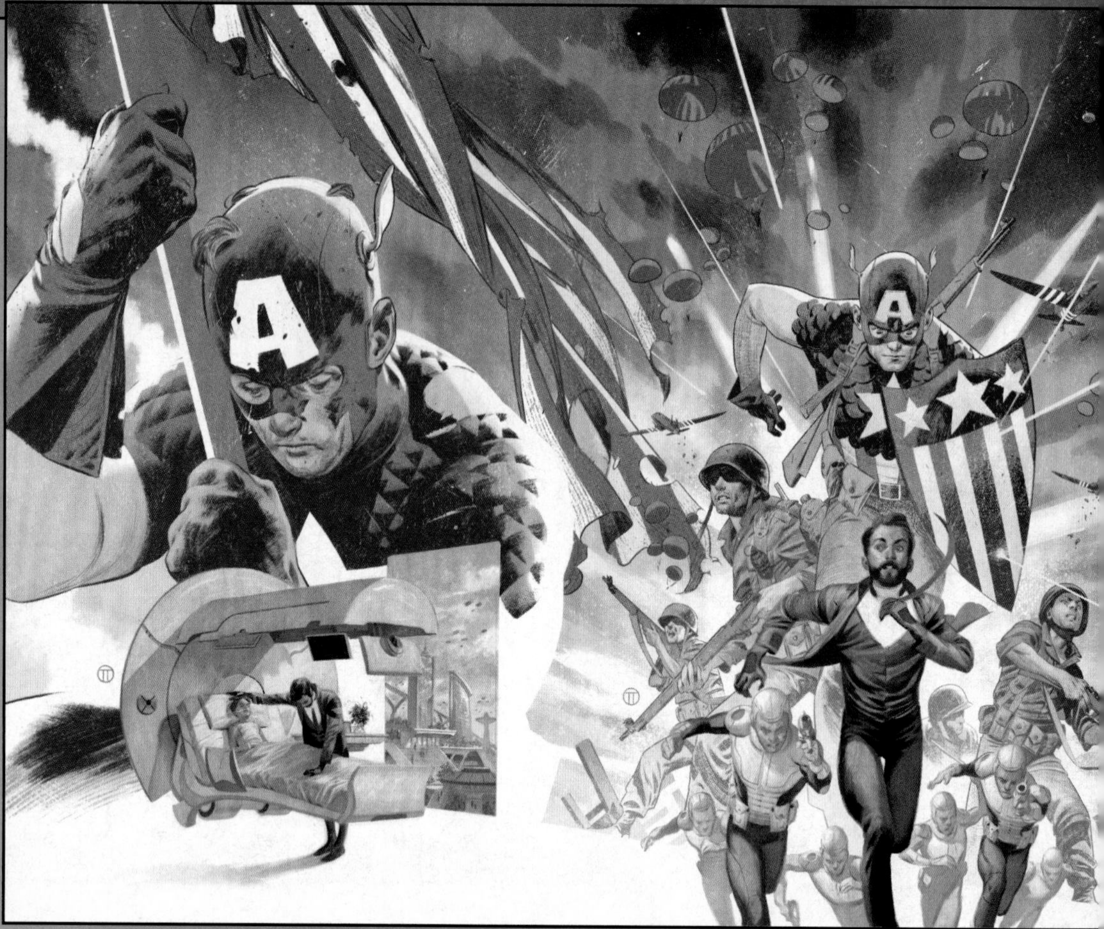

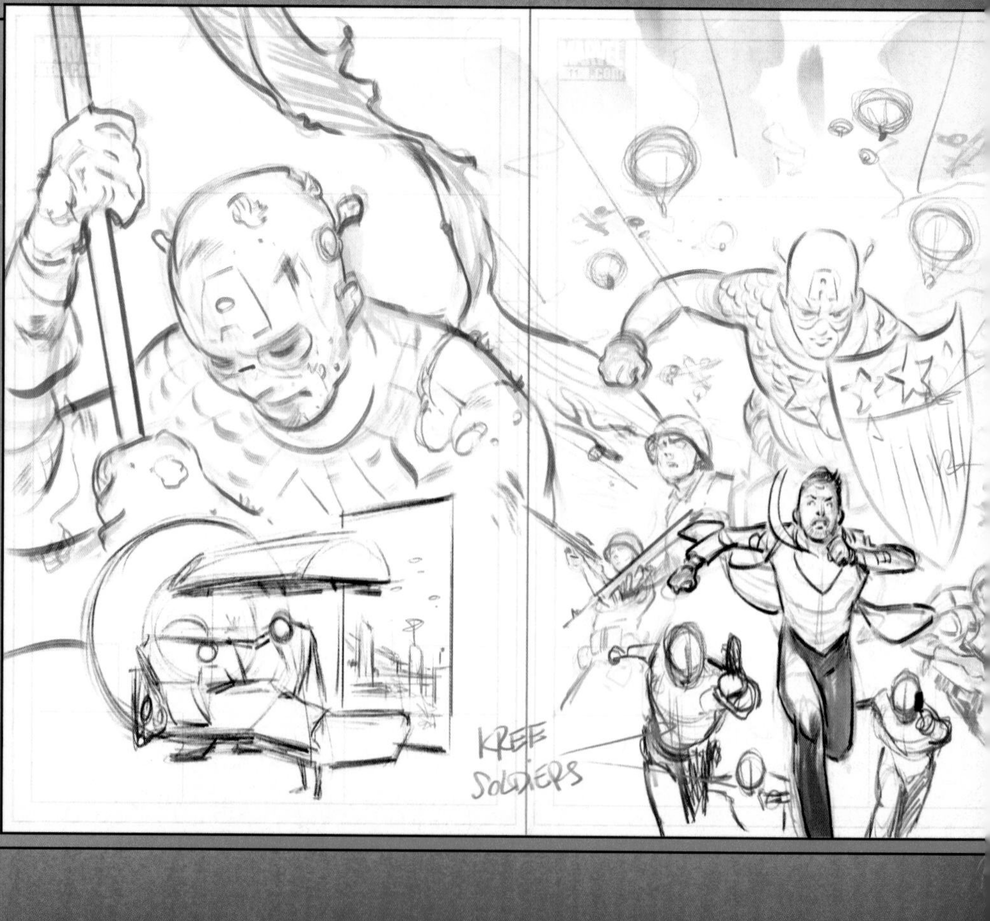
KREE
SOLDIERS

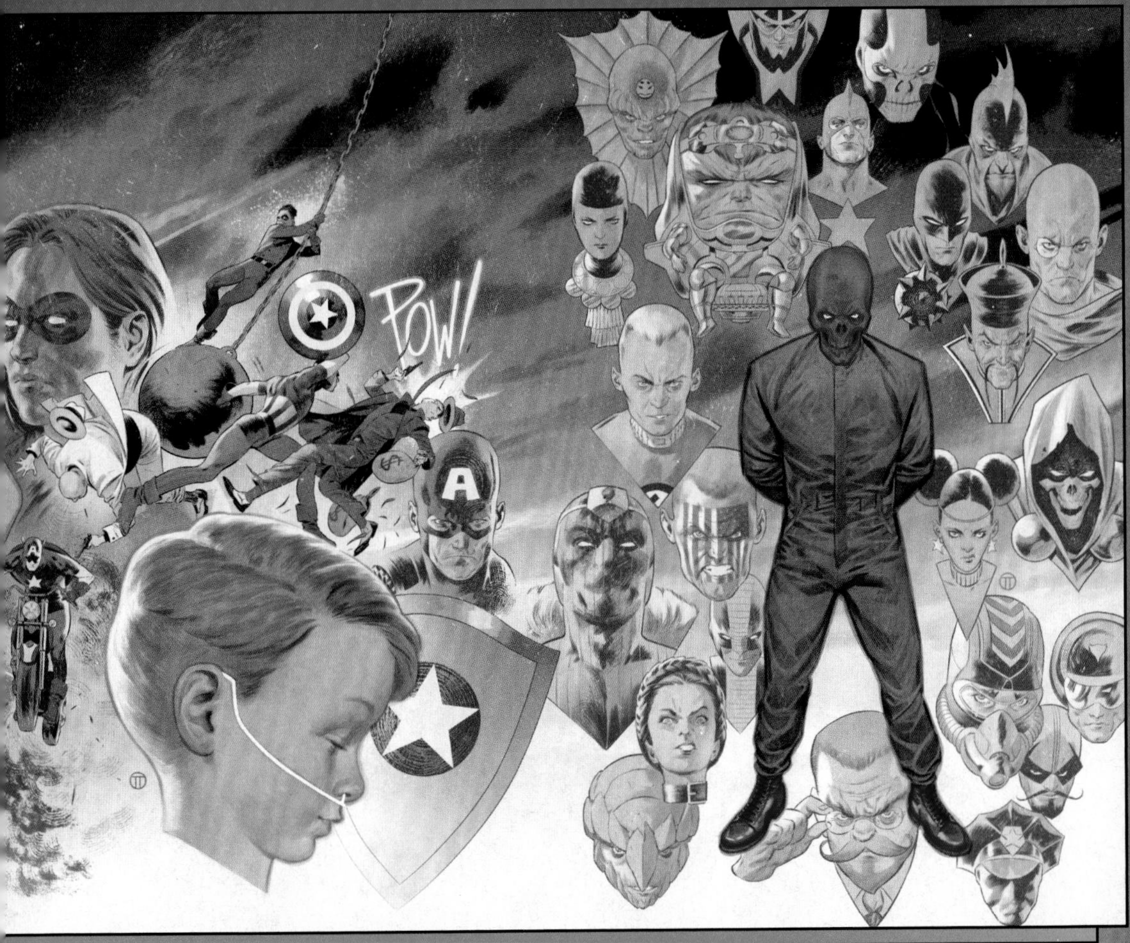
POW!

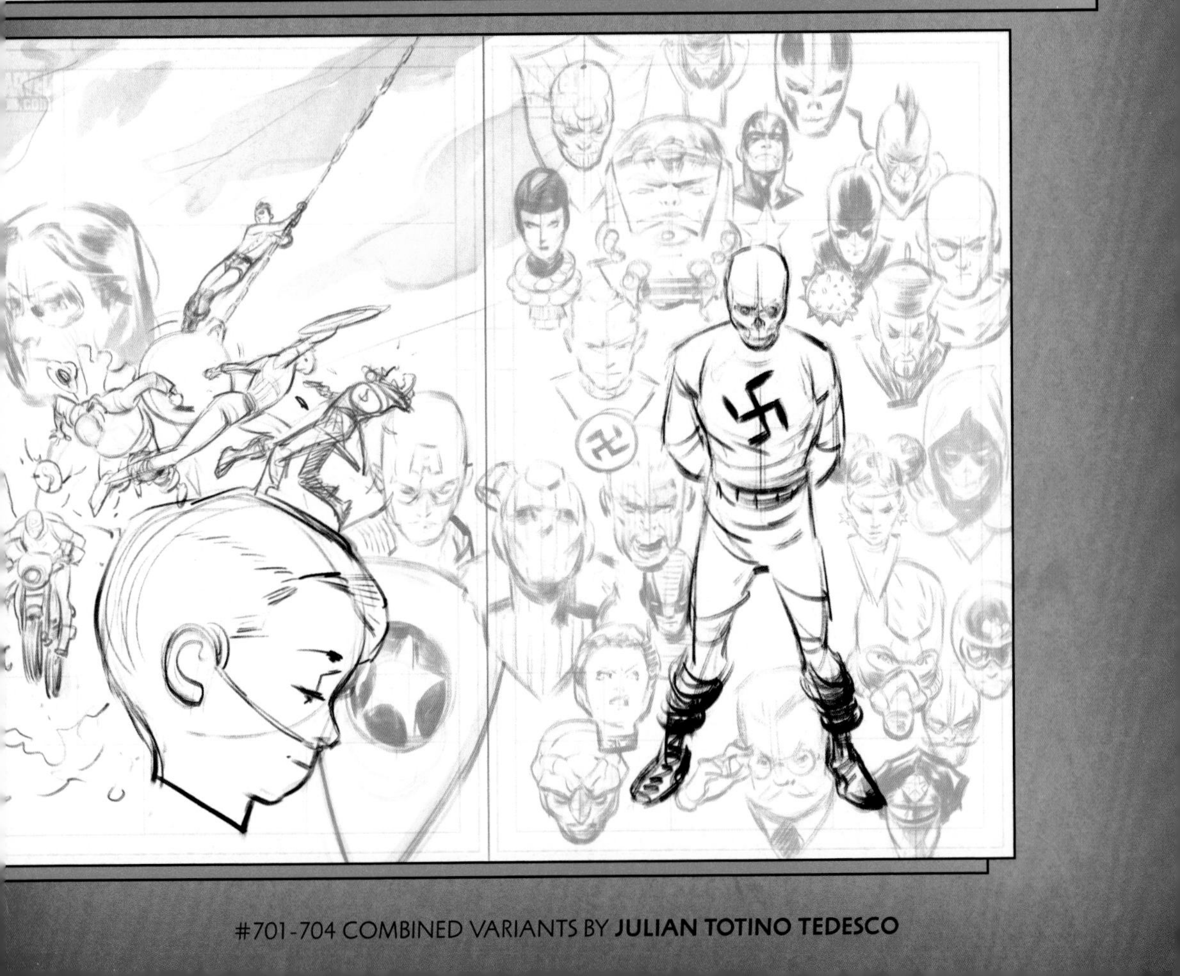

#701-704 COMBINED VARIANTS BY **JULIAN TOTINO TEDESCO**

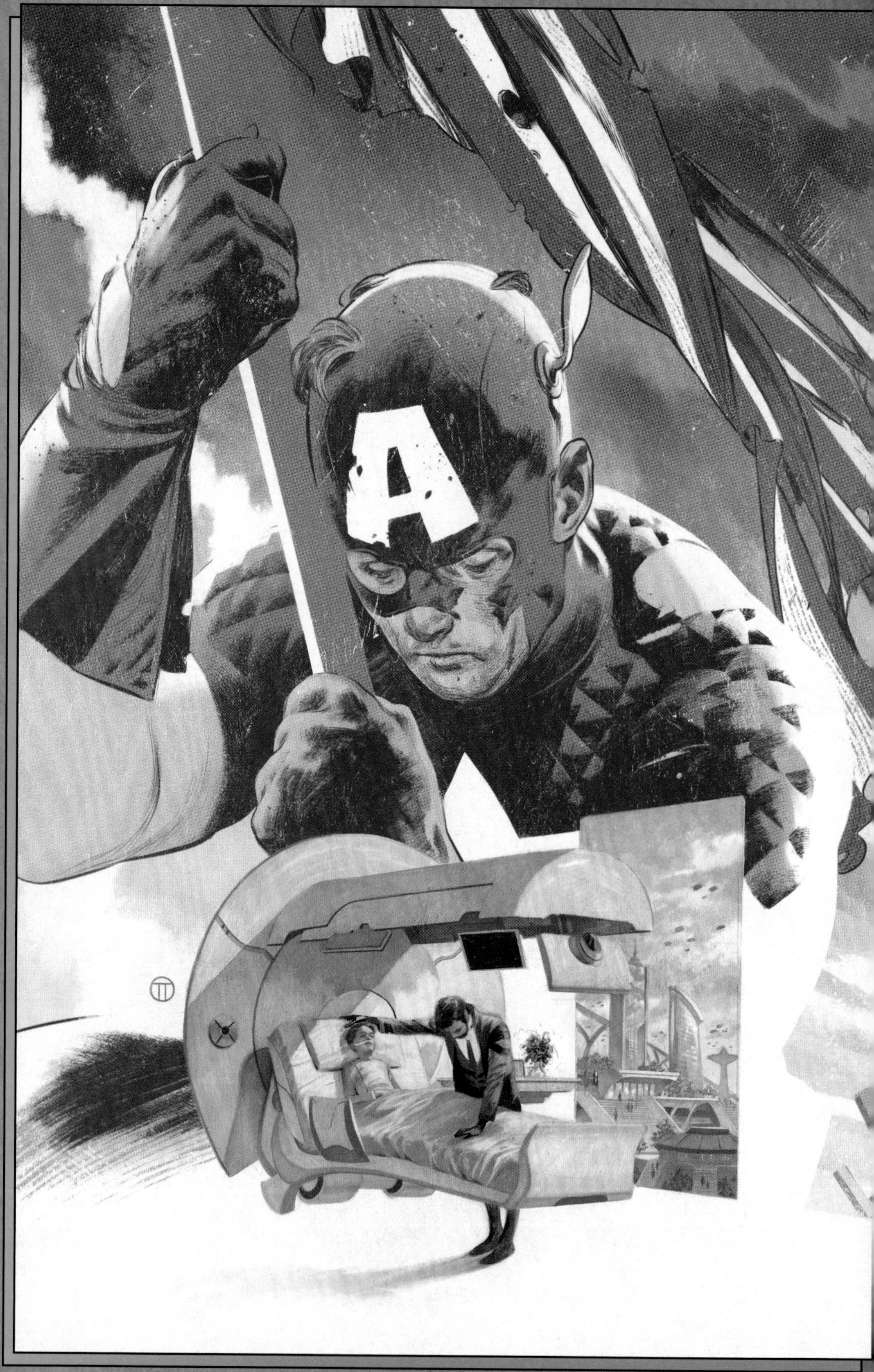

#701 VARIANT BY **JULIAN TOTINO TEDESCO**

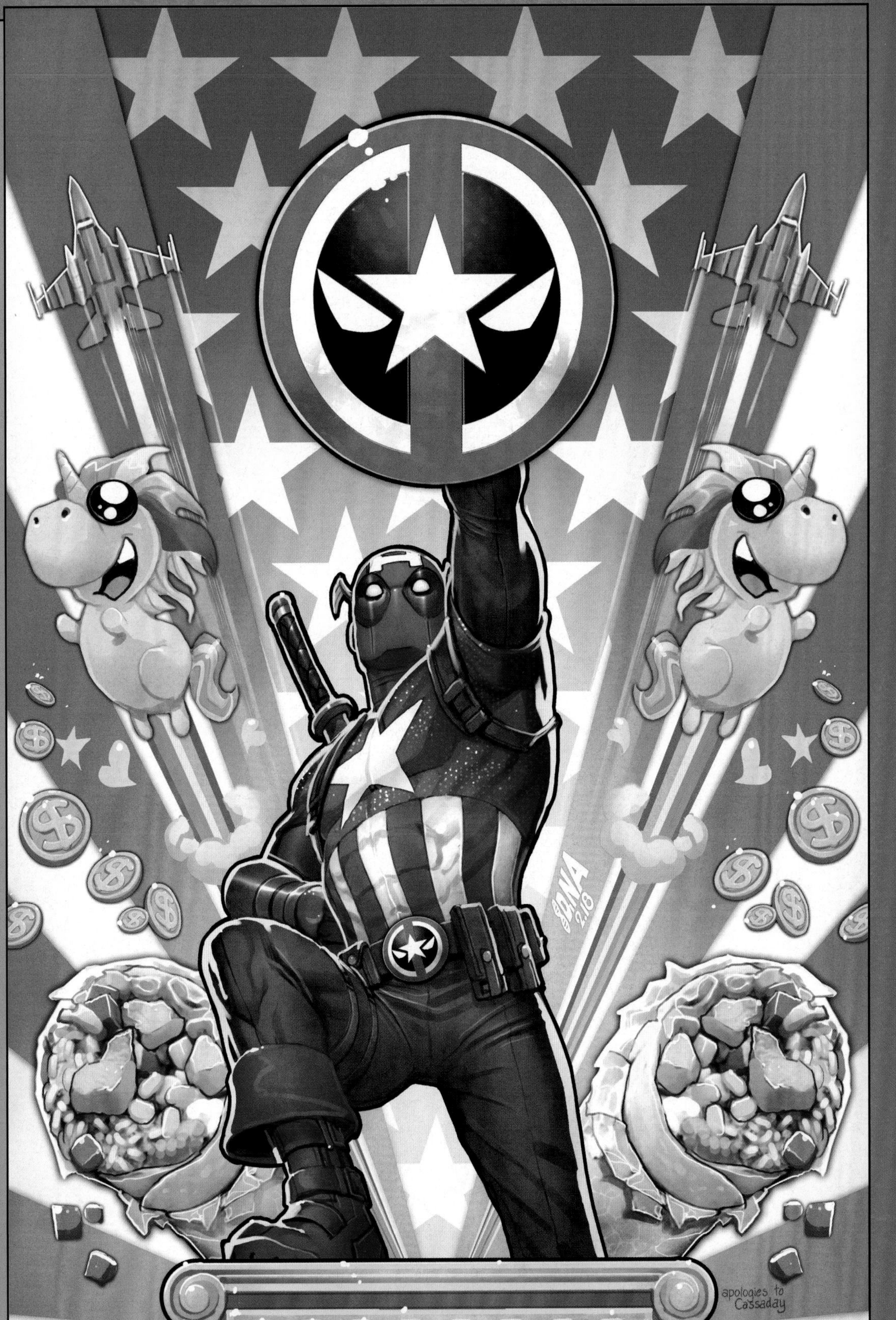
apologies to Cassaday

#701 DEADPOOL VARIANT BY **DAVID NAKAYAMA**

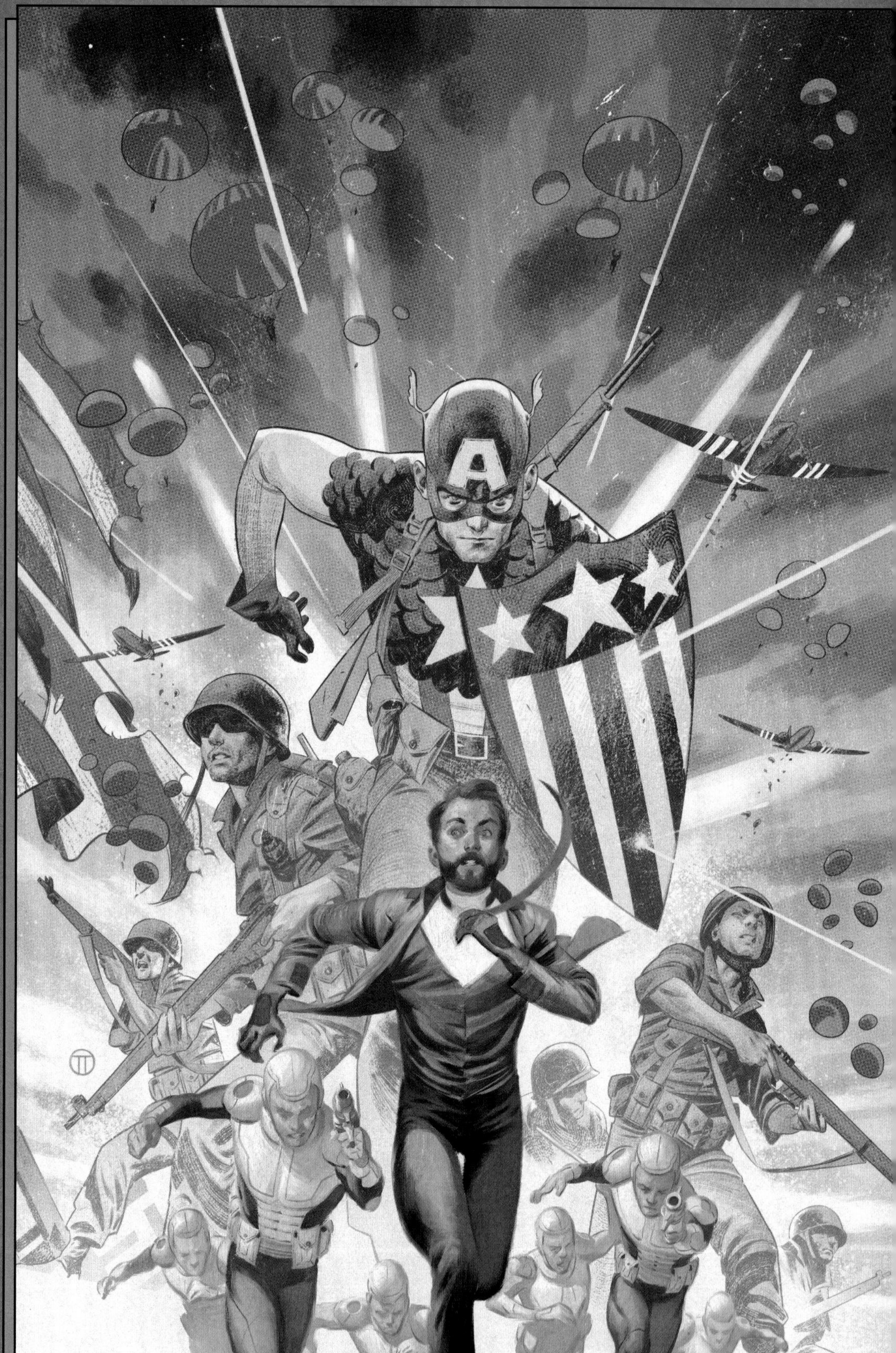

#702 VARIANT BY **JULIAN TOTINO TEDESCO**

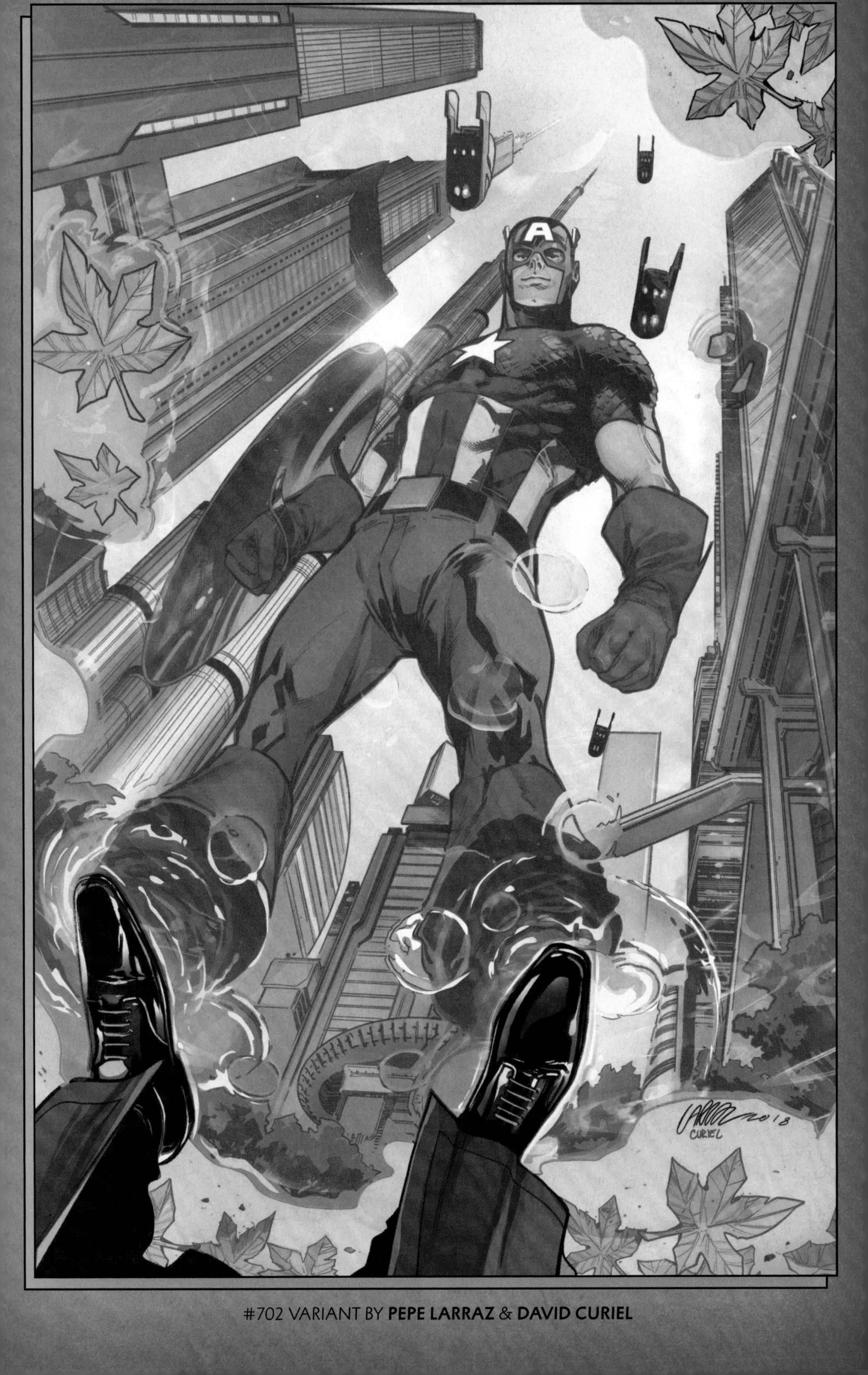
LARRAZ 2018
CURIEL

#702 VARIANT BY **PEPE LARRAZ** & **DAVID CURIEL**

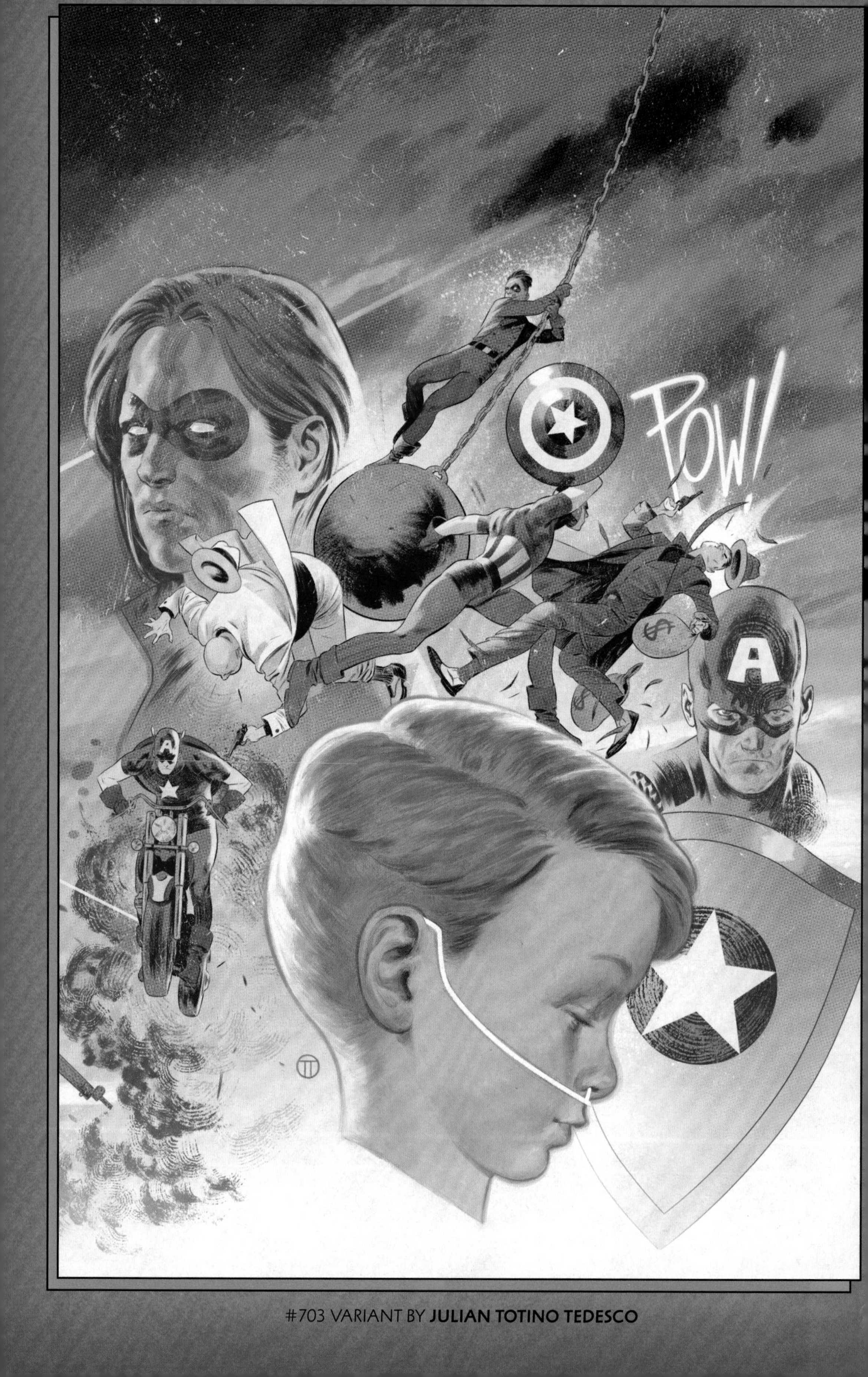

POW!

#703 VARIANT BY **JULIAN TOTINO TEDESCO**

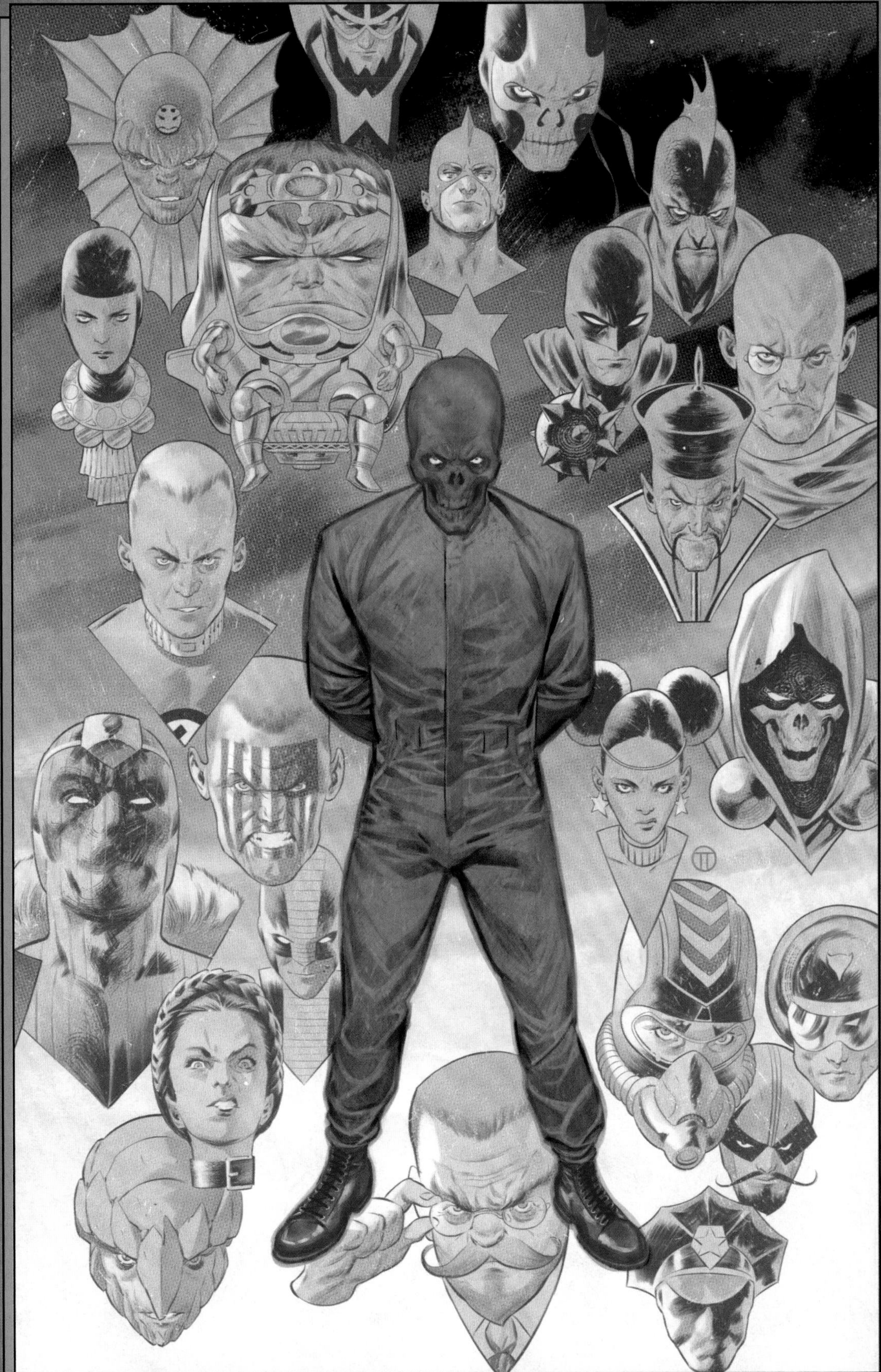

#704 VARIANT BY **JULIAN TOTINO TEDESCO**

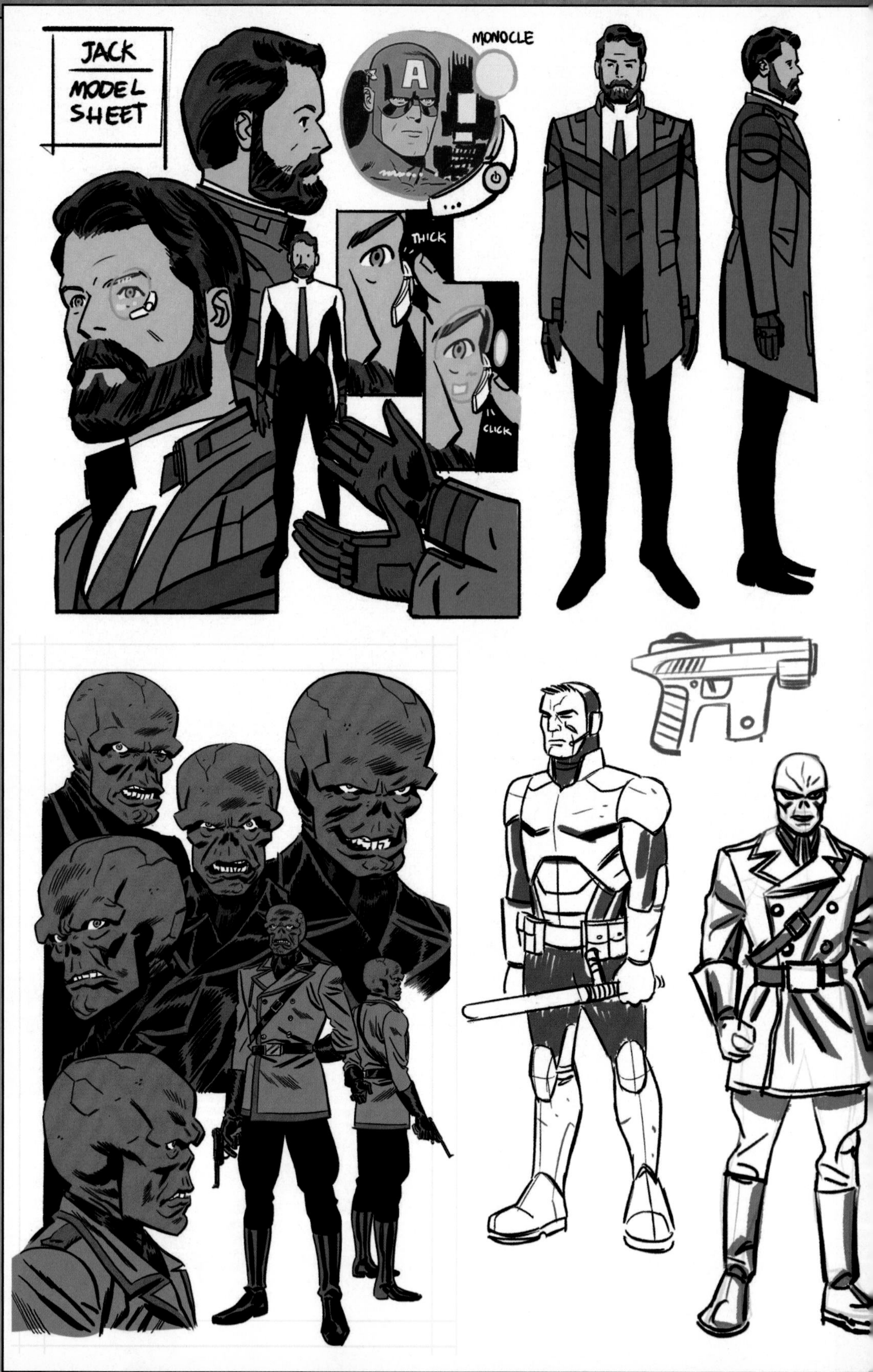
JACK
MODEL SHEET
MONOCLE
THICK
CLICK

DESIGNS BY **LEONARDO ROMERO**

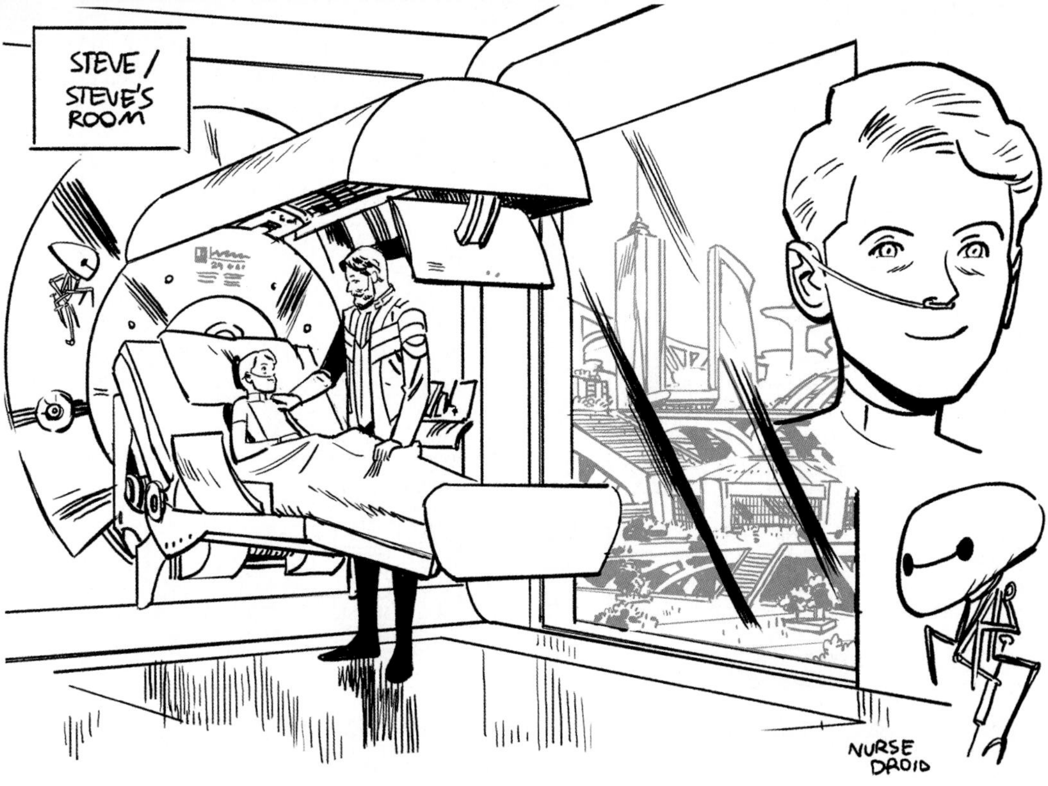
STEVE / STEVE'S ROOM
NURSE DROID

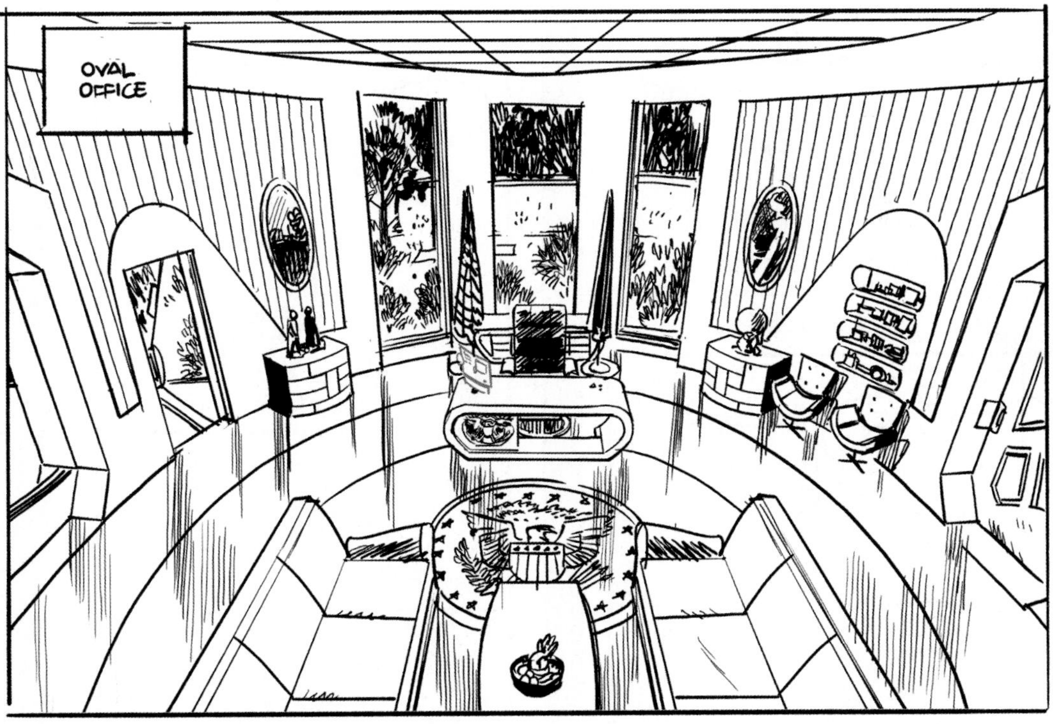
OVAL OFFICE

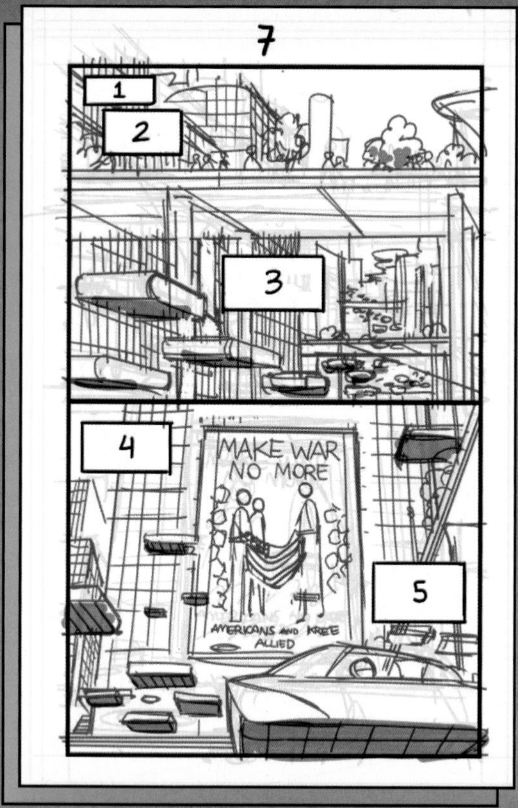
7
MAKE WAR NO MORE
AMERICANS AND KREE ALLIED

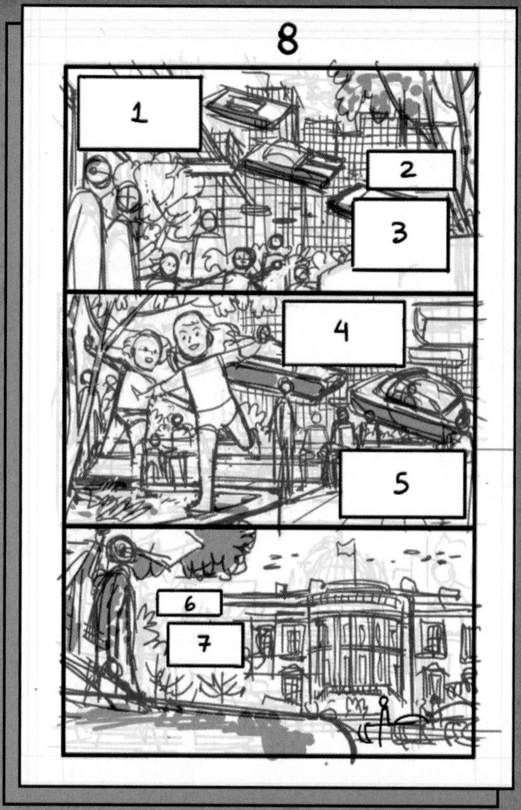
8

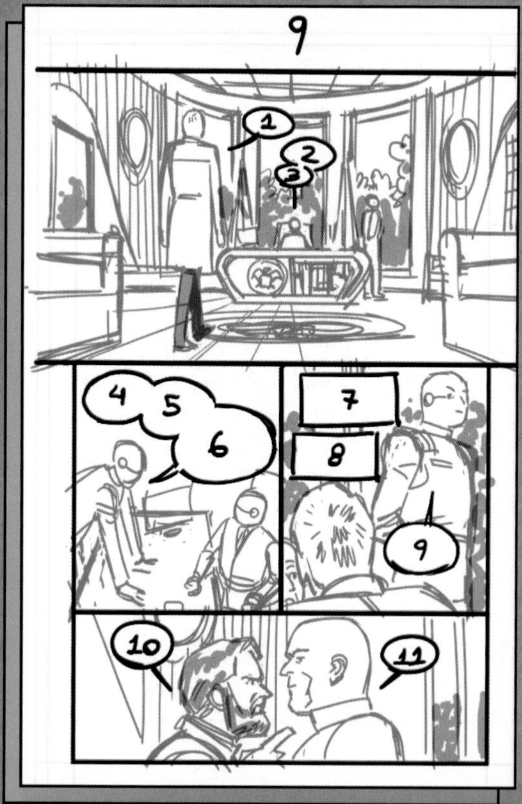
9

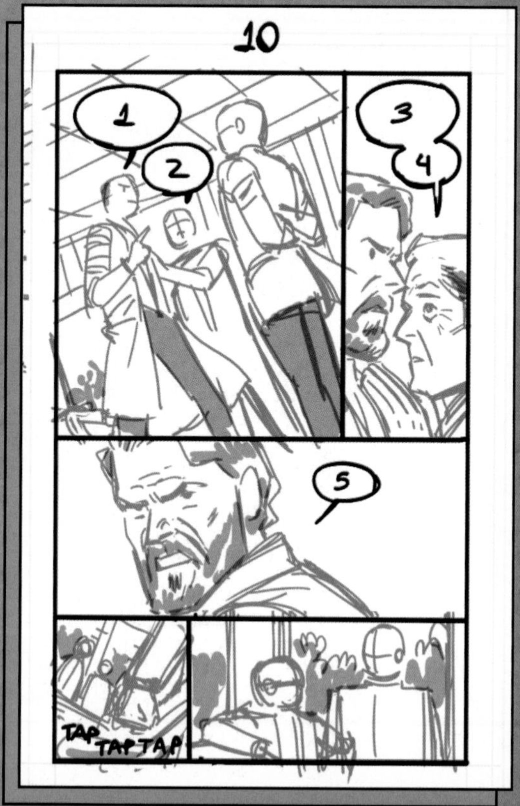
10
TAP TAP TAP

#701 LAYOUTS BY
LEONARDO ROMERO

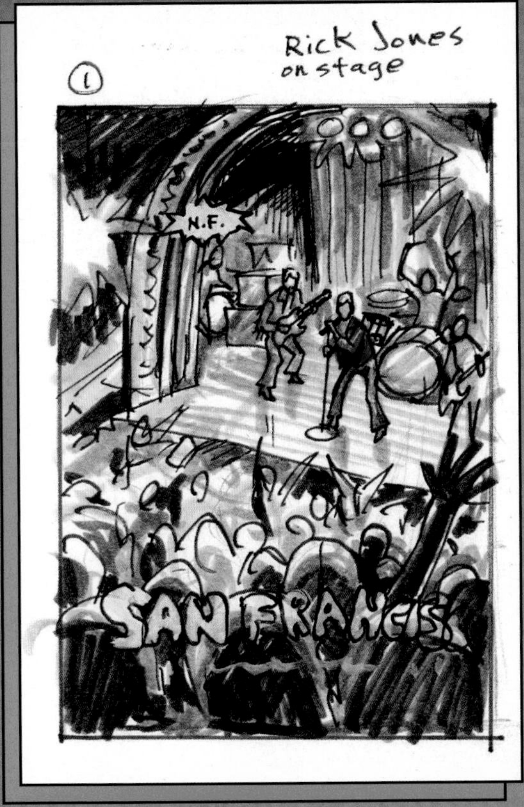
1
Rick Jones on stage
N.F.
SAN FRANCIS

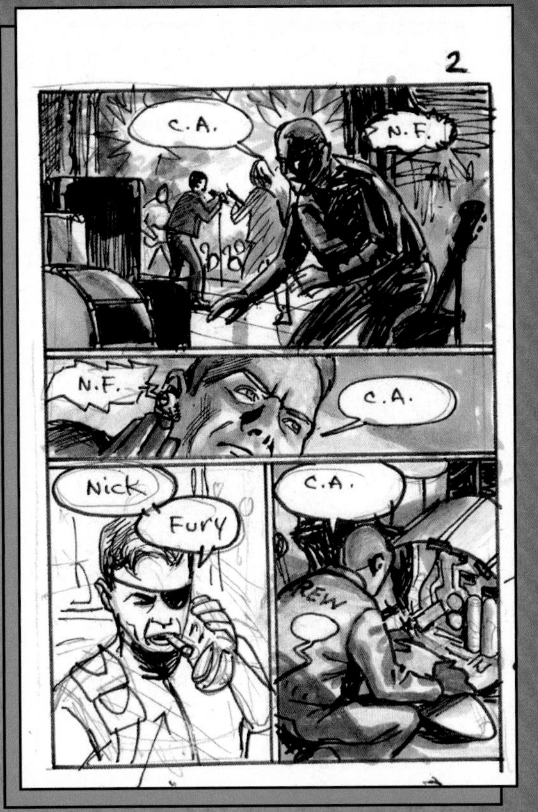
2
C.A.
N.F.
N.F.
C.A.
Nick
Fury
C.A.

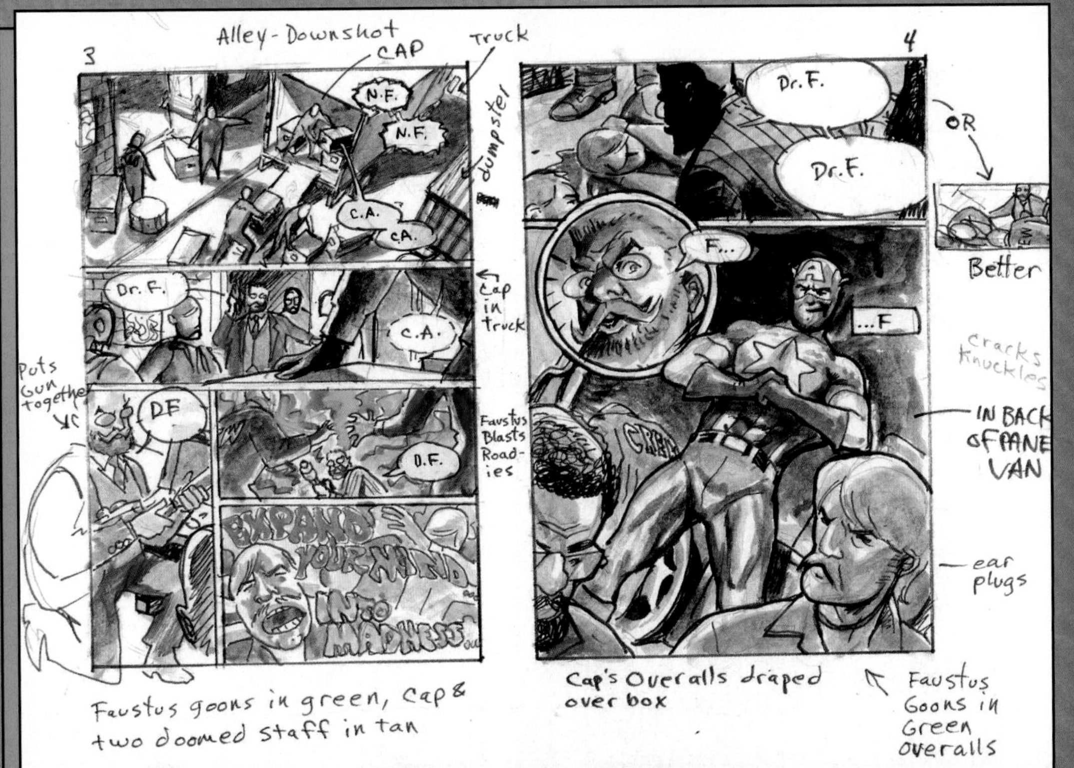
3
Alley-Downshot
CAP
Truck
N.F.
N.F.
dumpster
C.A.
C.A.
Dr. F.
C.A.
Cap in truck
Puts Gun together
DF
Faustus Blasts Road-ies
D.F.
EXPAND YOUR MIND INTO MADNESS
Faustus goons in green, Cap & two doomed staff in tan
4
Dr. F.
Dr. F.
OR
Better
F...
...F
Cracks knuckles
IN BACK OF PANE VAN
ear plugs
Cap's Overalls draped over box
Faustus Goons in Green Overalls

#701 LAYOUTS BY
J.G. JONES

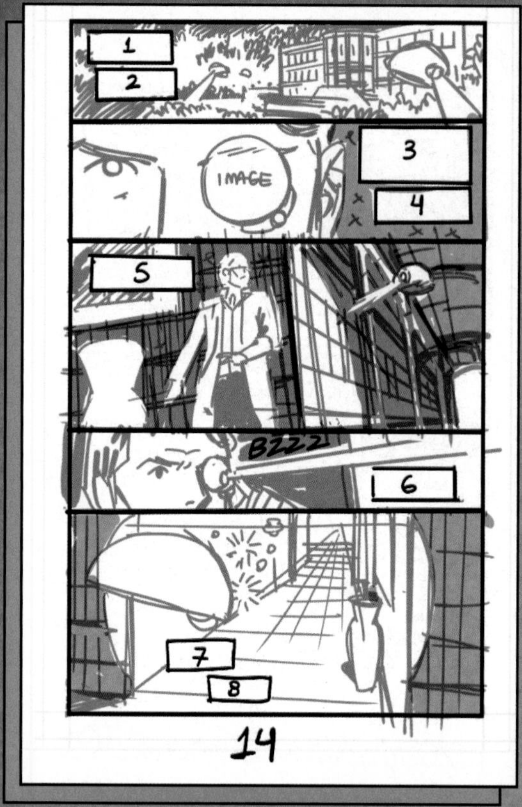
IMAGE
BZZZ
14

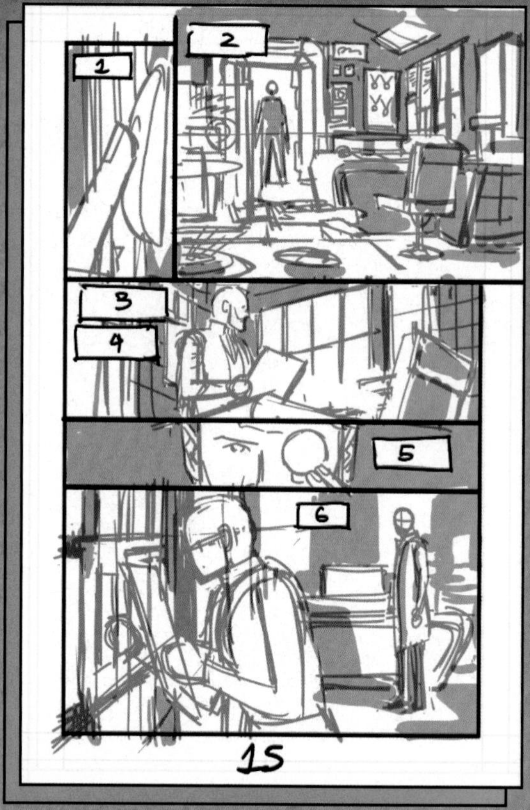
15

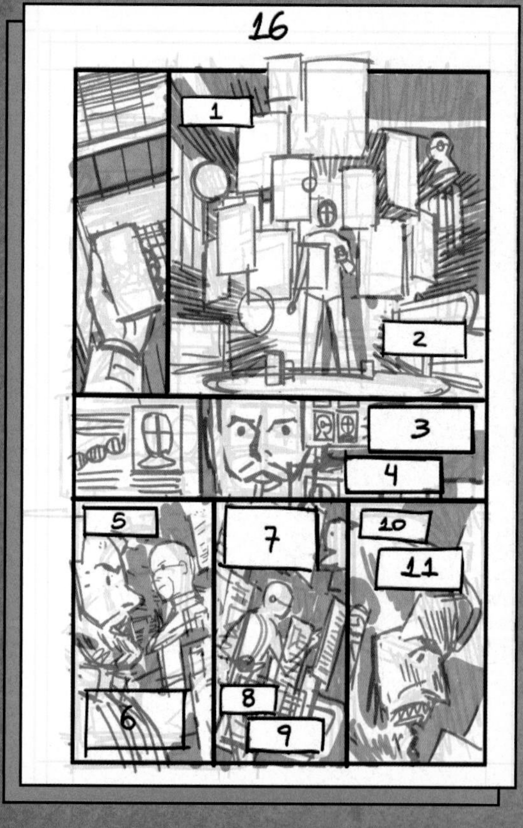
16

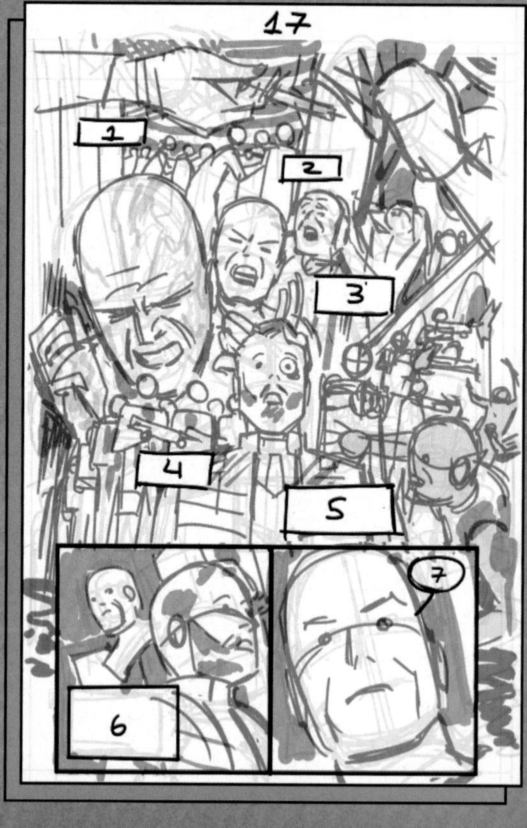
17

#701 LAYOUTS BY
LEONARDO ROMERO

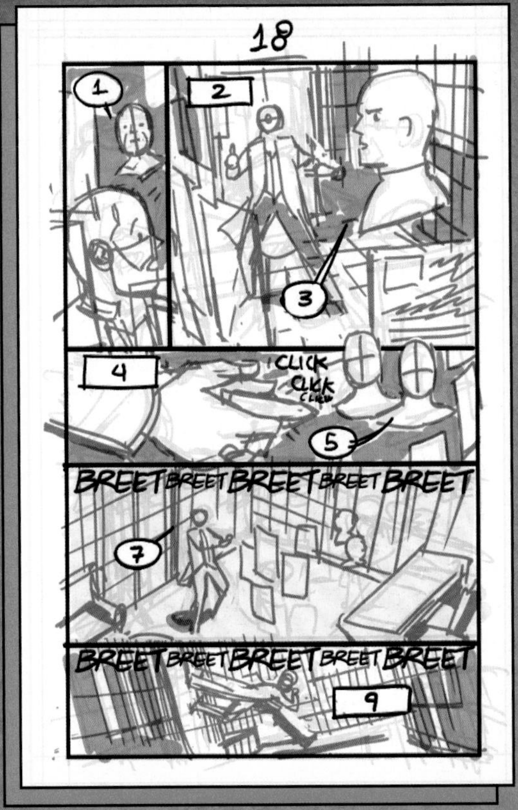
18
CLICK CLICK
BREET BREET BREET BREET BREET
BREET BREET BREET BREET BREET

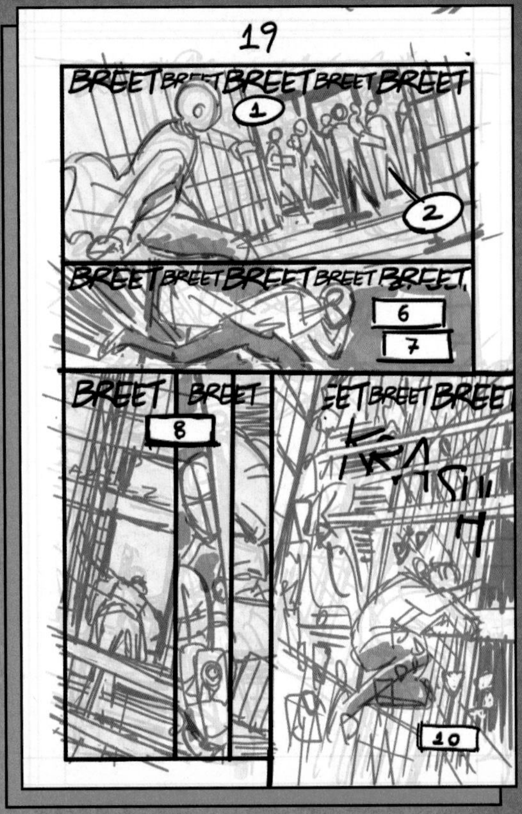
19
BREET BREET BREET BREET BREET
BREET BREET BREET BREET BREET
BREET BREET
BREET BREET BREET

#701 LAYOUTS BY
LEONARDO ROMERO

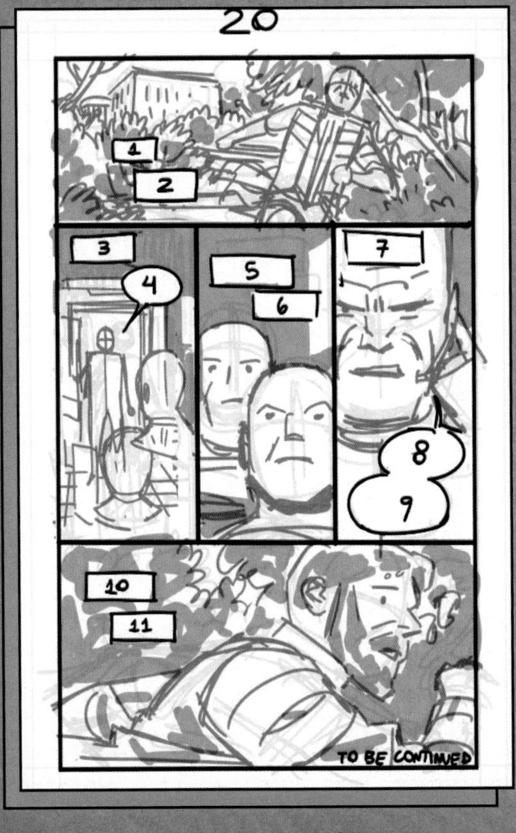
20
TO BE CONTINUED

#701 LAYOUTS BY
LEONARDO ROMERO

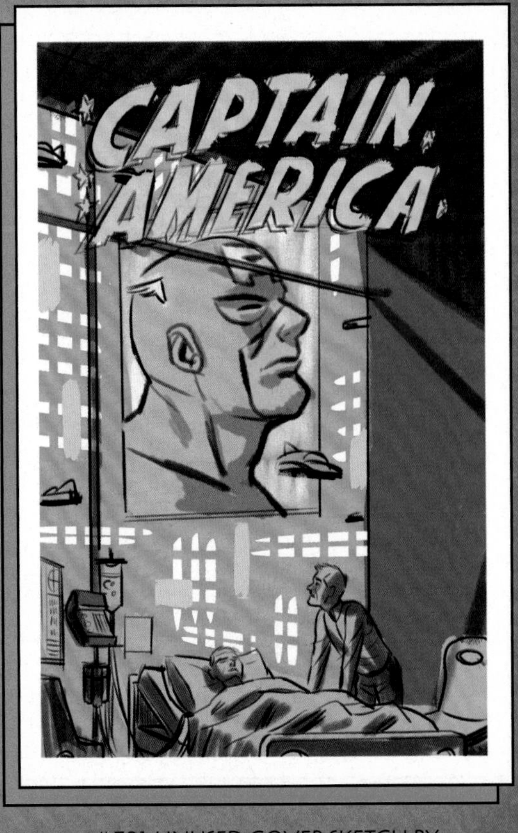
CAPTAIN
AMERICA

#701 UNUSED COVER SKETCH BY
MICHAEL CHO

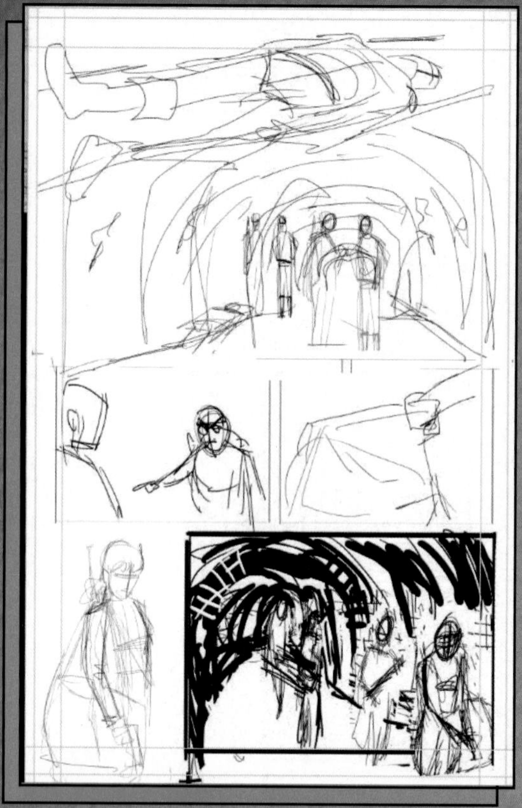

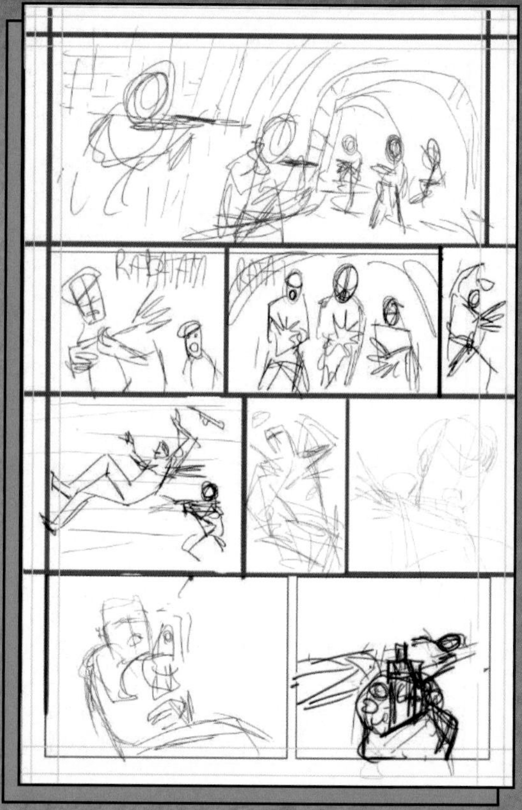

#702 LAYOUTS BY
ROD REIS

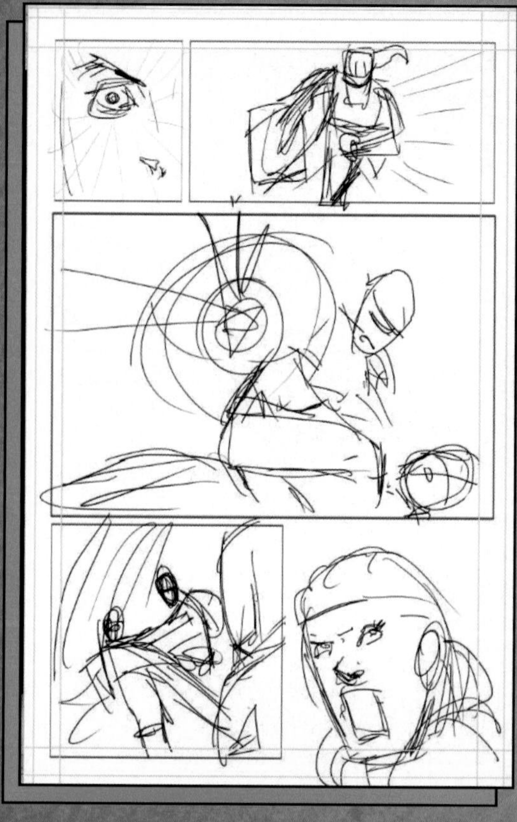

#702 LAYOUTS BY
ROD REIS

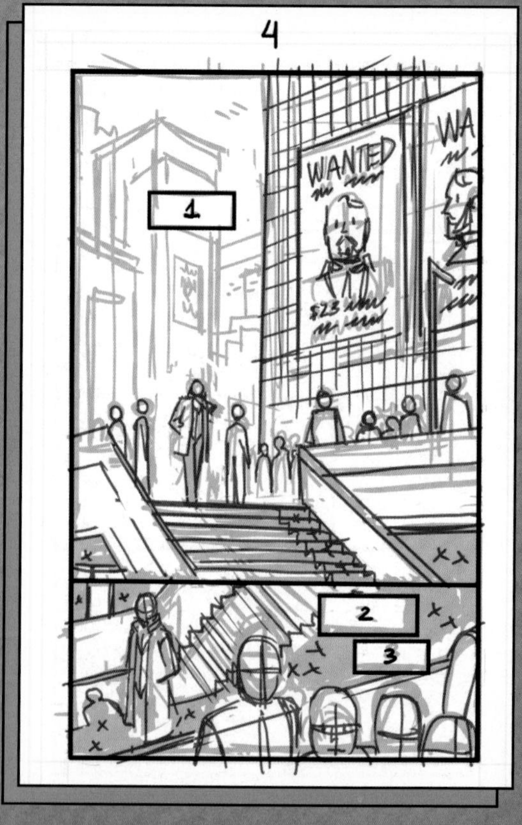
4
WANTED
1
2
3

#702 LAYOUTS BY
LEONARDO ROMERO

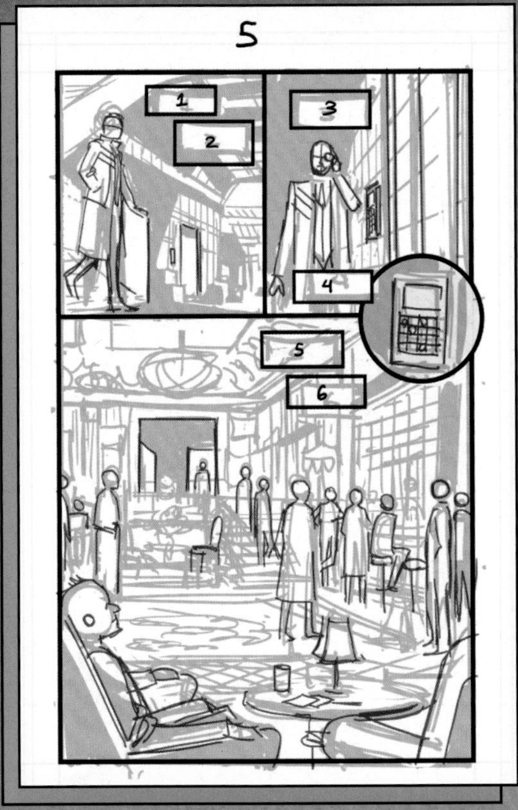
5

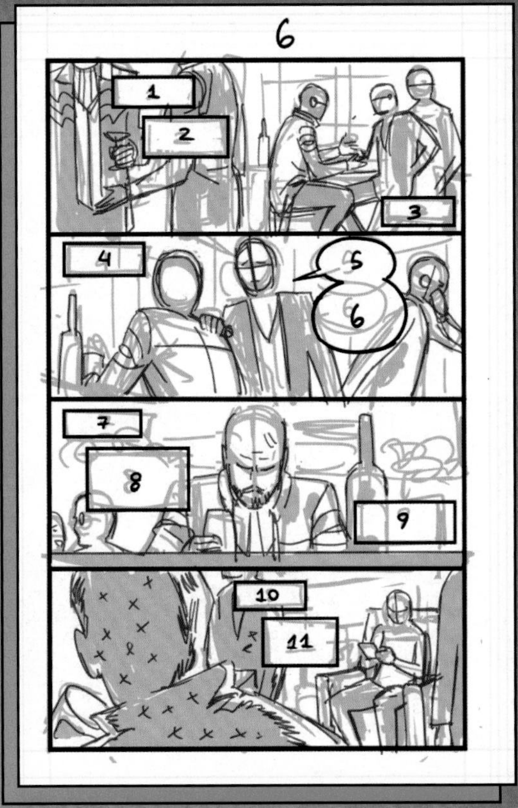
6

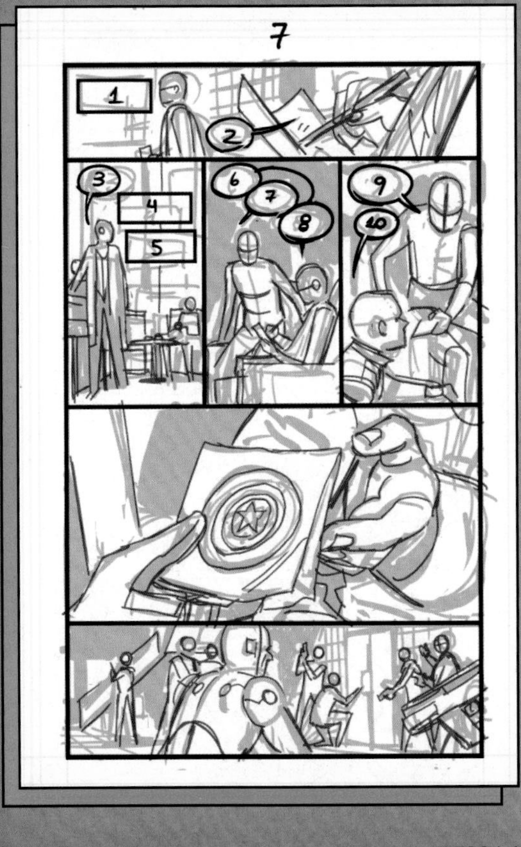
7

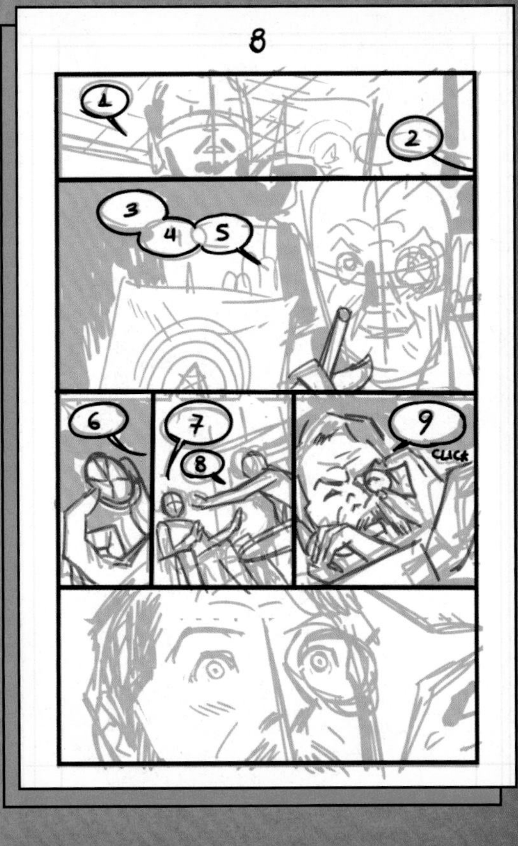
8
CLICK

#702 LAYOUTS BY
LEONARDO ROMERO

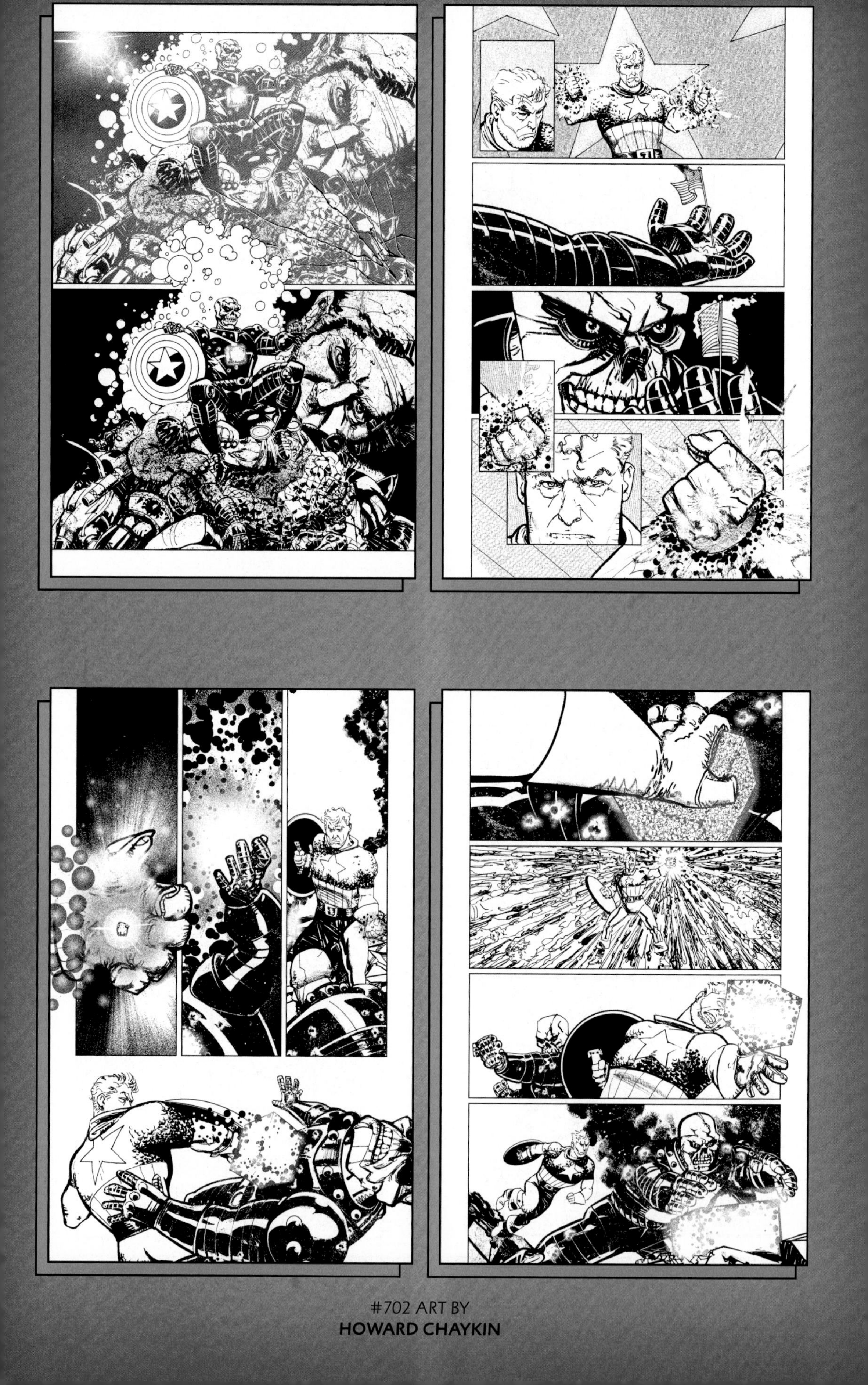

#702 ART BY
HOWARD CHAYKIN

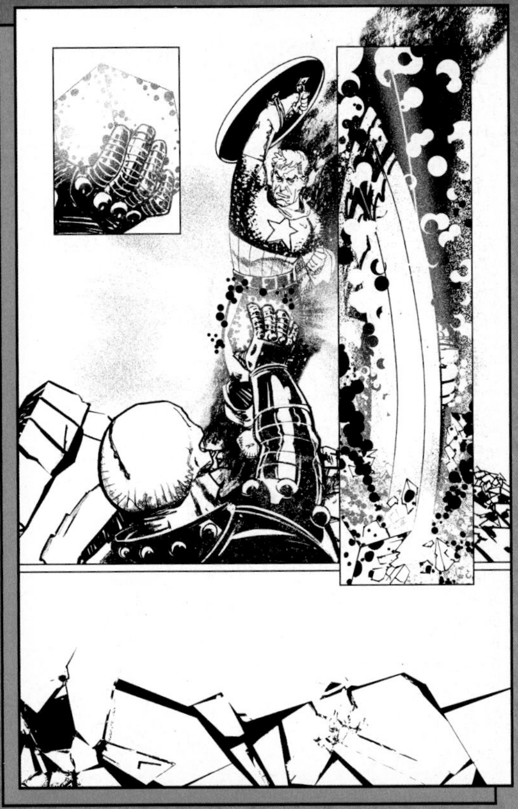

#702 ART
BY **HOWARD CHAYKIN**

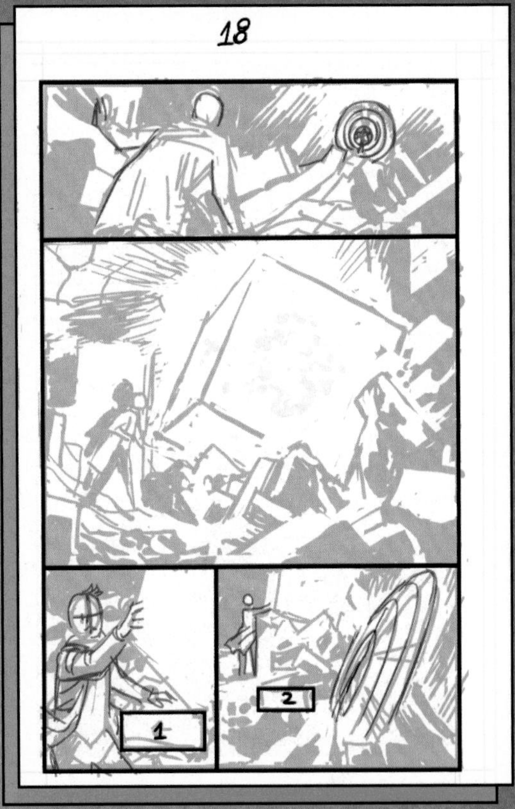
18
1
2

#702 LAYOUTS
BY **LEONARDO ROMERO**

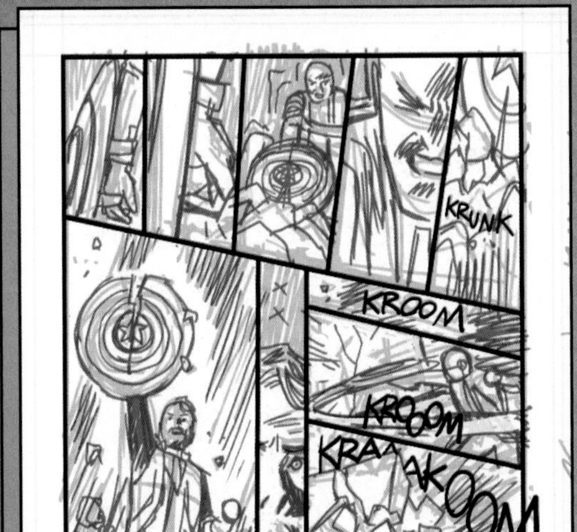
KRUNK
KROOM
KROOOM
KRAAAKOOOM
KRAAK
1
19

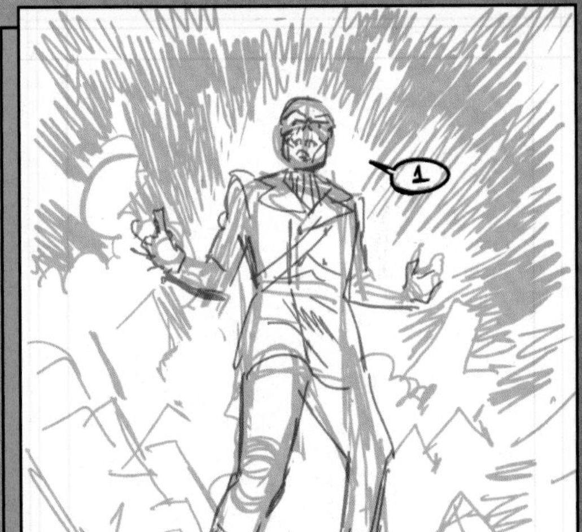
1
2
20

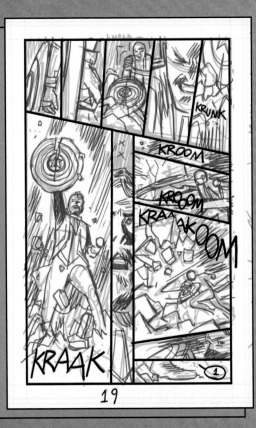

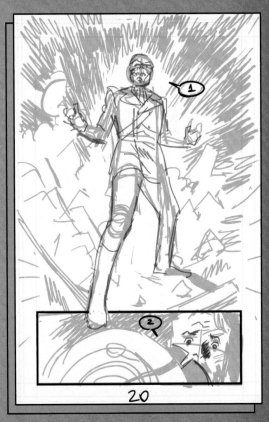

#702 LAYOUTS
BY **LEONARDO ROMERO**

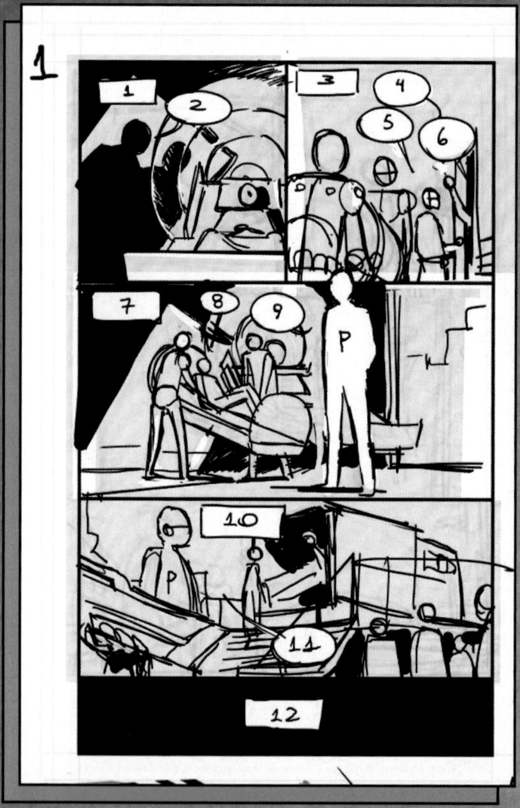

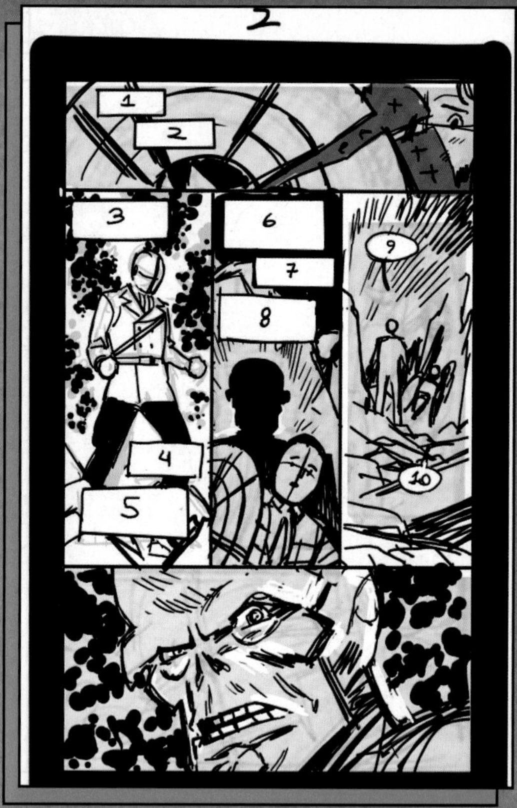

#703 LAYOUTS BY
BY **LEONARDO ROMERO**

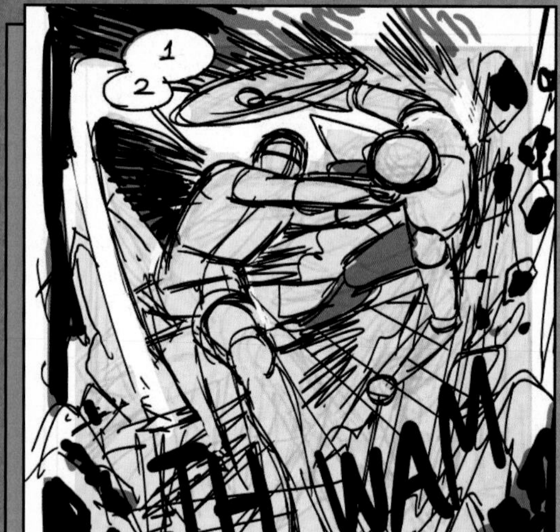
TH WAM

#703 LAYOUTS BY
BY **LEONARDO ROMERO**

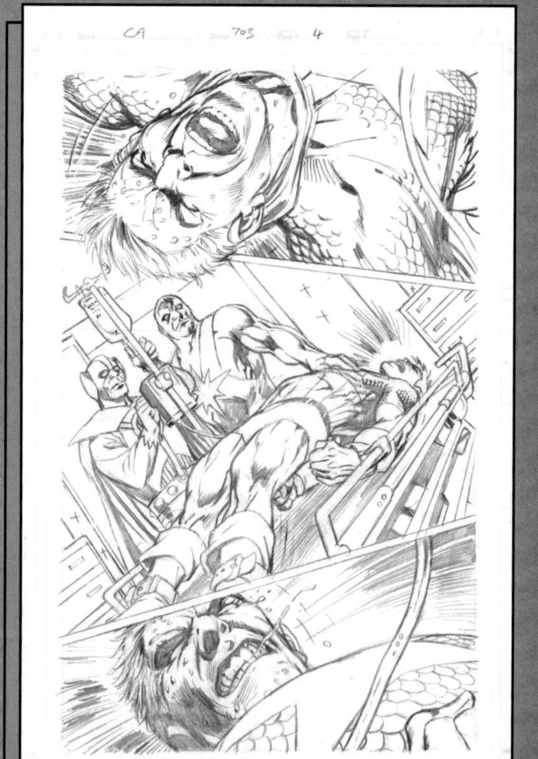

#703 PENCILS BY
ALAN DAVIS

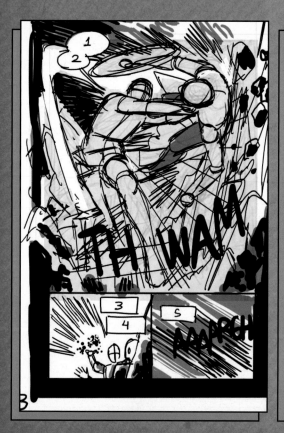

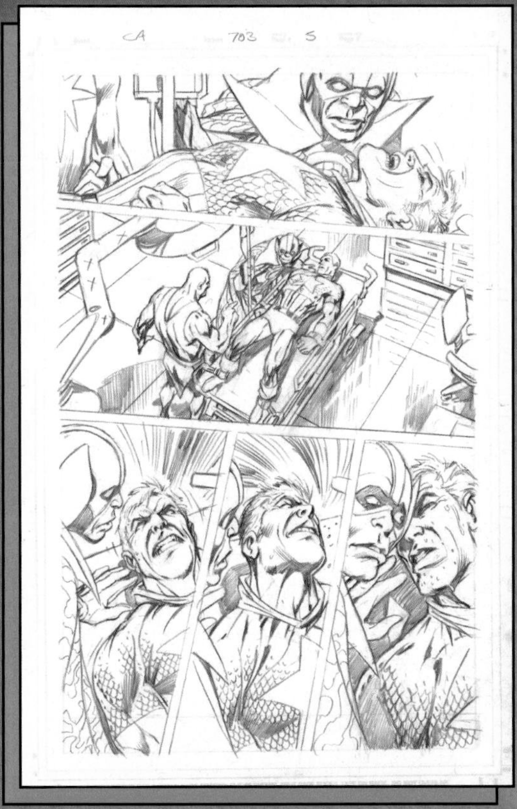
CA 703 5

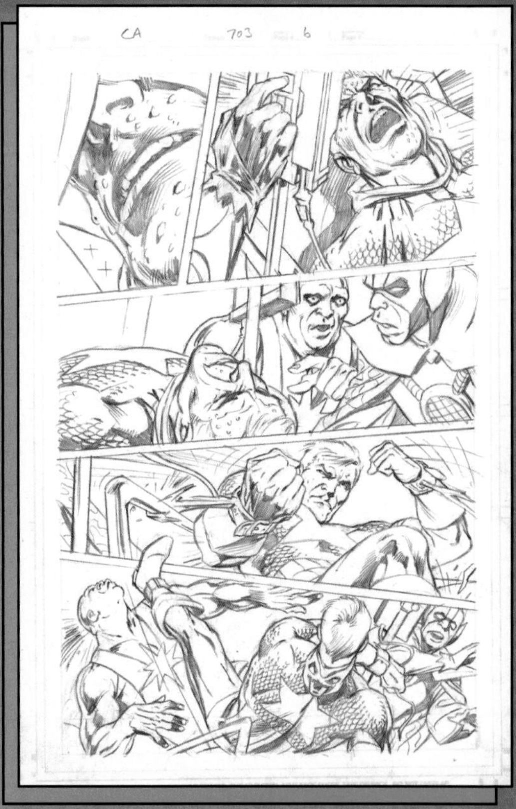
CA 703 6

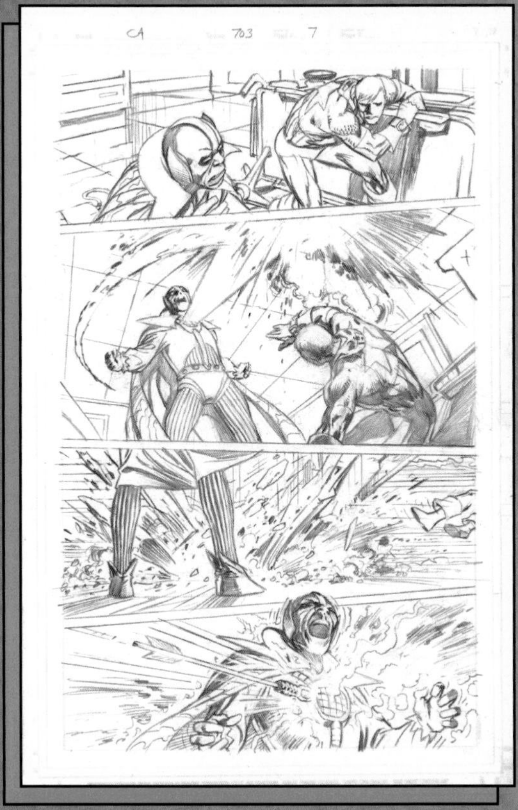
CA 703 7

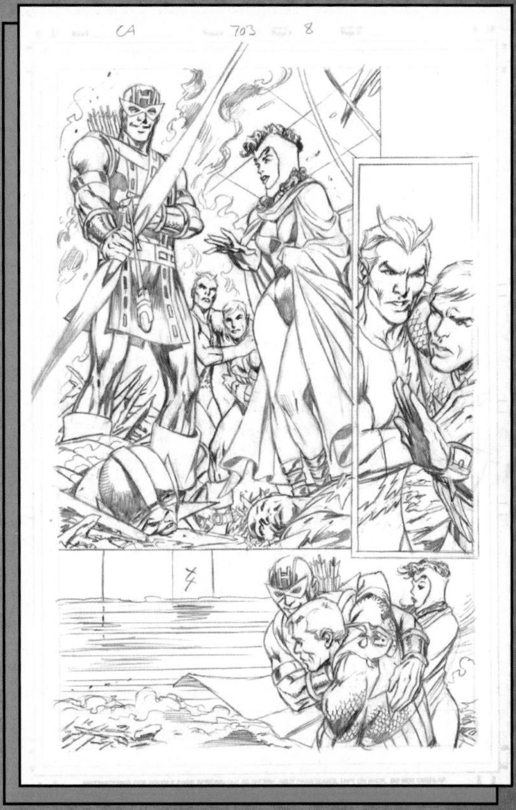
CA 703 8

#703 PENCILS BY
ALAN DAVIS

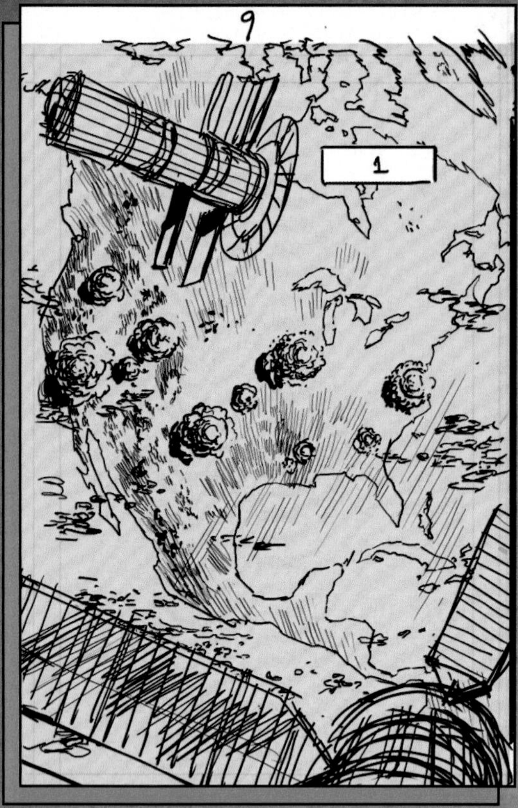
9

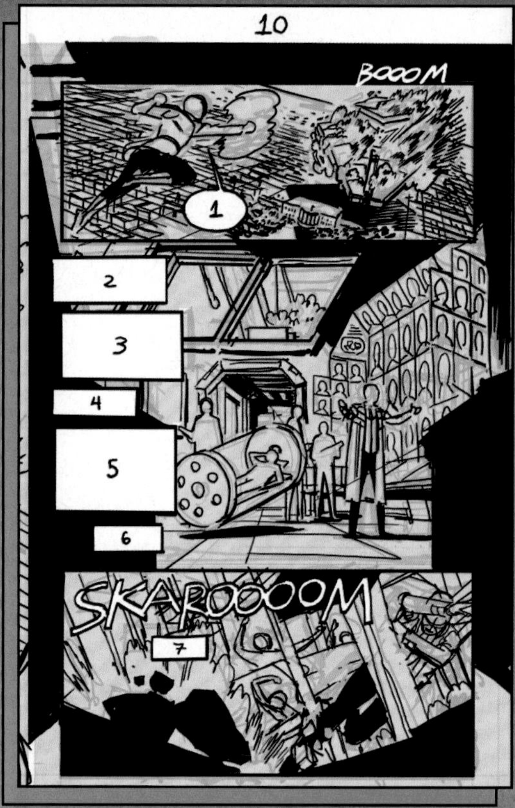
10
BOOOM
SKAROOOOM

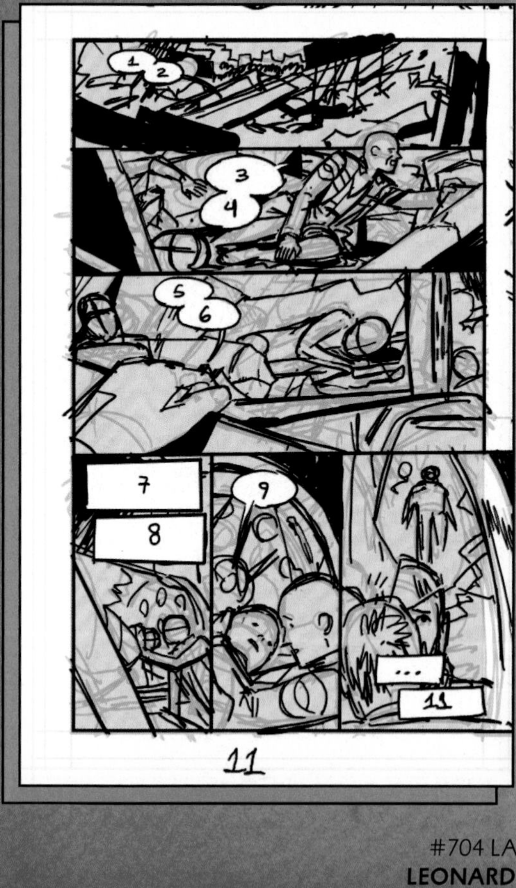
11

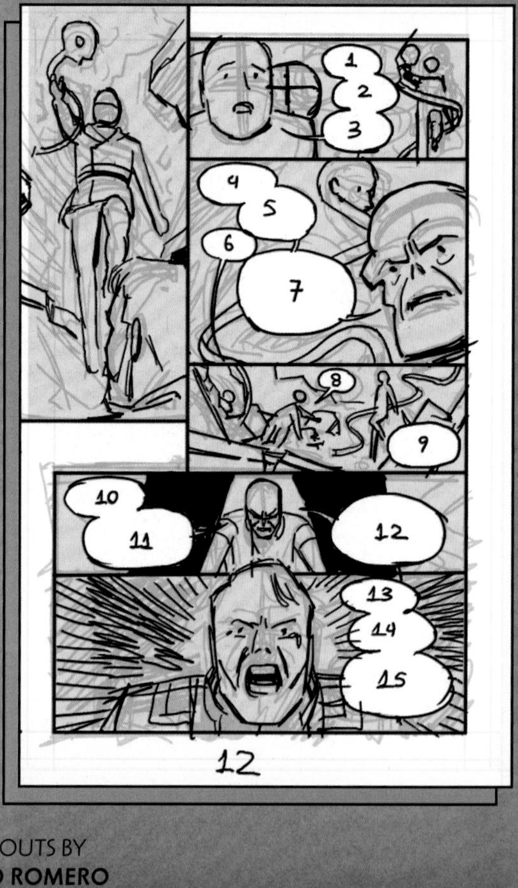
12

#704 LAYOUTS BY
LEONARDO ROMERO

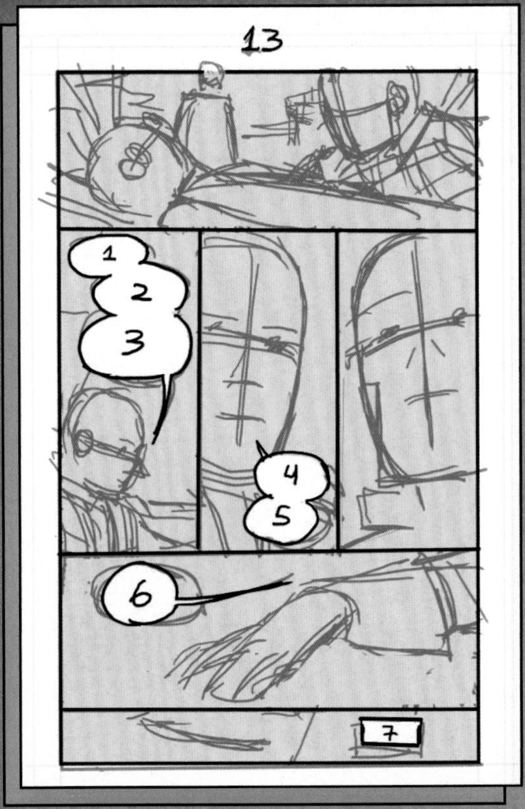
13

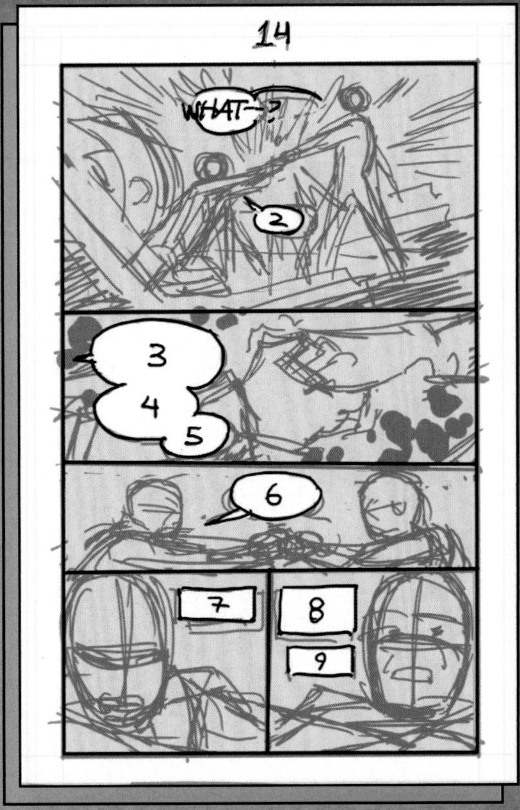
14
WHAT—?

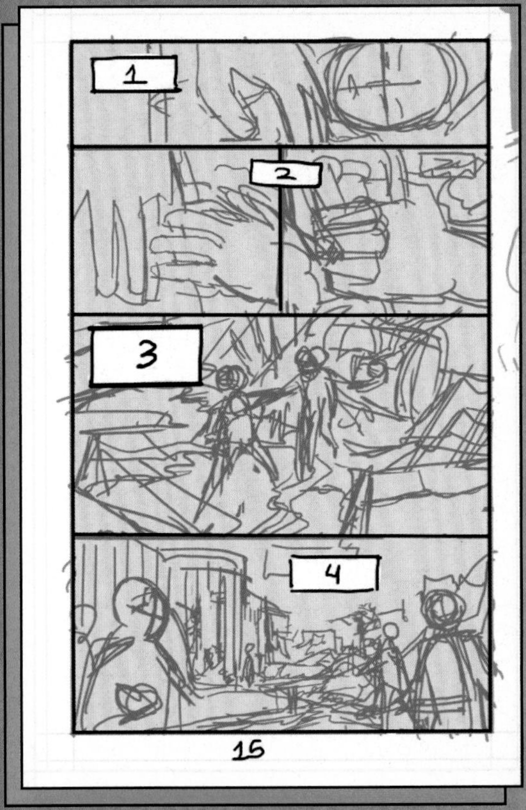
15

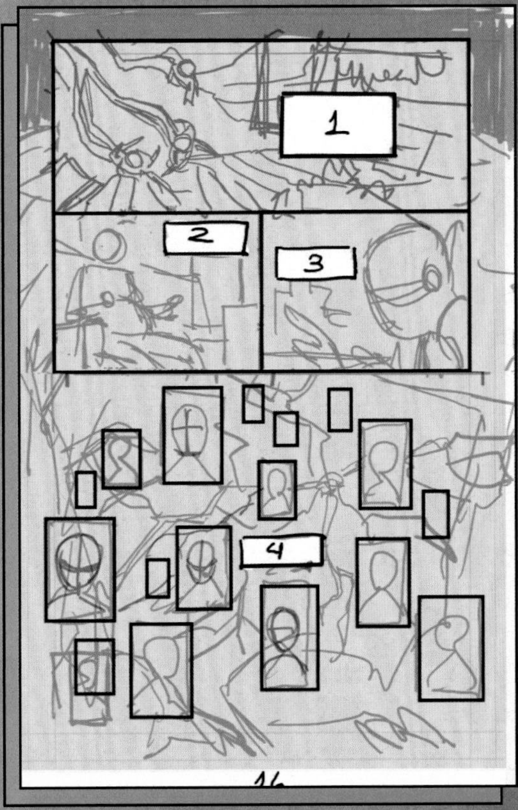

#704 LAYOUTS BY
LEONARDO ROMERO

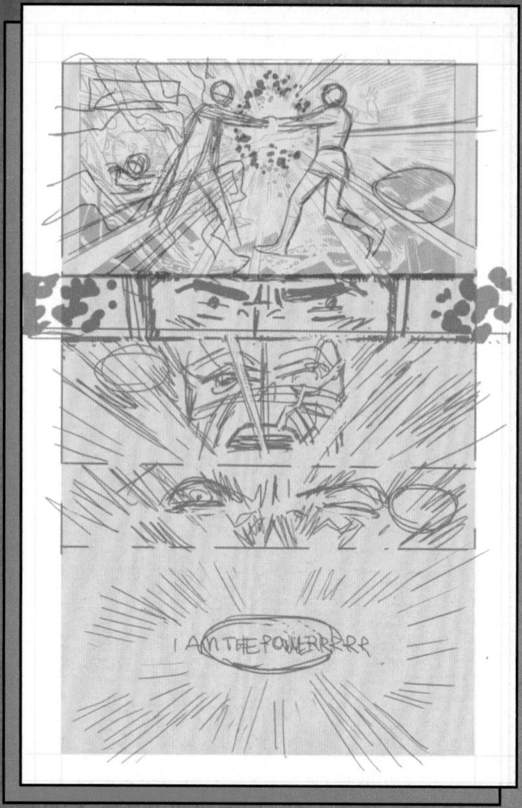
I AM THE POWERRRRR

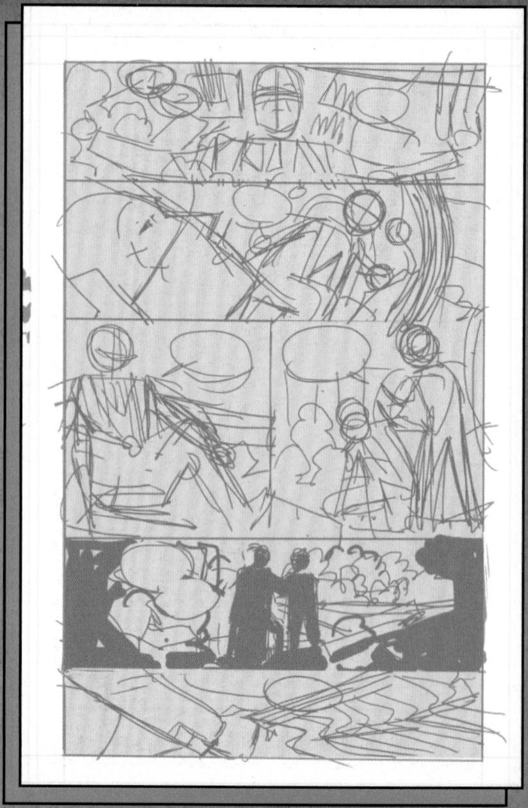

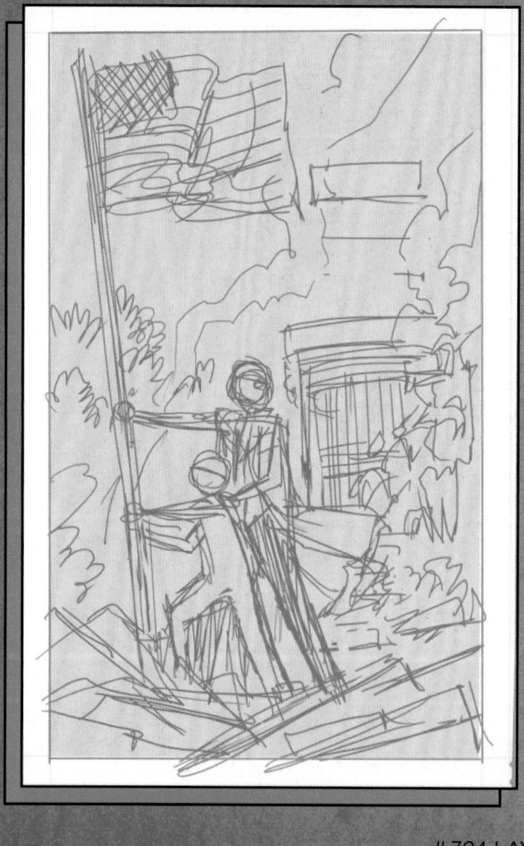

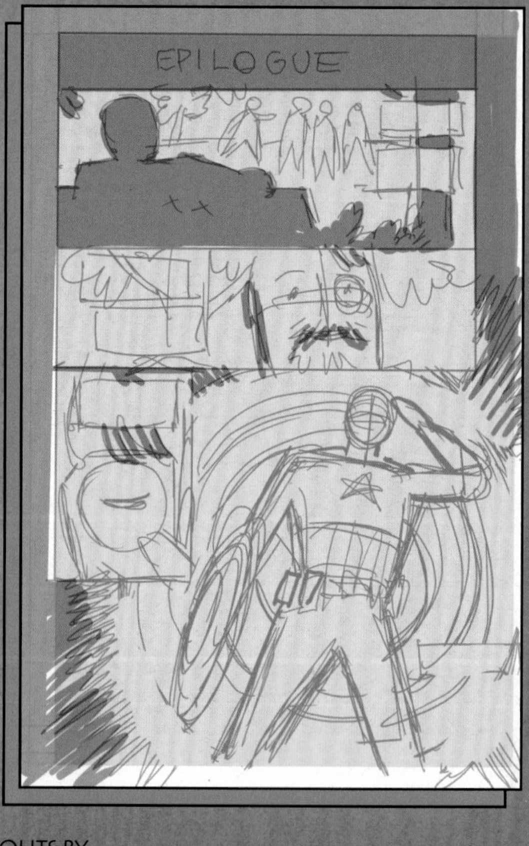
EPILOGUE

#704 LAYOUTS BY
LEONARDO ROMERO